A HISTORY OF PREGNANCY IN CHRISTIANITY

This book examines changing views of procreation and foetal development throughout the history of the Christian tradition. This is the first comprehensive study of cultural perceptions of pregnancy, an area of scholarship that has been understudied in the past. Pregnancy holds a central place in Christian ritual, iconography, and theology, including the dogma of the incarnation and the cult of Virgin Mary. This book provides a broad introduction to the changing attitudes and ideas within Western Christian communities by focusing on four periods of transition: antiquity, the Enlightenment, modernity, and the present day. It lays the groundwork for further study of the interactions between biological models, cultural preconceptions, and religious beliefs.

Anne Stensvold is Professor of History of Religions at the University of Oslo, Norway. She has written extensively on popular religion and religious change and is the editor of *Western Balkans: The Religious Dimension* (2009).

A HISTORY OF PREGNANCY IN CHRISTIANITY

From Original Sin to Contemporary Abortion Debates

Anne Stensvold

Routledge
Taylor & Francis Group

NEW YORK AND LONDON

618.2
Stensvold

First published 2015
by Routledge
711 Third Avenue, New York, NY 10017

and by Routledge
2 Park Square, Milton Park, Abingdon, Oxon OX14 4RN

Routledge is an imprint of the Taylor & Francis Group, an informa business

Library of Congress Cataloging in Publication Data
Stensvold, Anne, 1956-
A history of pregnancy in Christianity : from original sin to contemporary
abortion debates / Anne Stensvold. -- 1st ed.
pages cm
Includes bibliographical references and index.
1. Pregnancy--Religious aspects--Christianity. 2. Pregnancy--History.
3. Abortion--Moral and ethical aspects. I. Title.
RG525.S6927 2015
618.2--dc23
2014044583

ISBN: 978-0-415-85758-1 (hbk)
ISBN: 978-0-415-85759-8 (pbk)
ISBN: 978-0-203-79889-8 (ebk)

Typeset in Bembo
by Taylor & Francis Books

CONTENTS

ACKNOWLEDGEMENTS

Without a sabbatical from my workplace, the Department of Culture Studies and Oriental Languages (IKOS) at the University of Oslo, this book would not have seen the light of day. There are also many people who have had a hand in its creation. First of all, I would like to thank Kari Elisabeth Børresen and Ingvild Gilhus, who both exemplify in their own way the generosity of excellent scholarship. For Kari's persistent interest in the intellectual conditions of female life and Ingvild's emulation of Socrates in more ways than one, I am immensely grateful. Ingvild is also more directly (but unwittingly) involved in this book. In connection with her sixtieth birthday, we made a special issue of *Dīn: Religionsvitenskapelig tidsskrift* (*Journal for the Scientific Study of Religion*). The topic was Creation. Second, I would like to thank all the other contributors for commenting on the article which formed the starting point for this book: Siv-Ellen Kraft, Dag Endsjø, Christian Bull, Pål Steiner, Henny Fiskå Hägg, Ida Marie Høegh, Hugo Lundhaug, Sidsel Undheim, and Lisbeth Mikaelsson. Finally, my thanks go out to Hanne Trangerud, who carried out research tasks for me.

This book is dedicated to the memory of my childhood friend Christine Holm, who was diagnosed with uterine cancer the same week that I learnt I was pregnant and who died the day after my son's first birthday. It is also dedicated to my friend Maria Isabel Morales, who first introduced me to the intricacies of American abortion debates, when she worked in New York as a psychologist in the 1980s. Without our need to communicate, I would never have felt the urge to translate the article in *Dīn*, which I subsequently expanded and which I eventually turned into this book.

INTRODUCTION

What is a human being? Contemporary medicine forces us to rethink the meaning of human life. Stem cell research and in vitro fertilization (IVF) raises the question of when life starts. Respirators and heart machines blur the line between life and death; surrogate mothers and seed donors question traditional ideas about parenthood; and organ transplantation and abortion force us to rethink our conceptions of the individual.

The birth[1]
At a hospital in one of Rio de Janeiro's most densely populated areas, they treat more than a thousand patients a day, nearly all of them poor or extremely poor.
The doctor on duty told the following story to Juan Bedoian:
Last week, I had to choose between two newborn baby girls. We have one respirator. They were born at the same time, and it was up to me to decide which one of them should live.
It wasn't a choice for me to make, said the doctor, it was for God to decide. But God didn't say a word.
Regardless of what he decided to do, the doctor would be guilty of a crime.
Even if he chose to do nothing, he would be sentencing both of them to death.
There was no time to think. The two baby girls were already in the grips of death; they had already started to leave this world.
The doctor closed his eyes. One was destined to die, the other to live.

Faced with such dilemmas, we need words and metaphors to think with. One way of doing so is to look to the past and see what people in other historical circumstances thought and how they acted in relation to these matters. This is the purpose of this book. It puts the concept of human life to the test by focusing on pregnancy, birth, and abortion in the history of Christianity.

Abortion is on the political agenda in several countries, especially in North America where strong groups of Christian anti-abortionists challenge the liberal abortion laws that were introduced in most Western countries during the 1970s. The positions are locked, and debates turn into quarrels, sometimes ending up in all out violence and murder. The moral issues at stake here are high on both sides. But where the feminists' concern for women's rights often seem blind to the moral dilemma of abortion, anti-abortionists close their eyes to the needs of (newborn) infants being raised in poverty. The conflict may be described as a clash of values, a stalemate position between a religious and a secular view of life. So when anti-abortionists define the zygote as being endowed with a soul and argue for its human value, those in favour of so-called 'free abortion' insist on the autonomy of the pregnant woman and her right to decide over her own body. They speak about abortion, but talk about different things.

Pregnancy is a key symbol in Christianity, with the miraculous conception of Christ and Mary's pregnancy as the founding events of the religion. Pregnancy is not given much attention in the Bible, however. In the New Testament, Elizabeth, the mother of John the Baptist, is pregnant, and the Old Testament mentions couples with fertility problems, e.g. the story of Abraham and Sarah (Genesis 16). Interestingly, their problem of producing offspring is first addressed by introducing the servant Hagar to act as what we today would call a surrogate mother. But when Hagar refused to give up the child, God miraculously intervenes and makes Sarah pregnant at 90. Conception is described by metaphors and through implicit understanding – "A man knows his wife": "Now the man knew his wife Eve, and she conceived and bore Cain, saying, 'I have produced a man with the help of the Lord'" (Genesis 4:1).[2] This scene took place as soon as Adam and Eve were expelled from the Garden of Eden, making pregnancy the founding event of the history of mankind after the expulsion from Paradise. If seen together with the birth of Christ, it is possible to argue that pregnancy *could* have been conceptualized as a sacred event among Christians. But Christianity did not develop a cult of human pregnancy – or a veneration of motherhood for that matter. Instead, it transferred the reverence to Virgin Mary and developed a prolific tradition of theological reflections on human procreation. These reflections started within the context of late antiquity (200 CE – 500 CE) and were coloured by Graeco-Roman culture – its ideas about the human body; the hierarchical relation between man and woman; and its hierarchical social order.

Pregnancy is a physical state, a function of the female body, a fact of life. But it is also an experience shrouded in fear and expectation, a matter of endless speculation, rumour, and fantasy. However, the experiential dimension of pregnancy is not the topic of this book, which instead investigates the underlying assumptions and the taken-for-granted notions that condition the way we interpret and experience the world. Informed by the assumption that biological models condition religious ideas and theological reflections, this book approaches different ways of conceptualizing pregnancy within the Christian tradition. Its aim can be summed up as an attempt to understand how and why the conceptualization of procreation, pregnancy, birth, and abortion change over time.

In a Christian world view, there are two ways of bringing something new into the world: creation and generation. Augustine established a clear distinction between them and linked it to man and God: God was the sole creator; it was his privilege to create from nothing (*ex nihilo*). Man, on the other hand, was only an artisan who could shape and mould existing matter into new forms or multiply and generate that which already exists, e.g. sow seeds in order to harvest and generate his own offspring. On this view, human activities which we would categorize as creative acts, such as painting a picture, writing a novel, or making a child, are not creative activities at all, although the latter comes closest and is significantly referred to as "procreating", i.e. helping God realize or bring forth his creation. This theological understanding relied implicitly on an ancient Greek biological model which made a categorical distinction between creation and human generation. In Aristotle's understanding, generation involves a "transformation of existing material in such a way that a different substance is produced" (Pasnau 2002: 101). In other words, generation means to bring something or someone into being from something (material) which already exists, whereas creation means bringing forth something which did not exist before (*ex nihilo*).

The distinction between creation and generation was also of paramount importance in early Christian thinking, where it was correlated with the distinction between eternity and decay and between God and man. Only God could create. Eternity belonged to him. Human beings could only copy, reproduce, and generate in time, which means that all their produce has a limited duration. This explains the ease with which early Christianity adopted the Greek vegetative model of human procreation and human life.

Ageing was understood as a necessary counterpart to growth. Because all living things must die, growing must stop at maturity. When the fruit is ripe, so to speak, decay sets in. According to this logic, there was no difference between vegetative generation and human procreation, since both processes involved gradual growth and subsequent decay. Human procreation was a natural part of the world that God had created, and the lives of humans were therefore doomed to end. However, by God's grace mankind was singled out to receive a second chance at eternity in the Resurrection. The idea that life entails decay, that ageing is the other side of growth, and that birth necessarily entails death may explain the preoccupation with nutrition and growth processes. In ancient Greek thought, the distinction between plants, animals, and humans was superseded by the idea of life. According to this model, growth as well as generation among plants, animals, and humans were not different in kind, but rather constituted a continuum: As the seeds take nutrition from the earth and grow to fulfill their form, the human seed is nurtured in the mother's womb, where it would grow into a human form. The growth process involved in this transformation of seeds into grain was envisaged as being parallel to the transformation from semen to foetus and the birth of an animal or a human being. In the world view of early Christianity, there was no categorical difference between vegetative generation and animal procreation: Both were conceived of as different forms of propagation, generation, or making offspring.

The Christian correlation between generation and decay (death) stems from Greek thought, in which generation was associated with the female. According to the myth of Pandora, death was introduced to the world (of men) by a woman. Similarly, in Augustine's exposition of Genesis, it is Eve who introduces Adam to death. But in both instances – the myth of Pandora as well as Genesis – the ultimate responsibility is assigned to men: They broke the agreement with the god(s) and stole the fire/ate the apple. Pandora brought sexuality, generation, and death to mankind (here strictly understood as male). Since women were introduced into the world of men as punishment, their social status was decisively inferior. But in Christian mythology, the punishment was the expulsion from Paradise. Compared to women in Greek mythology, women in the Christian tradition were in a decisively better position: They went from being *the* punishment to being punished together with men. But both mythologies create a strong association between women and evil. Eve represents everything that is alien to God – death, decay, and moral corruption – in spite of the very concrete function which women had – for everyone to see – in the actual creation of and caring for new life.

Historically speaking, Christianity replaced the Graeco-Roman world view with a monotheistic one, which brought with it new ideas about God, sin, and bodily resurrection. However, it was not a simple substitution of one world view with another, but a complex cultural process whereby the Christian message was adapted into a Graeco-Roman context. In this respect, the history of Christianity – from its origins as the belief system of a Jewish sect to its emergence as the dominant religion of the West – is like all historical processes, that is, multi-layered and complex. The short version is that Christianity conquered European culture and transformed peoples from gentiles into Christians over a period of more than a thousand years. But when Emperor Constantine (306–337 CE) legalized Christianity in 313 CE, it did not imply the immediate death of old gods and the total annihilation of Graeco-Roman culture. Thus, the great theologian Augustine writes about Roman gods as if they had real power. He addresses his Roman audience and mocks their gods: "How can they (the gods) be regarded as anything but abominable evil spirits, eager to deceive mankind?" (*City of God* II, 13). Religious and cultural developments are never that simple. They involve clashes and compromise, contradictions and incompatible world views standing side by side. Thinking about religion and culture as discrete entities, therefore, is too simple and too crude. Instead, we can think about Christianity as a religio-cultural entity with its own ideas and practices. Inspired by Ludwig Wittgenstein who understands culture as the totality of the context of a given language (Wittgenstein 1957) – or by Hans-Johann Glock, who said that a form of life "is a culture or social formation, the totality of communal activities into which language-games are embedded" (Glock 1996: 125) – we can approach Christianity as a more or less integral part of Western culture, starting with its enculturation into the Graeco-Roman world, passing through a long peak of cultural dominance which lasted over a millennium, to the various forms of Christianity we find in contemporary culture, where secularization has marginalized religion and Christianity has dispersed into a variety of forms.

In a similar vein, I would say that an open-ended approach is needed if we are to make sense of the various views on pregnancy and procreation in con-temporary Western society, where some regard each fertilized human egg as a human person while others understand procreation in strictly biological terms. The phenomenon of modern mass media has made us aware of a whole range of such incompatible understandings and radically different world views. But Christianity still dominates Western popular culture, and Mary and Eve remain more or less explicit models for the representation of women in film, television, and interactive media (Frye 1982). This can partly be explained by what seems to be an inherent resistance to cultural change: As Jean-Pierre Albert asserts when reflecting on the logic of cultural innovation, the incorporation of new ideas is a fragile process. For a new religious idea or practice to become accepted and even popular, it must be recognizable as something new; it also has to somehow relate to the old end established order (Albert 1997). This does not mean that profound change is impossible. It means, rather, that cultural changes can bring something new or seem to occur *ex nihilo*, but that what is new must answer to a need.

Each culture and every period has its own system of meaning which is expressed and transmitted in language – verbal and visual. But only those ideas that have a resonance and appear plausible will survive. Thus, several categories of Greek thought are still with us (e.g. spirit/matter distinction), whereas others have been lost (e.g. faculty, which refers to an innate ability or quality). When Christianity was introduced into the Graeco-Roman world, it brought with it unknown categories (e.g. doom/salvation). During the Enlightenment, new distinctions (organic/mechanic) came to the fore. What contemporary culture has brought to the stockpile of cultural patterns is harder to discern apart from new interpretations of age-old categories (e.g. nature/culture, individual/society). The new social role of women, however, has made renegotiation of gender relations inevitable and has placed the pregnant body in the centre of contemporary political debates.

What is a human life? When does it begin? Where does it end? There is no final authority where life and death are concerned, and the meaning and purpose of a human life cannot be settled once and for all. For this reason, this book is written as a comedy, to paraphrase the medievalist Caroline Walker Bynum: "If tragedy tells a cogent story, with a moral hero, and undergirds our sense of the nobility of humanity, comedy tells many stories, achieves a conclusion only by coincidence and wild improbability, and undergirds our sense of human limitation" (Bynum 1992: 24). In a similar vein, this book does not try to reveal past truths or tell a comprehensive story about human procreation through the ages, but rather seeks to contribute to contemporary reflections on what it means to be a human being.

This book traces the conceptualization of pregnancy in Western Christian culture from antiquity until the present day and gives a broad introduction to the topic by focusing on four moments of transition in the Western conceptualization of pregnancy: antiquity, the Enlightenment, modernity, and contemporary abortion debates. The first chapter gives a brief introduction to the theoretical perspectives that inform this book. The remaining chapters are organized chronologically in four parts.

Part I, Beginnings (Chapters 2–5), starts with a brief presentation of theoretical approaches to pregnancy. An underlying assumption of this book is that biological models influence theology. This part discusses biological models from Greek antiquity and how they were adopted by Christianity. The focus is on Augustine, the development of Canon law, and folk traditions related to pregnancy. Part II, The Enlightenment (Chapters 6–8), focuses on significant changes of ideas and practices during the Enlightenment, when the human body was recast in scientific terms. Starting with the body of saints, this part traces the development of science. Informed by the assumption that science emerged within a Christian context, it looks at the interaction between religious beliefs and scientific theories about human procreation. Part III, Modernity (Chapters 9–11), starts with the emergence of modernity and ends with the Second World War. This part of the book looks at how Christian ideas and values came under siege by science and by various socio-political forces, focusing on the discovery of the mammalian egg in 1827, a peak event during the nineteenth century. It then goes on to discuss Christian reactions to major scientific developments more broadly, e.g. the discovery of heredity, the menstruation cycles, and methods of birth control. Finally, Part IV, Contemporary debates (Chapters 12–15), focuses on the twentieth-century debates about fertility, contraception, and abortion. It looks at contemporary abortion debates and traces how the reframing of the foetus by technological inventions such as IVF, surrogacy, and ultrasound influences the arguments of Christian and secular interest groups. Finally, this part focuses on the clash between conservative Christian values and secular ideals of gender equality and women's rights.

Notes

1 From *Les voix du temps* by the Uruguayan poet Eduardo Galeano (Montreal: Lux, 2011). Here cited from *Le monde diplomatique*, December 2011 (my translation).
2 Bible citations are from the New Revised Standard Version (NRSV).

PART I

Beginnings

Theory, late antiquity (200–500), and the medieval period (500–1500)[1]

1

CONCEPTUALIZING PREGNANCY

FIGURE 1.1 American film actress Demi Moore on the cover of *Vanity Fair*, August 1991. © Annie Leibovitz.

In 1991, Demi Moore made history when she appeared naked and pregnant on the cover of *Vanity Fair*. The picture was hard to decipher; an expectant mother or a sexualized body? Mary or Eve? It defied such distinctions and stated boldly that this woman was both: mother and sex symbol. The picture created havoc, but the posture soon became a standard for pregnant Hollywood celebrities – and others. Ambiguity was probably the reason for its success. When Demi Moore fixes the spectator with her gaze, she challenges them to acknowledge her body as her own. This is her belly, and the foetus inside it is hers.

In 1991, when the image was first published, American society was marked by heated debates on abortion. The pregnant Demi Moore must be seen in this context. Whether intentional or not, the image was an intervention in the abortion debates. Playing on Mary and Eve as cultural stereotypes, it was also a critique of traditional Christianity. Here was a celebrated film star and a successful professional woman who displayed her naked body in public. This was a new kind of feminist statement: A woman playing on cultural stereotypes willingly presenting herself as an object of desire. The cover image was ambiguous, to say the least.

In anthropology, ambiguity is associated with taboo and uncleanliness (Turner 1967, Douglas 1966). The typical reaction is to keep it apart and hide it away. In Western society today, it seems that the reverse is true. Mass media are permeated by ambiguous bodies which break with established oppositions – private vs. public, pretty vs. ugly, man vs. woman – thereby keeping ancient dualisms alive. Demi Moore played on these categorizations when she displayed her pregnant body in public. Unlike images of androgynous fashion models, her pregnant body is ambiguous because it contains more than one human being. This blurring of bodies makes the pregnant body a disturbing entity; it doesn't fit. This is particularly evident in the way that mass media normally present pregnant women: either as expecting housewife-mothers "who cannot wait to meet their child" or as busy career women with "a baby bump" who go jogging as usual. Mother Mary and sinful Eve have been recast as mother and career woman: both share a common fate in having a female body.

Ambiguity also dictates the way we speak about the foetus. It is hard to talk about because it surpasses the distinction that we normally rely on: It is not a human being, and nor is it *not* human. The uncertainty is reflected in ordinary speech. If the pregnancy is desired, we speak about the foetus as if it were already a full-born child – thereby magically helping to bring it safely into the world. But if the pregnancy is unwanted, we use words which allow us to think of the foetus as something external, invading, and foreign – something which can be removed. Both options rely on a false assumption that we can speak with certainty about something which remains unclear. A foetus is in the process of *becoming* a human being – or not. It is hard to talk about because it is hidden and unreachable beyond normal human relationships: Except for its mother, it remains unknown to others until it is born. The introduction of ultrasound images from the mid-1980s changed all this; as Clare Hanson puts it: "The ultrasound has become widely accepted as a crucial rite de passage in pregnancy, the point at which the embryo becomes (at 11 to 13 weeks) a 'real baby'" (Hanson 2004: 158). The ultrasound image served as proof, as it were, of the foetus' existence. Nevertheless, the reality of the foetus still remains inaccessible in principle because its existence can only be observed indirectly via the mother's expanding belly. Hence, pregnancy remains a complex cultural phenomenon, and the life of the foetus remains surrounded by uncertainty. Although the process of foetal development is well known by now and scientific documentation is available to everyone, each individual pregnancy is unique. Or put differently: The beginning of life is as difficult to monitor as the end.

Over the last decades, pregnancy has increasingly become a matter of medical expertise and manipulation – from IVF to surrogacy. But apart from these inventions, pregnancy has also remained a function of the female body. Whether a pregnancy ends with the birth of a healthy child or by spontaneous abortion – and whether a pregnancy is wanted or not – it is an experience of existential dimensions, leaving its marks on the female body as a remembrance. Therefore, it is rather surprising that pregnancy has played such a small part in feminist theory. Feminist theory has been closely attached to the political project of female liberation from the start, and feminist theory has therefore had strong normative trends and has to a large extent been judged just as much by its political merits as by its academic achievements. In short, the socio-political situation of women has been its focus, and social oppression, rather than biology, has been its main concern. This is also the case in religious studies, where feminist scholars have typically focused on women's religious practices and on the conceptualization of womanhood in sacred texts (King 1995, Juschka 2001). Among Christian feminists, the picture is slightly different, since intellectual achievement is often combined with activism and motivated by a wish for internal church reform. Liturgical studies of gender-inclusive language and historical research on the first Christian communities are examples of feminist research areas motivated by a wish to change (male-dominated) normative Christianity. Taking the patriarchal tradition of the Catholic Church into account, it is no surprise that Catholic feminists are at the forefront of feminist theology (Schüssler Fiorenza 1983, Ruether 1983, Børresen 1968 and 1995). Criticizing the theological basis for the Church's overt denial of women's equality to men, they have been less concerned about theoretical debates about gender.[2]

Toril Moi suggests (Moi 1998) that the leading French feminist Simone de Beauvoir had a liberating mission when she coined the cultural-constructivist concept of gender ("*On ne naît pas femme on le devient*" – "You are not born a woman, you become one"). By introducing the idea of sexual roles as culturally construed rather than biological facts, Beauvoir gave the subordination of women a less compelling character. It is perhaps significant that Beauvoir herself did not experience motherhood. Nevertheless, the idea of pregnancy – the possibility of it – conditions the self-understanding of women from the first menstruation onwards. Whether or not pregnancy is actually experienced, it is a fact of women's lives – a possibility – from the age of puberty to menopause. Regardless of whether it is something you hope for or wish to avoid – something you expect to happen or a distant memory – pregnancy shapes women's lives.

Although pregnancy and birth are foundational events and the birth of the Saviour is a central theme in the Christian calendar and cultural representation, pregnancy does not receive much attention. It has a surprisingly small place in art; whereas portraits of the Virgin and Child abound, depictions of Mary as an expectant mother are extremely rare. Birth is also conspicuously absent in Western fiction and mostly described from a male perspective, as in scenes in which the father listens to the cries of pain, scenes describing how women suffer, and scenes explaining the fear associated with a dramatic delivery. "I need to address my gratitude to someone or something", my friend said when she wanted to explain why she, a non-religious person, wanted to have her newborn child baptized in church. Such perspectives are conspicuously absent from Christian art. The Internet revolution has hardly had any impact in this regard. The quantity of information on pregnancy and birth has grown exponentially, but not more so than other topics of a personal nature. On social media sites such as Facebook, the number of pages dedicated to pregnancy is overwhelming, but the presentations are strikingly poor and are nothing other than repetitive displays of cultural clichés. At the same time, the messages are surprisingly private in character. It is "my pregnant body" and "my birth experience". This privatization of pregnancy and birth may be explained as a result of the long history of male dominance and female invisibility in public. But it is also possible to say that the poverty of expression and the lack of words reflect the wordless quality of the interaction between the woman and her unborn offspring. It is also strangely emblematic of the fragility of that relationship.

Because of this cultural silence, we lack words and metaphors which would allow us to reflect and develop our understanding of pregnancy. This has far-reaching consequences, not least for the political debates about abortion, where the lack of an adequate vocabulary is striking. The feminist Julia Kristeva is an exception (Kristeva 1986). In an article written during her own pregnancy, she tries to capture the experience, and she describes it as a deeply disturbing and ambivalent one. Her intervention comes as a response to the feminist emancipatory project. Starting with Simone de Beauvoir who wrote about pregnancy in negative terms (Beauvoir 1989), feminist academics have largely treated pregnancy and motherhood as a political challenge rather than as a bodily experience and an emotional relationship. But whereas Beauvoir was critical because her project was female emancipation, Kristeva tries to capture the significance of the mother–child relation. Interestingly, when she writes about pregnancy, she uses much the same imagery as Beauvoir used when writing about the sexual relationship between man and woman.

To Beauvoir, motherhood was the main obstacle to female emancipation. Her ideal was the male artist – the only truly free person in the Paris of her day. She protested against a patriarchal society which forced women into passivity and idealized motherhood, and put up a male ideal for women to aspire to. To Beauvoir, freedom was paramount and motherhood was its negation. While men were free to make an imprint on the world, women were victims of their biology. They were locked up in the home, where they led restricted lives robbed of their freedom and independence. Women lived in a perpetual state of annihilation, a condition epitomized by pregnancy. She claimed: "With her ego surrendered, alienated in her body and in her social dignity, the mother enjoys the comforting illusion of feeling that she is a human being *in herself*, a *value*. But this is only an illusion. For she does not really make the baby, it makes itself within her" (Beauvoir 1989: 496). A thoroughly political feminist, Simone de Beauvoir embraced gender equality and sexual emancipation, but regarded pregnancy as an abomination because of the social implications it entailed for women. To her, sexuality was a more interesting topic because it signified transgression and therefore liberation. She described sexual intercourse as a truly transgressive act: "There is in erotic love a tearing away from the self; transport, ecstasy; suffering also tears through the limits of the ego, it is transcendence, a paroxysm" (Beauvoir 1989: 390). To men, it involves transcending the limits of their own body, whereas women desire the dissolution of the distinction between you and me, subject and object. In Beauvoir's analysis, the male sexual act is related to men's propensity for action – and creativity.

When Beauvoir denounced women's aspirations to marriage and motherhood, it was because she was a political writer addressing the oppression of women in French society in the postwar period. She regarded motherhood as a form of self-denial, using the concept of suffusion, of total identification with the foetus, to illustrate her point. In pregnancy, the suppressed housewife–woman has the illusion of owning her own body, as the child takes over from the husband (Beauvoir 1989: 496). Here, Beauvoir describes motherhood as a distorted kind of sexual desire – the woman's longing to melt in the man's embrace is subsumed under her wish to remain as one with her child. Pregnancy and motherhood become synonymous with alienation (Beauvoir 1989: 477). This was also what marriage implied for women, namely, the surrender of their subjectivity. To become a wife and mother was what Beauvoir's audience (1940s French women) aspired to. Like many defenders of conservative family values, Beauvoir saw pregnancy as a symbol of marriage and – unlike the former – therefore as a symbol of repression. With her critique of marriage in mind, the pregnant body was a symbolic prison that entailed a life in slavery to biological functions rather than a celebration of the freedom she valued.

Although Beauvoir's scepticism towards pregnancy was somewhat exaggerated – she described it as a female self-sacrifice – it does underscore the fact that pregnancy implies a fundamental change for the female body. When the female body hosts another human being, and when its belly starts to swell, it takes on a life of its own, so to speak: It loses its subjectivity and gains an additional meaning. It is a pregnant body and therefore not exclusively 'mine'. This blurring of distinctions between mother and child is also the focus of Julia Kristeva's reflections on pregnancy and birth as she strove to come to grips with the experience. Writing about the foetus in her womb, Kristeva contradicts Beauvoir when she describes her attitude as being deeply ambiguous and expresses estrangement and wonder:

> The other (the child) is inevitable, she seems to say, turn it into a God if you wish, it is nevertheless natural, for such an other has come out of myself, which is yet not myself but a flow of unending germinations, an eternal cosmos. The other goes much without saying and without my saying that, at the limit, it does not exist for itself.
>
> *(Kristeva 1986: 168)*

What Kristeva describes is not suffusion, but rather the contrary: distant adoration and incessant but failed attempts to grasp the reality of the unborn child. With a clear reference to Beauvoir ("turn it into a God if you wish"), she dismisses her exposition of motherhood as irrelevant. The pregnant female body does not fit into a strictly dualistic system of either/or, man or child, but remains a residual category – a personal experience and a social fact at one and the same time. It is a mute phenomenon veiled in mystery and therefore not expressed in language. In order to break this silence, Kristeva brings forth the only culturally acceptable or speakable pregnant woman, the Virgin Mary. The title of Kristeva's essay is "Stabat Mater", a title which evokes religious as well as aesthetic associations to the Virgin's suffering at the feet of the Cross and the music and paintings dedicated to this theme of pain and beauty in Christian art. Writing about the period shortly after delivery, Kristeva describes giving birth as a physical separation. It is not the woman who attaches herself (desperately) to the child as Beauvoir maintained. The woman's relation to her child is blurred, chaotic, and urgent – so much so that we are uncertain of who she refers to when writing "my body": Is it the foetus, the newborn, or her own body? We do not know:

> My body is no longer mine, it doubles up, suffers, bleeds, catches cold, puts its teeth in, slobbers, coughs, is covered with pimples, and it laughs. And yet, when its joy, my child's, returns, its smile washes only my eyes. But the pain, its pain – it comes from inside, never remains apart, other, it inflames me at once.
>
> *(Kristeva 1986: 167)*

Kristeva's poetic rendering of the experience of pregnancy and motherhood is one of surprisingly few. It would seem that the entry of a large number of women into the blogosphere would mean that women's experiences and women's points of view would have gained an unprecedented focus. But so far, the Internet revolution has only increased the cultural exposition of women's bodies as passive objects in advertising, fashion, and film.

It is possible to go beyond criticism of misogynistic Western culture and approach the cultural absence of pregnancy from a different angle. Inspired by structuralist anthropology, we could describe the pregnant body as disturbing. It is disturbing because it deviates from the normal body, which by definition belongs to *one* person. The pregnant body defies this; it is different, out of the ordinary, ambiguous, and therefore culturally embarrassing and often ignored. An important argument in structuralist anthropology (Lévi-Strauss 1963, Douglas 1966, Ortner 1973) is the claim that cultures cannot withstand ambiguity and will typically try to place ambiguous phenomena into a binary structure or else exclude them by making them sacred or taboo. Writing about primitive (oral) culture, Claude Lévi-Strauss argued that every culture has a classificatory system based on opposites (left/right, cold/hot, dark/light). This dualism conditions our thought and inspires myths, i.e. stories that explain cultural categories. Myths are stories we tell in order to make sense of our lives, and the driving force behind them is the dualism of culture and language, which "always progresses from the awareness of oppositions towards their resolution" (Lévi-Strauss 1963: 224). If transposed to more familiar terrain, we can easily find confirmation of this in Christian theology, where those articles of faith that do not easily fit into the system attract more attention. Take, for instance, the Christian doctrine of the incarnation, which states the logical impossibility that Christ was both a man and God. The bishops' council at Nicaea (325) first tackled the problem by declaring the dogma of Jesus' double nature: true God and true man. They seemingly created a synthesis, but in fact only established a contradiction to be a truth. Since the dogma did not in fact resolve the contradiction, it continues to be food for thought for Christian theologians. Similarly ambiguous is the Virgin Birth – an improbable and self-contradictory event – which has continued to intrigue and fascinate Christians and which has secured for the mother of Christ a central position in Christian devotion.

In addition to the most clear-cut categories (e.g. life/death, light/darkness), every culture must tackle a number of inherently ambiguous categories. And some phenomena resist resolution, e.g. the pregnant body which is neither one nor two, neither you nor me. According to Lévi-Strauss' theory, phenomena which do not fit into the prevalent system of binary oppositions function as blind spots in the system. They draw attention to themselves, create embarrassment, silence, and protest. That is why the ambiguous invites reflection and is, as Lévi-Strauss put it, food for thought. The British anthropologist Mary Douglas has a different take on the things that fall outside of the cultural pattern of categorization. Since no system can encompass all phenomena, there will always be a residual of concepts and objects that do not fit, anomalies which threaten the system of meaning. To illustrate her point, Douglas relates E.E. Evans-Pritchard's story of how the Nuer deal with "monstrous birth". They define them as "baby hippopotamuses, accidentally born to humans and, *with this labelling*, the appropriate action is clear. They gently lay them in the river where they belong" (Douglas 1966: 39, my italics).

When transposed to contemporary abortion debates, we can see the importance of labelling. While neo-conservative Christians refer to "the unborn child" and place it within the system of divine creation, liberals (Christians as well as secularists) label it as a foetus and appeal to human rights in support of a woman's right to choose.

Lévi-Strauss claimed that cultural categories are expressed in myths. In this context, the concept of myth must be understood not as a specific literary genre, but as a key story, a story – long or short, fiction or fact – which is known to everyone in a given culture. Elaborating on this line of thinking, American anthropologist Sherry Ortner argues that stories (myths) may be effective expressions of shared ideas and values when they contain certain key symbols. Key symbols are, like any element of language, culturally specific and must be studied in context (Ortner 1973). According to Ortner, key symbols provide a possible point of entry into invisible, implicit, and taken-for-granted cultural values. In this book, I approach the pregnant body as such a key symbol. Informed by structuralist anthropology, we may say that pregnancy is a disturbing phenomenon because it breaks the pattern which organizes the world into binary structures (e.g. hot/cold, old/young, cooked/raw, white/black, man/woman). But this is also why it merits attention. Because pregnancy does not fit into a binary structure, it offers a glimpse into the deepest ideas and values which inform our culture. Reflecting on gender relations, Ortner observes that every known culture gives women a subordinate position. "What could there be in the generalized structure and conditions of existence, common to every culture, that would lead every culture to place a lower value upon women?", she asks (Ortner 1974: 71). It seems odd to her that women, who literally carry the survival of our species, are not valued as equals to men. Ortner's answer is biology: Menstruation, pregnancy, and lactation associate women with their bodily functions, and hence to nature. But we need culture, skills, and intelligence to survive, and that is why (male) skills are more highly valued. Yes, human existence relies on nature – and any species needs offspring in order to survive – but we value culture more. And when Christianity teaches that God made Adam the custodian of the earth and responsible for "all living things", this is what underpins the hierarchical relation between man and woman in the Christian tradition and defines it as one of dominance and subordination. Moreover, the relationship was regarded as static and biologically founded in natural body functions; it designated the female as nurturing and caring, and associated her with home and family life. However, scientific inventions undermined traditional notions and made the biological arguments largely irrelevant. When the contraceptive pill regulates female fertility and the morning-after pill allows women to enjoy their sexuality without paying for the consequences with their life, we may say that culture has changed nature and made women structurally equal to men. Antiquity defined the child and the pregnant woman as the father's property. Christianity placed the holy child in the centre and introduced the notion that children were a gift from God. During the Enlightenment, pregnancy became a function of the female body, and modernity approached pregnancy and birth as medical conditions. To these understandings we must now add the contemporary idea that the unborn child is an individual with human rights. All of these ideas, however, leave the pregnant woman in a dire situation. Even in contemporary discourse, pregnant women are not regarded as autonomous selves, but are instead subjected to their biological condition.

Notes

1 Gender and biological perspectives come together in contemporary American religious studies of women's experience (Saracino 2011) and women as religious agents (Hill Fletcher 2013).
2 All dates cited in this book are CE unless otherwise indicated.

2

PATTERNS OF MEANING
Pregnancy in late antiquity

In the Graeco-Roman world of late antiquity (200–500), Christianity gradually developed into a dominant religion. Although the Christian message broke radically with the ancient Graeco-Roman world view, the change did not take place as a radical conversion, but rather as a reorientation and a shift of scenery. The influence of the Graeco-Roman context on early Christianity is hard to measure. In one area in particular, traditional ideas were particularly influential, namely, in the conceptualization of the human being (anthropology). Christianity brought new ideas about the meaning of life, but apart from notions such as sin and resurrection it had little to add to taken-for-granted ideas about sexuality and the human body. As Peter Brown puts it: "Like long-familiar music, the *idées recues* of the ancient world filled the minds of the educated Christians when they, in their turn, came to write on marriage and on sexual desire" (Brown 1988: 9).

Theories about how human procreation takes place are inevitably framed by biological assumptions about the functioning of the human body. Christianity is no exception, and the biological models which informed early Christianity derived from its Graeco-Roman context. According to ancient Greek thought, human generation was no different from the rest of nature. Ancient Greece was an agrarian society: The mother's womb was understood as a parallel to the earth, and the father's semen was like the seeds which the farmer spread on the soil (Dean-Jones 1994). Seeds and fertility, which we think about as metaphors, were used as descriptive terms in antiquity. Life resided with the father. It was his seed that produced the offspring, and the mother was simply a passive receptacle. Although her menstrual blood served as building material for the foetus' body and provided the nutrition which allowed it to grow, the mother's importance was regarded as being inferior to that of the father. She simply provided passive matter and served as host for the foetus. It was the man's semen that brought life.

These ideas were refined and developed by Aristotle (384–322 BCE), whose theory of human procreation was subsequently included in the theological reflections of Christianity. In fact, it was Aristotle's theory that provided the logical basis for the dogma of Original Sin. According to Aristotle, the father was the creator because his semen contained the human *eidos*, the idea of the human being (Gilhus et al 2009: 25). The child was a replica of the father and consequently belonged to him. The mother's role was subordinate and instrumental. She served as an instrument for male proliferation.

Aristotle used the term 'soul' to designate the creative faculty of the male seed: "(I)t is the soul which is the cause and first principle of life … Qualitative change, also, and growth are due to the soul" (*De anima* II, 415b, 8). It is worth noting

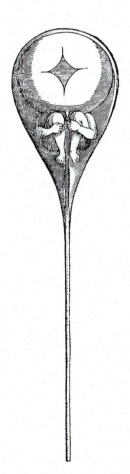

FIGURE 2.1 The miniature human inside the sperm. Drawing by N. Hartsoeker, *Essay de dioptrique*, 1694. © Wellcome Library, London. Wellcome Images/ Wikimedia Commons.

that Aristotle did *not* associate the soul with the spiritual realm. To Aristotle, the soul (*anima*) was the sum of mental faculties and the life principle which ensured that the seed of a man resulted in a human being. It should also be noted that Aristotle saw the foetus as a *potential* human being – a being in the process of becoming, of realizing its proper form, which it received from its father. It was the soul which directed the process in which the foetus acquired its human form, according to Aristotle. This male-oriented theory posed a problem: If the child was a replica of the father, how could a man create a daughter, i.e. a creature which is unlike him? Aristotle's answer was that the female was an undeveloped male. A daughter was a failed son due to unfortunate circumstances during pregnancy. It was the mother's fault:

> Women who are with child should be careful of themselves; they should take exercise and have a nourishing diet. The first of these prescriptions the leg-islator will easily carry into effect by requiring that they shall take a walk daily to some temple, where they can worship the gods who preside over birth. Their minds, however, unlike their bodies, they ought to keep quiet, for the offspring derive their natures from their mothers as plants from the earth.
>
> *(Aristotle, Politics, 7, 16)*

In a similar manner, the Greeks explained why a child could resemble the mother. It was because the mother's body left its imprint on the child during the pregnancy. If a child looked like its mother, it was a reminder of the pregnancy. These ideas reflected the subordinate position of women in antiquity's patriarchal society. A woman was for all practical purposes dependent on men and was considered weak and irrational. However, men and women shared a common humanity even if women were regarded as imperfect men, more sensitive, and less rational. Women had the same spiritual qualities as men – only to a lesser extent. A similar view of gender relations was also present in early Christianity.

But there was also another, competing theory of procreation in late antiquity. It received little attention from theological authorities, but it dominated medical practice, where it influenced common ideas about health and sexuality far into the modern era. Its most important exponent was a Greek medical scientist by the name of Claudius Galenus, who is often referred to by scholars as Galen (129–210). He was a uniquely influential follower of the Hippocratic tradition, who informed Western medicine with a theoretical framework and practice from antiquity through the middle ages to modern times (Dean-Jones 1994). On this note, it is also possible to argue that Hippocratic understandings inspire much of the alternative medical practices and contemporary so-called 'new' religious ideas about the human being (Hunt 2003). In the present context, Galen's view on sexuality and procreation is particularly interesting. Unlike theological and phi-losophical theories, Galen's theory gives the mother an active role. Remaining a kind of popular undercurrent in European folk tradition, Galen's theory did not influence Christian theology directly, but it did somehow exist undisturbed in the wider cultural context of popular Christianity.

Galen challenged Aristotle's theory of human sexuality and procreation in several respects, the most important being that he maintained that women, like men, emit seed and have orgasm. Galen belonged to the Hippocratic tradition and understood the body in terms of temperature, moisture and balance between the four basic elements: fire, water, earth and air. According to this theory orgasm was a necessary precondition of procreation for the female as well as the male. For Galen orgasm was not primarily a sign of sexual pleasure or fulfilment. It was a sign that the body produced enough heat, and heat was necessary because heat produced during intercourse would "cause the finest parts of the blood to be concocted into semen" (Laqueur 1987: 4). Heat was a key element in any transformation, and in order to be able to procreate, the male and the female body must produce sufficient heat to allow a transformation of one kind of matter (body fluids) into another (seed). Undoubtedly, this had an important impact on sexual practice among ordinary people, as is illustrated by the fact that Galen's link between female orgasm and procreation remained an unquestioned truth in European popular culture (Darmon 1977).

In Galen's model of the body, the male and female reproductive organs have parallel functions. Thus, in European folk culture the female reproductive organ was understood as an inverted male organ. While the latter was so hot and strong that it had to remain outside the torso in order to keep cool, the female organ was interior because it needed the heat from other organs. But the parallelism did not stop there. Like the male organ, the female organ also produced seed during orgasm, which was emitted in the womb, where it intermingled with the male seed. According to Galen, the mother's seed was not different from the father's in form and function, and both parents contributed to the body as well as the soul or mind of the child. However, the female seed was weaker and contributed to a lesser extent than the male seed (De Renzi 2004: 208). According to this model, then, the foetus was the joint product of active participation from the mother as well as the father.

Why did official Christianity ignore Galen? The simple answer is that his medical theory was incompatible with Christian values: not because it seemed to give women a more active role in procreation, but because it was based on a strictly materialistic understanding of procreation. To him, the human being was a physical reality, as was its soul, which he located in the brain. The soul was part and parcel of the body, and it lived and died along with it (Kusukawa 2004a: 6). To Galen, the soul developed together with the rest of the body during its time in the womb. And because the soul was able to grow, it too was also subject to decay and death like the rest of the body. Such a materialistic understanding was incompatible with Christian notions. Galen's theory of procreation was overlooked by theologians and had little impact on official Christian teachings. In fact, it would seem that it existed side by side with official views in some kind of peaceful division of labour between Christian theory and medical practice. Even though normative Christian teachings were underpinned by elaborate theological arguments and moral deliberations, they did not give rise to actual medical practices. In practice, then, it was Galen's techniques that were used by physicians, but in theory, Christian ideas reigned.

The Graeco-Roman culture of late antiquity was permeated by dualism: Male was opposed to female, and spirit was opposed to matter. The entire world was ordered in binary oppositions within a hierarchical order. The split between spirit and matter was at the core of the system and was also reflected in the relation between man and woman: Man was associated with spirit and rationality, whereas woman was associated with matter and death. These ideas and values were expressed socially in the patriarchal system which defined women as structurally subordinate to men. The societies of late antiquity were hierarchical, with strict divisions between social groups. And within each social group – citizens, slaves, artisans, farmers, etc. – women were subordinate to men. In ancient Athens, women were not recognized as citizens and were banned from taking part in public life. They had no independent status but belonged to male households – under the control of their fathers and then their husbands (Songe-Møller 1989, Vernant 1982).

This was patriarchy in its purest form. Women remained in a subordinate position throughout their lives: first as daughters to their fathers and then as wives to their husbands. Thus, when they married, they acquired a similar status in law to that of their own daughters. The male head of the family was the master, and women and children were for all practical purposes his property. It should be noted that this description applies to the elite free citizens of Athens. There is, however, no reason to think that the subordinate position of women was less prominent among the slaves or in the lower strata of Athenian society. Relations between men and women across the class divide were regulated according to social hierarchical concerns. In fact, women of the elite citizen class were socially higher and therefore in a position of dominance over men from the lower strata of society. It should also be noted that where slaves were concerned, free women were in a position of absolute dominance.

The legacy of Graeco-Roman patriarchy was integrated into Christian thought from the start. There are different theories about patriarchy and the systematic subordination of women. Sherry Ortner sees it as a universal trait and explains it as a reflection of women's closer relation to bodily processes (e.g. menstruation, pregnancy). In addition to these cultural ideas, the physical restraint on women's activities following multiple pregnancies and lactation also plays its part. Viewed like this, it is hardly a coincidence that the demand for equal rights and political and economic power for women coincided with the invention of modern contraception devices in the twentieth century.

The Greek model of procreation was perfectly tailored to the patriarchal system, where the wife was an instrument in the service of her husband. The *paterfamilias* had responsibility for his household – including his servants and slaves – and ruled over it. The *paterfamilias* also decided whether a newborn child should live or die. Abortion as well as infanticide were widely practiced in antiquity, and many Greek and Roman writers found the Jewish practice of prohibiting infanticide and accepting all children born into the community to be quite strange (Wiedemann 1989: 37). The Greek model of procreation legitimized infanticide. Since the male was the sole progenitor of his offspring, it followed from this that he had ownership of and responsibility for the foetus as well. Roman society was not altogether misogynistic; it did in fact allow women to own property and function as *patresfamilias* in the absence of a male head – although this was indeed an unusual situation, and women's '*paterfamilias*' powers were limited. More interesting in the present context is the fact that her authority did not include the children who remained the responsibility of the father's family (Saller 1999: 188). A similar limitation can be seen in the rules concerning Roman citizenship. It was normally transferred from father to child, but if the mother was unmarried, the child would receive the mother's status – as free citizen or slave. It was only paternal citizenship that could provide the child with full citizen status. Children of unmarried mothers could not inherit property or become a *paterfamilias* in their own right. Yan Thomas explains this by referring to the Roman idea that in the absence of a (known) father, the child was literally rootless. The word 'root' should be understood literally as the family's origins in the soil (*autokefal*). According to this idea, man originated from the soil and sexual procreation was only introduced with the arrival of women. This belief remained a tenet of Greek and Roman culture as illustrated in the notion that children born to an unmarried woman did not belong to a lineage; therefore, without real parentage, "the child who has no legal father derives his primary origin from his mother, and this origin is counted from the day he comes into the world" (Thomas 1992: 125–26).

A fatherless child was in a dead-end situation, so to speak. Cut-off from his unknown or unacknowledged father, fatherless children were regarded as persons without physical origins. Deprived of a male progenitor, the child of an unmarried mother was unable, not physically but by law, to create his own lineage. Under normal circumstances, a male child would be given citizenship in the family's city of origin counting backwards from father to grandfather and so on, going as far back in time as possible in an effort to trace the lineage. In order to become a fully recognized citizen, a man literally had to be able to trace his family roots. Citizenship could be transmitted by a free unmarried mother to her fatherless child, but said citizenship would apply not to her hometown but to the city in which her child was born. This makes perfect sense when one takes the prevailing theories of procreation into account. Since the child of an unmarried mother was *not* the offspring of her father, it had no roots in its mother's family home. But these were exceptions. The bulk of these legal provisions which regulated the status of children were based on taken-for-granted ideas about procreation which reflected the social and legal superiority of men.

A similar family model explains an old Norse tradition: A newborn child was accepted as a child of the family through the 'kneeing' or knee-seating ceremony, where the father took the newborn child in his lap and declared it to be his son or daughter (as the case may be). The ceremony was obligatory and functioned as a final stage of the birth process. Interestingly, the same ceremony was used in connection with adoption. If the ceremony was not performed, it was equivalent to a death sentence: The child would be killed or left to die. This was the other side of the *paterfamilias* position. Else Mundal argues that it is unlikely that the *paterfamilias* himself would perform infanticide, since the word used in the oldest Christian laws in Norway (*maðr*) does not necessarily refer to a man (Mundal 1989). Taking the legal context into consideration, the word should be translated as 'someone', she claims. On this basis, Mundal argues that anyone in the household – husband, wife, or slave – could be the one who actually had to perform the infanticide and carry the newborn child out of the house and into the forest, where it would be left to die. Mundal also points out that the stipulated penalty in Christian law, which criminalized the Norse practice was five hundred times higher for the head of the household than for other members of the household in the case of a guilty verdict. Thus, the law reflected the patriarchal system by giving the head of the household the main responsibility for infanticide – or as Mundal puts it: "The husband was regarded as the main suspect and held to be the person responsible for infanticide" (Mundal 1989: 123, my translation).

The strict prohibitions against infanticide that were introduced into Norse society by Christian law meant a restriction of the *paterfamilias*' authority, since he was no longer allowed to decide over life and death in his own household. A passage from Aristotle's *Politics* leaves no doubt that a similar custom existed in Greece: "As to the exposure and rearing of children, let there be a law that no deformed child shall live" (*Politics* 7, 16). Apart from the brutality of such customs, it is worth noting that this form of infanticide which Aristotle refers to as 'exposure', and Nordic sources call '*barneutbæring*' (lit. "bring the child outside"), was structurally opposed to the kneeing ceremony, which Onians defines as an Indo-European custom: "A child was placed upon the knee of his father or foster father as a sign that he was acknowledged" (Onians 1988: 175). As mentioned above, adoption was a common practice in pre-modern agrarian societies. Structurally, it corresponded to the kneeing ceremony, which served as the final, legal part of pregnancy and birth, and which put the father's stamp on the entire process.

In his etymological explanation of the kneeing ceremony, Onians traces the custom back to the idea that the knees and thighs were the seats of life. Knee, *genu* in Latin and *genou* in French, has the same root as *genus* (Latin, birth) and *genitalis* (Latin, fruitful), he claims, and 'knee' is interchangeable with the term for 'generation' in many Indo-European languages: "I suggest, with the name they bear witness that the knee was thought in some way to be the seat of paternity, of life and generative power, unthinkable though that may seem to us" (Onians 1988: 175). However, tracing the meaning of the reproductive organs (*genitalia*) to the life force in the bone marrow and linking this to Roman house gods (*genii*) tell us little about the relation between parents and children. Onians' etymological explanations notwithstanding, his main thesis is fruitful: that the ideas associated with the body inform the way we act and the way we understand the human condition.

Dualism was a pertinent feature of ancient Greek thought; male was defined as the opposite of female; the body was defined as the opposite of the mind; and human was seen as the opposite of animal. These dichotomies were again organized into a hierarchy of moral values, where woman was subordinate to man, the body was subordinate to the mind, and animal was subordinate to human. Gilhus calls this a rigid system which lacked a middle ground (Gilhus 2006: 40). There simply was no room for ambiguity, and the system was therefore rigid and unable to handle difference except by radical separation or exclusion. At the centre of the Greek view of man was an idea of the male as the perfect human and an idea of the woman as a deviation from this norm (Songe-Møller 2002). There was one standard or norm for humans, and it was male. As a consequence, the female was "wrong" and therefore had to be segregated and kept away from public life. All positive values were attached to the male, the most important being the capacity for rational thinking. Man was closely associated with the realm of ideas, whereas woman was closely associated with irrationality, emotions, death, and decay.

The cultural codes of the Graeco-Roman world were by and large adopted and integrated into Christianity, notably in the continuity of the norms and rules that regulated gender relations. In spite of the Christian emphasis on the equality of man and woman when it comes to salvation, in this world patriarchy continued uninterrupted (Børresen 1995). This discrepancy between the real and the ideal was a feature of early Christianity, as Antoinette Clark Wire shows in her analysis of the congregation in Corinth (Wire 1990). In a historical analysis of Paul's rhetoric, Wire focuses on the role of a special category of religiously active women and female prophets, and paints a nuanced picture of the dialectic of Paul's Hellenistic-Jewish teachings and how they were received in Corinth. She then reconstructs Paul's audience – as well as their views and norms – arguing that his "persuasion is insistent and intense" and that he is not confirming the norms of the Corinthians, but rather "struggling for their assent" (Wire 1990: 9). Paul's letter to the Corinthians includes a number of patriarchal measures to limit women's participation in public life: "Women should be silent in the churches. For they are not permitted to speak, but should be subordinate, as the law also says. If there is anything they desire to know, let them ask their husbands at home. For it is shameful for a woman to speak in church" (1 Corinthians 14:34–35). According to Wire, Paul's emphasis on female subordination shows that these norms were indeed not traditionally adhered to by the Corinthians. In fact, Wire maintains that the first Christian congregations in Corinth practiced an egalitarian religion. Feminist church historians have pointed out that the first Christians radically broke with these patriarchal norms, arguing that several institutional functions were open to women (Schüssler Fiorenza 1983). But as soon as the institutionalization process of Christianity was under way, male dominance was in place (Esler 1994). In a radical critique of patriarchy, feminist theologian Elisabeth Schüssler Fiorenza maintains that Christian institutional religion has enforced gender models and power structures which are historical constructs and which go against the grain of the Christian message:

> Reproducing societal patriarchy, Christian religious patriarchy has defined not only women but all subjugated peoples and races as "the Other", as "nature" to be exploited and dominated by powerful men. Obedience, economic dependence, and sexual control are still sustaining forces of societal and ecclesiastical patriarchy.
>
> *(Schüssler Fiorenza 1992: 203)*

Criticizing this "power of dominance", Schüssler Fiorenza claims that traditional dichotomies reproduce and sustain the system of patriarchal power. Dualism is based on a logic of radical exclusion of "either/or", she argues – either man or woman, human or animal, slave or free, superior or inferior. Schüssler Fiorenza's ideal church is an egalitarian community, an 'ekklesia of women', which "empowers and invigorates life" and which she proposes as an alternative to a male-dominated church system which she refers to as 'kyricalism' (Schüssler Fiorenza 1992: 192). Christianity is imbued with dualism – man/woman, good/evil, man/animal – which "has mediated ancient patterns of patriarchal submission". Writing with an emancipatory zeal, Schüssler Fiorenza analyzes patriarchy as the source of male power in the Catholic Church. She contends that there is no alternative but to abolish the culture of dominance within institutional Christianity (kyricalism) and replace it with a radical democratic church (ekklesia of women). This utopian ideal aside, the patriarchal power structure of Graeco-Roman antiquity has been preserved within organized Christianity. In tune with the structural dualism of Graeco-Roman culture, the Christian scriptures emphasize male dominance and female subordination, e.g. the apostle Paul's rules of conduct for women:

> But I want you to understand that Christ is the head of every man, and the husband is the head of his wife, and God is the head of Christ ... For if a woman will not veil herself, then she should cut off her hair; but if it is disgraceful for a woman to have her hair cut off or to be shaved, she should wear a veil ... For a man ought not to have his head veiled, since he is the image and reflection of God; but woman is the reflection of man. Indeed, man was not made from woman, but woman from man. Neither was man created for the sake of woman, but woman for the sake of man.
>
> *(1 Corinthians 11:3,6–9)*

These passages illustrate how women were assigned a subordinate position in Paul's hierarchical world; and their subordinate status would eventually become official Church teaching. Effectively excluding Christian women from taking part in official church business (and public life), Christianity continued the patriarchal tradition.

The categorical distinctions between man and woman, matter and spirit, and flesh and soul had a huge impact on the Christian conceptualization of the human being, especially its moral teachings on and attitudes towards sexuality. The human body was an ambiguous entity: part holy – destined for resurrection and eternal life – and part sinful – in need of strong measures to control its natural drives, especially sexuality. Seen from a Christian point of view, the pregnant female body was a body in open defiance of ascetic ideals and a symbol of life as well as sin. Ironically, but perfectly understandable from Lévi-Strauss' observation that cultural ideas are organized as binary structures which are necessarily incomplete and are therefore "good to think" (Lévi-Strauss 1963, 1969), Mother Mary became the focal point of early Christian popular culture. Her ambiguous status as woman and Mother of God, human and holy, a mother but also a virgin, did not fit and therefore held people's imagination. A similar case could be made for sexual abstinence and celibacy, which became a core issue in moral theology even though the majority of Christians lived in marriage and motherhood and the birth of Christ were central motifs in the foundational story of Christianity.

Christian conceptions of the human body found an outlet in asceticism as expressed in clerical celibacy and monastic institutions. The body was both feared and valued, a fact well illustrated by Saint Antonius, who died in 356 and who allegedly had thousands of followers visit him in his lonely abode in the Egyptian desert. By the end of antiquity, both male and female ascetics lived secluded lives in religious contemplation after having renounced pleasure. Asceticism was an option for the religious virtuosi, who could withdraw from the ways of the world and dedicate their lives to Christ. But asceticism was countered by another aspect of Christian faith, most notably by the positive valuation of Christ's body as the centre of devotion, which was expressed symbolically in the Eucharist and aesthetically in the veneration of sculptures and paintings of the crucified messiah. Christian ideas about the body were expressed in two ways: in the dogma of the Incarnation and in the doctrine of bodily resurrection after death. Both ideas were equally hard to grasp for people who were socialized into the Graeco-Roman culture and world view. Christianity upset old distinctions and cut across established categories. It broke with the established body/soul dichotomy and was received with incredulity by most people: "When they heard of the resurrection of the dead, some scoffed; but others said, 'We will hear you again about this'. At that point Paul left them" (Acts 17:32). But Christian attitudes towards the body were also ambiguous.

Ascetic techniques and self-imposed suffering ensured that the mystic came closer to God and experienced a totally self-negating union with God, *unio mystica* (James 1997). Another aspect of the Christian attitude towards the body found expression in the cult of saints, where the dead bodies of saints were ascribed spiritual

worth and served as intermediaries between man and God (Brown 1988, Weinstein and Bell 1982). Holy men and women attracted devotees already in the
fourth century, and there is evidence that their bodies were venerated (Brown
1988). The doctrine of sainthood implied that each Christian was potentially a
saint, but official Church recognition was restricted to dead saints because it was
only *after* death that the saint's body attained perfection and became sacred. The
logic which accounted for this transformation was based on the notion that the
saint's body was sanctified by his or her perfect moral life. Hence, the cult of
saints illustrates the idea that there was an intrinsic link between body and soul.
These ideas and practices were incompatible with the Greek world view, where
the young, male body was venerated for its beauty, but did not have an intrinsic
worth. On the contrary, the body was a living thing, a subject of growth and
decay and ultimately death (Kuriyama 1999). Seen from this angle, the Christian
veneration of the body appeared contradictory.

According to Greek tradition, all bodies, whether vegetative, animal, or human,
were doomed to decay and death. The only entity that could 'survive' was the
immaterial, namely, the soul. Unlike Christianity, which held that the body and
soul have the same ontological status because both were created by God, Greek
tradition regarded the soul as infinitely more valuable than the body. It was the soul
which had ultimate value: It was the soul which in the last instance distinguished
man from other beings. It constituted the essence of man, and unlike the body it
was not subject to decay and death. Aristotle formulated the Greek view in terms of
a clear subordination of the body to the soul: "All the natural bodies are instruments
of the soul: and this is true for the bodies of plants as those of animals, showing
that all exist for the sake of the soul" (*De anima* II, 415b, 8). Despite these overwhelming discrepancies, early Christian theology related actively to the Greek body/
soul dualism. Put bluntly, we may say that Christian theologians appropriated
Greek concepts and put them to their own use. Where the body/soul dualism
was concerned, body and soul remained opposites, but the opposition was subsumed under God, so to speak – first by defining man, body, and soul as God's
creation, and second by the dogma of Bodily Resurrection. Each person was
therefore a unity of body and soul, as expressed in the story of man's creation, in
which God first forms the body and then gives the body life: "Then the LORD
God formed man from the dust of the ground, and breathed into his nostrils the
breath of life; and the man became a living being" (Genesis 2:7). The story tells
about the perfect beginning before Adam and Eve committed sin and were
thrown out of Paradise. In this state of bliss, there was peace and harmony
between the spiritual and material realms. But as soon as sin entered, the harmony
was broken. Sin destroyed the unity and made life a battle within each person.
Life was a fight between spirit and matter, rationality and desire, high morals and
lowly instincts. According to Christian doctrine, the harmony could only be
restored by salvation. Salvation would bridge the gap between body and soul and
restore all men to their perfect form – as they were in the moment of creation.

The cult of the saints developed this new teaching further by allowing for dead human bodies to be sanctified.

In Christianity, the soul was an entity directly associated with God and created in his image: "Then God said, 'Let us make humankind in our image, according to our likeness; and let them have dominion over the fish of the sea, and over the birds of the air, and over the cattle, and over all the wild animals of the earth, and over every creeping thing that creeps upon the earth'" (Genesis 1:26). From this text, we see that godlikeness was embedded in the body as well as the soul, but in practice the soul gained the upper hand and became the godlike aspect of the human being. We see it, as mentioned earlier, in asceticism. Although theologically based on the idea that body and soul constitute a unity, the manner in which a person becomes holy was as an effect of spiritual and moral purity, on the one hand, and denial of bodily desires on the other. Nevertheless, the unity of the person was maintained by the unity of body and soul, and expressed in the dogma of Bodily Resurrection: "For if the dead are not raised, then Christ has not been raised. If Christ has not been raised, your faith is futile and you are still in your sins. Then those also who have died in Christ have perished" (1 Corinthians 15:16–18). It promised the reconstitution of the individual, the reunion of *this* body and *this* soul. Thus, Christianity understood death as a temporary separation of body and soul in open defiance of Graeco-Roman thought. We may say that Christianity tried to surpass the entire problem of death by defining it as a temporary condition, an intermediary state between life on earth and eternity.

Although the dogma of Bodily Resurrection was clearly incompatible with the devaluation of the body in Greek dualism, the hierarchy between spirit and matter, and soul and body persisted, as is illustrated by the ascetic practice of monks and nuns who tormented the body for the benefit of the soul. By and large, the ascetic tradition – from extreme masochistic flagellation rituals to abstinence from excessive food and drink – ensured that the Christian body remained associated with the negative. Impurity and decay remained associated with the body – especially with the female body. Thus, the Greek body/soul dichotomy survived in the new Christian ideas and practices. One such idea was the relation between man and woman. As mentioned earlier, patriarchy continued uninterruptedly after Christianity became the dominant religion of the Graeco-Roman world. But Christianity represented continuity in other respects as well, as patriarchy held sway and the social hierarchy and the subordination of women continued – even though man and woman had the equal opportunity to be saved: The Church found a compromise and postponed equality to the afterlife. Hence, gender equality did not apply to life here and now. Nevertheless, on an individual level Christianity did represent a positive change for women, since the doctrine of equality before God allowed them to develop a new sense of self-esteem:

> Although Christianity did not end sexual discrimination in the late Roman Empire, it did offer women the opportunity to regard themselves as

> independent personalities rather than somebody's daughter, wife or mother. According to the Acts of the Apostles, it enabled women to develop self-esteem as spiritual beings who possessed the same potential for moral perfection as men.
>
> *(Wemple 1992: 172)*

Religion does not exist in a vacuum. When Christianity became a world religion, it happened within the confines of the Graeco-Roman world. Graeco-Roman society was (for the most part) an agrarian society, and agriculture provided the most readily understood metaphors with which to express ideas about life, spirit, body, and death. It was also a society without a monotheistic deity or a myth of a God who created the world with men and women with a free will. Although humans were inferior to the ancient gods, there was no sense of sin and final judgement. Such ideas were introduced into the Graeco-Roman world by Christianity, which also brought new ideas about the relation between man and woman, and the meaning and purpose of human life. The spiritual equality of all human beings was potentially a revolutionary force. But in practice, it was kept at bay and transformed into the image of Christian patriarchy in the process. Or to paraphrase Elisabeth Schüssler Fiorenza, the Church became a kyriarchy; it sided with the dominant power and legitimized the hierarchical order of society (Schüssler Fiorenza 1992).

3

CHRISTIAN PROCREATION ACCORDING TO AUGUSTINE

The basic tenets of Christian doctrine were developed in late antiquity, the period from 200 to 500. Christianity's inculturation into Graeco-Roman culture was a complex process which changed the former as well as the latter. The Christian message was framed and interpreted with Graeco-Roman concepts and ideas, and the evolution of Christian norms and beliefs changed attitudes and practices. In his exposition of the body in early Christianity, Peter Brown argues against the idea that Christianity introduced a set of negative attitudes towards bodily pleasures into a hedonistic culture which valued sex and celebrated gluttony: "Pagans and Christians alike, the upper classes of the Roman Empire in its last centuries lived by a code of sexual restraint and public decorum that they liked to think of as continuous with the virile austerity of archaic Rome" (Brown 1988: 21–22). The most important among Christian thinkers in this period was Augustine of Hippo (354–420). Best known for the doctrine of Original Sin, he linked Christianity with Greek thought and incorporated Greek dualism into the Christian conception of man. He also prepared the ground for the development of Christian monasticism with its valuation of celibacy and ascetic practices.

When Augustine converted to Christianity in Milan in 387 at the age of 32, he also gave up the family life he had been living for 15 years with his concubine and their son. He spent the greater part of this period living in Italy and teaching rhetoric, with his Christian mother Monica sharing his house. She died in 387, the same year that Augustine converted, and two years later his son Adeodatus died at the age of 18. It was more or less at this time that Augustine decided to live as a celibate.[1] His impact on Christian theology was vast and reflected his own rich life: a philosopher born and raised in Carthage, North Africa, trained in Greek thought, teacher of rhetoric in Milan, and a Manichean (member of a sect teaching strict dualism) before he converted to Christianity at the age of 32, spending the rest of his life as a bishop in Hippo (in today's Tunisia). He was a prolific writer of theological texts and penned an acclaimed autobiography; after his death, he was venerated as a saint and celebrated as one of the main teachers of Christian theology. His position in Catholic theology is symbolically expressed by his title as *doctor ecclesia*, and he is counted among the four eminent Doctors of the Church (along with Ambrose, Jerome, and Gregory the Great). Augustine holds an equally exceptional position in Protestant theology as an indisputable authority. A philosopher converted to neoplatonic Christianity, with a dualistic world view relying on dichotomies such as good/evil, light/darkness, and sin/eternal bliss, Augustine epitomized Europe's transition from antiquity to Christianity.

Central to Augustine's teaching was the biblical tale of how Adam and Eve ate the forbidden fruit and how they were subsequently expelled from Eden because of their disobedience: "The woman said to the serpent, 'We may eat of the fruit of the trees in the garden'; but God said, 'You shall not eat of the fruit of the tree that is in the middle of the garden, nor shall you touch it, or you shall die'" (Genesis 3:2–3). The same prohibition, in almost the same words, was given to Adam in the previous chapter of Genesis, leaving no doubt about its importance: "And the Lord God commanded the man, 'You may freely eat of every tree of the garden; but of the tree of the knowledge of good and evil you shall not eat, for in the day that you eat of it you shall die'" (Genesis 2:16–17). To Augustine, the main point was not God's rage, however, but its consequences: Sin changed the inner constitution of Adam and Eve so fundamentally that their nature was transformed – hence Augustine's concept of Original Sin. It was this faulty nature, according to Augustine, that was transmitted via Adam's seed to all future generations. His explanation of how and why Adam's sin was transmitted relied on a biological theory of procreation. Based on the biological knowledge available to him, Augustine built his theory on the assertion that the child is a true copy of its father: "The seminal reason of the child dwells with the seed of the father, as the causal reasons of all beings exist from the moment of creation" (Børresen 1995: 43). Thus, Adam was literally the prototypical man (Børresen 1968: 131). The logic was something like this: Since Adam's part in Original Sin made him imperfect, his seed was automatically affected and the imperfection passed on to his son, and so on. This was Original Sin, according to Augustine: Adam's seed was the transmitter, and sexual orgasm was the mechanism through which it spread. It was Adam (not Eve) who was responsible for the human condition. His seed contained the procreative power, and therefore it was male desire which was ultimately responsible for transmitting this sinful human nature to each new human being.

Augustine is associated with a negative attitude towards sexuality, but in his writings he refers to human procreation as *bonum originale*, original good. It was good because it served a divine purpose, allowing man to fulfill God's command to multiply: "God blessed them, and God said to them, 'Be fruitful and multiply, and fill the earth and subdue it; and have dominion over the fish of the sea and over the birds of the air and over every living thing that moves upon the earth'" (Genesis 1:28). But procreation became fundamentally problematic when Original Sin changed everything and Adam's seed became the means by which it was transmitted to the entire human race. Building on the biological theories of antiquity, Augustine made his own adjustments by assigning an active role to God. In his model, the male generative power was not contained entirely in the semen; it also relied on God's direct participation in every act of generation, which was a manifestation of divine creativity (Børresen 1995: 41). Referring to 1 Corinthians 3:7, "So neither the one who plants nor the one who waters is anything, but only God, who gives the growth", Augustine shows that the creative source is God alone.

Despite his valorization of procreation, Augustine was sceptical of its moral effects. In his theological reflections, he describes the male sexual drive as an insatiable and uncontrollable desire for the female body, an instinctive force or primal power which escaped attempts at rational control. Hence, it should be shunned like the plague, he advised, except when put to use in procreation. In Augustine's view, all passions were suspect because they disturbed rational thinking, created emotional chaos, and, worst of all, they took man's attention away from God. But unlike other sins like greed and jealousy, sexual desire cannot be kept under control, because it resides in a physical organ which exposes its inherent desire in a shameful way (*City of God* XVI, 23). Obviously, Augustine was writing about males. But women were equally sinful, if not more so, because the female body was the cause of male desire. One may wonder why Augustine did not condemn procreation altogether or why he did not recommend celibacy and sexual abstinence for everyone. But this was not a solution. According to Augustine, everything existed for a reason, and sexuality was no exception. Despite its negative side, sexuality was part of God's plan "whereby he might complete the fixed number of citizens predestined in his wisdom" (*City of God* XIV, 26). Therefore, Augustine did not regard the sexual organs as impure or sinful as such. They were part of God's creation and served a God-given function. According to the same logic, procreation was not a sin as such; although the sexual desire that spurred it on was the most hateful effect of Original Sin, the result – offspring – was good. Therefore, Adam and Eve would have become parents in Paradise, Augustine reasoned, if they had stayed there long enough (*City of God* XVI, 24). But why did God want human beings to procreate? Augustine's answer was sainthood: When God created the human species, he arranged for a certain number of saints to emerge throughout the ages (*City of God* XIV, 23). Thus, God created sexual organs and sexual desire for a reason, namely, to ensure that procreation takes place and that the necessary number of saints come to life. Therefore, sexual desire must never be pursued as a goal in itself – that would be a sin – but valued for its function in reproduction. In this connection, Augustine distinguished between sexual desire and sexual activity. The divide resonates with the categorical split between the physical and the mental, body and soul, and emotions and rationality: ideals on the one hand and physical reality on the other. Augustine tried to resolve this ambiguity by distinguishing between legitimate and illegitimate sexual pleasure and between sexual desire and procreation.

Writing about Adam and Eve in Paradise, Augustine describes bliss as "perfect health in the body, entire tranquillity in the soul" (*City of God* XIV, 26). It is worth noting that "tranquillity in the soul" would not be disturbed by the act of procreation, because in Paradise procreation would have taken place without sexual passion, or, as Augustine puts it, "those parts of the body were not activated by the turbulent heat of passion but brought into service by deliberate use of power when the need arose, the male seed could have been dispatched into the womb" (*City of God* XIV, 26). But after the Fall, man became sinful and everything changed: Sexuality became the most prominent symbol of Original Sin and the female body its most explicit symbol. While they were in Paradise, Adam and Eve committed the primordial sin of following their own desires instead of obeying God's command. This act of rebellion made man a slave to his passions. This loss of freedom, to be a slave to bodily desire, is what sin ultimately means to Augustine. However, desire is not sinful in itself. It is only when it is abused, when man loses sight of the function or purpose it is designed to fulfill, that it becomes sinful. Rationality is the only defence which helps keep desire at bay. This applies to all bodily desires: hunger, thirst, rest, sleep, and sex. If hunger is left unchecked, it leads to sinful gluttony, and sexual desire may lead to adultery. But like hunger, which was designed by God to keep you alive, sexual desire also serves a higher purpose when it is used for its intended purpose: procreation.

In order to grasp Christianity's ambiguous view of procreation, it is necessary to take a closer look at Augustine's interpretation of the myth of creation (Genesis), which laid the grounds for a continuation of patriarchal gender models. There are two versions of creation in the Bible, which to some extent contradict each other. Genesis does not constitute one homogeneous text, but an immense connected narrative. According to one scholar, "it matters little whether one is more interested in the great individual narrative sources that make up the book or in the composition as a whole, which arose when a final redactor skilfully combined these individual sources" (von Rad 1972: 13). Since the first Christian exegesis, these texts have been approached as if they constitute a comprehensive whole; scholars tried to find underlying meanings in order to synthesize apparently contradictory paragraphs. In order to arrive at an unambiguous biblical anthropology, therefore, Augustine tried to harmonize the two versions of creation. The more recent version emphasizes that both man and woman were created in God's image (*imago dei*): "So God created humankind in his image, in the image of God he created them; male and female he created them" (Genesis 1:27). The older version tells the story of how God first created Adam and then Eve from Adam's rib because he was lonely and needed a companion: "So the Lord God caused a deep sleep to fall upon the man, and he slept; then he took one of his ribs and closed up its place with flesh. And the rib that the Lord God had taken from the man he made into a woman and brought her to the man" (Genesis 2:21–22). Basing his argument on the more recent myth (Genesis 1:27), Augustine maintained that man and woman were equals in terms of their relation to God, since both were created "in the image of God" (*imago dei*). He argued that they therefore had equal opportunity for salvation. Bringing the two creation myths together, Augustine held that woman's likeness to God (*imago dei*) was restricted to the soul: "The whole of his argument emphasizes the fact that woman's *imago dei* dwells in her rational soul, which is identical to that of man" (Børresen 1995: 29). Børresen explains how this interpretation relies on Augustine's distinction between two stages of creation (*informatio* and *confirmatio*) corresponding to the two versions of creation: "According to Gen. 1:27, the *informatio* both for Adam and Eve occurs simultaneously ... Gen. 2:22 points to another divine operation, which makes the one causal and instantaneous act efficacious in time. The difference in which our parents were formed, *confirmatio*, has therefore no influence on the dependence of each in regard to God, but, on the other hand it has great importance for the relationship of the two sexes to one another, since the relation between the two members of the first couple remains the prototype" (Børresen 1995: 17). While men were created "in God's likeness", women's godlikeness did not include the body. However, the older myth (Genesis 2:21–22) states that Eve was created from Adam's body, and this clearly meant that Adam had priority: Eve was created from his body, so Adam was the original human being: His body was the source of her body. To this exegesis, Augustine added the Greek model of procreation, which identified the man as the sole progenitor. Hence, Adam (not Eve) was the prototypical human, primordial man, the origin of humanity. Despite the Christian promise of salvation and bodily resurrection for men and women alike, Augustine built on traditional Greek ideas about the female body as lowly, chaotic, dark, and demonic, and construed the bodies of Christian women as equally deplorable.

In Augustine's view, there was one legitimate form of sex, namely, sex between man and woman within the framework of marriage. It is worth noting that marriage in Augustine's time was not a Church sacrament, but a legal contract and a building block of the patriarchal order, which regulated property ownership and inheritance. Marriage was a legal contract which ensured that the sexual union between man and woman took place within the framework of the family. It was marriage that rendered sexual intercourse a legitimate Christian activity – but only if it was motivated by the wish to procreate. It is important to remember that Augustine was a citizen of the Roman Empire and took male dominance for granted. In the family, the *paterfamilias* was responsible for everyone under his protection, and according to taken-for-granted biological notions he was also their source. This understanding was compatible with Christianity, which introduced one particularly important addition, namely, the all-powerful God at the peak of the hierarchy. In the Genesis story, God acknowledges Eve by stating a right of property and naming her: "'This at last is bone of my bones and flesh of my flesh; this one shall be called Woman, for out of Man this one was taken'" (Genesis 2:23). Augustine formulated his teaching on Christian marriage on this basis, describing it as a physical union of man and woman: "They are said to be 'one' either on account of their being joined together in marriage, or because of woman's origin, since she was created from the man's side" (*City of God* XIV, 22). The biblical myth expresses this notion of the married couple as "one flesh": "Therefore a man leaves his father and his mother and clings to his wife, and they become one flesh" (Genesis 2:24).

In late antiquity, abortion was both legal and relatively widespread – in spite of the dangers to the pregnant woman. It was the husband or *paterfamilias* who decided over life and death in his own household, and an aborted foetus would fall into the same category as the newborn child who was not accepted – for whatever reason – by the *paterfamilias* and placed in the forest to die (child exposure). The Christian idea that all human beings are created in the image of God changed this. It restricted the power of the *paterfamilias* by defining God as the father of all humans, the ultimately powerful. The concept of God redefined women as belonging to Him rather than her husband. But it took time before this idea was translated into practice. In late antiquity, only female monastics escaped the power of the *paterfamilias* (Bynum 1992).

Augustine's preoccupation with sin and sexuality also caused him to reflect on the beginnings of life. In *Enchiridion* (Latin, handbook), also known as Augustine's catechism, he discussed whether children who die in the mother's womb will be resurrected, and he arrives at the conclusion that they will – if they were "fully formed", i.e. had acquired a human shape: "For, if we say that there is a resurrection for them, then we can agree that at least as much is true of foetuses that are fully formed. But, with regard to undeveloped foetuses, who would not more readily think that they perish, like seeds that did not germinate?" (*Enchiridion* 23, 85). The connection here to Aristotle's theory of foetal development is evident. For a Christian thinker like Augustine, the distinction between the unformed and "fully formed" foetus pointed to the crucial point when a foetus becomes a human being: "To deny, for example, that those foetuses ever lived at all which are cut away limb by limb and cast out of the wombs of pregnant women, lest the mothers die also if the foetuses were left their dead, would seem much too rash" (*Enchiridion* 23, 86). On this basis, Augustine included the foetus in the Resurrection. In Augustine's view, the Resurrection implied not only the re-awakening of the dead, but also that every human being is restored to their perfect form:

> Thus, the perfection which time would have accomplished will not be lacking, any more than the blemishes wrought by time will still be present.

Nature, then, will be cheated of nothing apt and fitting which time's passage would have brought, nor will anything remain disfigured by anything adverse and contrary which time has wrought. But what is not yet a whole will become whole, just as what has been disfigured will be restored to its full figure.

(Enchiridion *23, 85)*

Despite his harsh judgement of sexual desire as ultimately a sign of human weakness, Augustine held the human body in high esteem. This is clearly expressed in his description of the Resurrection, when God shall recreate all humans with the sexual difference between male and female intact (*City of God* XXII, 17). Each person's body and soul will be reunited in its perfect form: Small children will resurrect as adults, and every deformity will be gone (*City of God* XXII, 19). Christian ideas about the body changed the anthropology of the Graeco-Roman world. They replaced the idea of man as split in two: the eternal soul on the one hand and the decaying body on the other. In Greek thought, the soul was incorporal and immortal, whereas the body was doomed to die. This discontinuity was typically expressed in the idea of reincarnation, whereby the soul takes on new forms and is reborn, either as an animal or a human being.

Unlike Greek thought, which cut the human person horizontally in two, Christianity introduced a new and integrated concept of the human being. With its teaching on bodily resurrection and mortal sin, Christianity split the person along a vertical line. The historian Gedaliahu Stroumsa explains: "The great divide was no longer between lofty spirit and base matter but cut through the subject itself" (Stroumsa 1990: 30). The Christian idea of man as a sinful being split the person in two: on one side was the sinner, and on the other side was the man "made in God's image" (*imago dei*). On closer scrutiny, Stroumsa's exposition of the Christian body does not take the special position of the female body into account. Unlike the male body, which mirrored God, the female body was not godlike, but imbued with sin. Therefore, it was necessary that the Saviour was born male. This was the logic which eventually legitimized male dominance and excluded women from the priesthood. For Christian women, the Greek split between body and soul remained, and instead of replacing it, as Stroumsa claims, Christianity added a new dimension to it. On this view, Christianity did not replace Greek anthropology, but developed it one step further. As we have seen, Augustine regarded the female body as more sinful than the male body and limited woman's "likeness to God" to refer only to her sexless soul. Male godlikeness, however, also included the body. Thus, Christianity did not redefine women in the same manner as it redefined men by adding something new to an existing model. Instead, the horizontal split between body and soul remained unchallenged where women were concerned, and to this was added a vertical axis cutting across the sin–innocence divide.

When Christianity replaced the body–soul divide with a new emphasis on the whole person (body and soul), it did not include women. Instead, Christian women were burdened with an imperfect body and faced the impossible charge of integrating it with their godlike soul. The obvious solution to this dilemma was denial; annihilation from her bodily functions. Nowhere are these ideals more apparent than in the veneration of female martyrs, where virginity and faith blend into a fatal mix of violence and suffering. The most influential saints' stories are found in the *Golden Legend* (*Legenda Aurea*) by Jacob of Varazza (Iacopo da Varazze), a contemporary of Thomas Aquinas. He compiled these stories in northern Italy at the end of the thirteenth century. There are few pregnant martyrs among the saints (and female saints with children for that matter), but the slave girl Felicity is one. She was pregnant when she was arrested along with her mistress Perpetua (died in Carthage ca. 203). Impatient to enter her martyrdom, she gave birth in prison at eight months "for fear that because of her pregnancy her death would be delayed" (Roman law prohibited the death penalty for pregnant women). Her mistress, Perpetua, had a small son (referred to as baby and infant) who she kept with her (for breast-feeding?) in prison. Perpetua and Felicity were sent out to the lions naked, which was the custom for female law-breakers (Shaw 1993: 8). The typical female martyr was a young girl, who, in defiance of her own family or in resistance to social pressure to marry a pagan man, died for her faith (e.g. Agnes died in Rome ca. 304). Christianity took shape in its encounter with the Graeco-Roman world. Augustine was an inter-mediary figure, a catalyst who shaped the new (Christianity) in such a way so that it made sense to his contemporaries. He managed to integrate the absolute authority of the Almighty by giving Him creative monopoly and placing man (and woman) in a position of humility, dependency, and gratitude. This he did by designating God as the sole source of everything and making man aware of his own dependency through the concept of Original Sin, which was transmitted through procreation.

Associating the human body with sin and punishment, the doctrine of Original Sin forged a sceptical attitude towards the human body, but more towards the female body, which was further removed from perfection than its male counterpart. By implication, the female body became a veritable burden to the Christian woman. Her best option was to alienate herself from her body and identify with her godlike soul. For men and women alike, the female body was a disturbing object which had to be kept under control. With its doctrine of salvation for all – men, women, citizens, and slaves alike, Christianity was a potentially disruptive element with its millennial expectations for a new world. But by the end of antiquity, millennial expectations had been culled and Christian norms and ideas were increasingly seen as being compatible with Roman patriarchal society. The threat that Christian ideas of equality between men and women and between social groups was contained institutionally in a range of new practices: the veneration of virginity, asceticism, and monastic seclusion; in addition, a Church organization ruled by celibate men ensured that the hierarchical order of and male dominance in the Church largely remained the same.

Notes

1 There are several sources to Augustine's life, above all his autobiography, *Confessions*. For a biography treating Augustine in a historical and wider cultural context, see Brown 2000.

4

PREGNANCY AND ABORTION IN MEDIEVAL SOCIETY

The medieval period, which lasted roughly from the end of late antiquity (ca. 500) to the early renaissance (ca. 1400), was a religiously prolific time. Europe was dominated by religion, as Christian precepts, practices, and authority provided the framework for a rich and varied popular culture. In many ways, it was a culture closed in on itself, but within medicine things began to stir from the late eleventh century onwards. The source of new ideas was the reintroduction of classical Greek texts, via new translations from Arabic, notably those of Aristotle. The reintroduction of classical Greek texts from Arabic came about through encounters with Muslim cultures in this period. First such encounters occurred in Moorish Spain, Al-Andalus (711–1492), but they also took place in the aftermath of the Christian crusades to the Holy Land (1095–1291), i.e. the establishing of religious houses by the largest religious orders and their contact with Muslim and Orthodox Christian traditions in the Middle East. Commenting on this contact Monica Green points to the importance of the religious houses for the transmission of medical knowledge:

> The "twelfth-century Renaissance" in medicine in fact begun in the middle decades of the eleventh century, when a handful of writers began to compose new texts out of late antique Latin or contemporary Greek sources. The most important prelude to Salerno, however, was the series of translations from Arabic into Latin made between the 1070s and 1090s at the monastery of Monte Casino.
>
> (Green 2002: 2)

Catholic theology during this period is foremost associated with Thomas Aquinas (1225–1274), whose importance for Catholic tradition only compares with that of

Augustine. But it was not only the learned elites that were affected. Arabic-Greek ideas about the human body, nutrition, and health were included in practical medical manuals and became part of European folk culture. This was a period of dramatic change, but also of religio-cultural consolidation. At the start of the period, Western Christianity was restricted to the Roman Empire in the Mediterranean basin, with some Christian enclaves existing among the Germanic tribes. By the end of the period, however, Europe had been thoroughly Christianized and institutionally united under the canopy of the Roman Catholic Church. When Christianity was established as a social institution all over Europe, the process of consolidation started. In order for Christianity to become a dominant social force, it had to exercise power over people's lives. The Church did so by elaborating rules of conduct and enforcing its own moral precepts. The power of Catholicism affected high and low, elite and folk traditions. Life and death as well as pregnancy and childbirth were among the things that came under Christian jurisdiction. The Church tried to enforce Christian morals, and one way of doing so was to introduce strict punishment for new sins, among them abortion. In the thirteenth century, Thomas Aquinas developed a theory on the foetus' gradual development, and it formed the authoritative basis for the Catholic view on pregnancy and abortion for the next 600 years.

Thomas Aquinas continued Augustine's reflections on life and procreation. Known for his efforts to reconcile Aristotle's theories to Christian doctrine, Aquinas elaborated and refined Christian anthropology. As Augustine and Aristotle had done before him, he regarded the father as the source of his children's lives and held that the soul resided in the semen. In the same vein, he gave women an entirely passive role in procreation, restricting their contribution to providing shelter and nutrition to the foetus and to being the subsequent 'birth machine'. What made it possible for theologians to persistently discuss procreation from a male perspective was not only the biblical texts, but also patriarchal ideas and values embedded in cultural practices. Christian ideals of celibacy and monasticism meant that normative Christian theology was developed in strictly male enclaves far removed from female influence.[1] These men's knowledge of women or women's issues was limited to the Virgin Mary, who played a larger role in male monastic devotion (Bynum 1992). Aquinas' theory of procreation and foetal development did not significantly challenge the traditional male perspective, but it gave a theological explanation of foetal development which explicitly combined Aristotle's biological theory with Augustine's theology, and provided a basis for Christian laws concerning abortion for the next 600 years. Thomas Aquinas' unique standing in the Catholic Church became evident in 1323 – only 50 years after his death – when he was declared a saint for his impeccable moral conduct and outstanding contributions to the Church. In 1567, Pope Pius V declared him a Doctor of the Church, thereby granting Aquinas a particularly authoritative position in Catholic theology.

Thomas Aquinas was a Dominican friar and built his theology on Augustine's work, but his most lasting influence was his re-evaluation of Aristotle's works

(Fitzgerald 1999). Aquinas maintained that human procreation was gradual and far more complex than a mere reproduction of Adam in Eve's womb. In 1567, he was given the same title as Augustine, *doctor ecclesia*, Doctor of the Church, in acknowledgement of his contributions to knowledge about the truth.[2] In the present context, his elaboration of the Church's teaching on human procreation is particularly important. His re-evaluation of Greek philosophy, notably Aristotle, prepared the ground for the Enlightenment and the subsequent development of non-theological theories about the human body. Although Aquinas' direct influence was restricted to learned circles, the hegemonic position of the Church and his dominant role within it gave his theories broad impact. Like Augustine before him, Aquinas held that the female body was one step further removed from God than its male counterpart. Since the body was not a part of woman's godlikeness, which only included her (sexless) soul, he regarded the hierarchical relation between man and woman to be analogous to that between God and man: "Like God is the beginning and end of the created world, man is the beginning and end of woman". He maintained that woman's godlikeness was restricted to her soul. But since the dogma of Bodily Resurrection implied that woman's godlike soul would be reunited with her female flesh in heaven, Aquinas postponed the bodily godlikeness of woman to the Resurrection, when the body would emerge in its ideal form (Børresen 1995: 248–50). In Aquinas' view, the Fall did not only affect the soul, it upset the human body and rendered it imperfect. Hence, human godlikeness was conditional: God had created man in his image, giving him a resemblance to God or a godly model. However, after the Fall man (and woman) was no longer a divine copy, but an imperfect image. In this way, Aquinas provided the Christian conception of the human body with a firm notion of imperfection. Where the female body is concerned, Aquinas regarded it by definition as less perfect than the male body.

Aquinas' reflections were heavily informed by Aristotle, who approached the soul as a kind of life power inherent in the father's semen. Its main function was to initiate and direct the life process. Following Aristotle, Aquinas envisaged the human soul, which was inherent in the male seed, as the source of human life. The father's seed initiated the growing process of the embryo inside the mother's womb and directed it through three stages: first, the semen entered the womb, a place with optimal nutritive conditions. At this first stage, the embryo has no decisive form; it is undifferentiated matter derived from the mother's menstrual blood – it is alive and furnished with a vegetative soul. After some time, the embryo enters into the second stage, in which the limbs start to appear and the vegetative soul develops into an animal soul. In the third and decisive stage, the foetus acquires a human form and a rational, human soul. The reference to 'soul' in this context is evidence of Aquinas' debt to Aristotle, whose theory of correspondence between form and content is a premise for his theory of embryonic development (Børresen 1995: 219). This process of development, as Aquinas saw it, involved radical transformations or metamorphoses:

Some have claimed that the vital operations that are apparent in the embryo do not come from its own soul, but instead come either from the mother's soul or from the formative power that exists in the semen. Both of these alternatives are false, because works of life such as sensing, being nourished, and growing cannot come from an extrinsic principle. Therefore, one should claim that the nutritive soul exists in the embryo from the beginning, and later the sentient soul, and, last of all, the intellective soul ... So, then, one should claim that the intellective soul, which is simultaneously sentient and nutritive, is created by God at the end of human generation, and that the preexistent forms are corrupted.

(*Aquinas,* Summa contra gentiles *2, 88–89)*

In Aquinas' view, the rational human soul was unique. It did not grow and pass through stages where it had the qualities of an animal's soul as Aristotle maintained; rather, it was given by God directly when the foetus reached a human-like form. He referred to this act as 'infusion' or 'ensoulment': "The body then of man is formed at once by the power of God, the principal and prime agent, and by the power of the semen, the secondary agent. But the action of God produces the human soul, which the power of the male semen cannot produce, but only dispose thereto" (Aquinas, *Summa contra gentiles* 2, 88–89). This theory, which is often referred to as 'delayed hominization', is important because it introduces a principle for distinguishing between two stages of foetal development: before and after the foetus acquires human status. According to this view, God's infusion of a rational human soul occurs once the foetus has acquired a human form.[3] The logic behind his refusal of Aristotle's evolutionary soul is as follows: Since the human soul is immortal, it is not subject to change and hence cannot develop. Consequently, the human soul must, at one stage, be introduced ready-made directly from God (the creator) into the human. It is God's act of infusing the soul, which in Aquinas' theology ensures the godlikeness, *imago dei*, of the human person.

Contrary to Aristotle, who maintained that foetal growth correlates with the evolution of the soul, Aquinas held that the *human* soul is perfect and eternal, and therefore does not develop, but stays the same. He retained parts of Aristotle's theory, however, and maintained that the soul is an active entity which is inherent in the semen from the start. Its function is to initiate growth and control development from one stage to the next. But Aquinas assigned a final role to God, who, at a given moment in the foetus' development, infuses a human soul which replaces the animal soul or rather relegates it to a lower position in charge of bodily processes. The human soul is responsible for rationality, which sets humans apart from the rest of God's creation. Like Aristotle, then, Aquinas also regarded the soul as the governing principle which granted that the creature develop into its intended form or essence, but, unlike Aristotle, Aquinas gave God a decisively important role in the history of each human being.

For Aquinas, form and content were necessarily bound together because form was the outward manifestation of content. Therefore, the foetus was not a human-in-the making before God had infused it with a human soul. Because form and essence (meaning or content) were intrinsically linked with each other in Aristotle's theory, the growth process also involved a change of essence. What Aristotle described – and Aquinas confirmed – was a spiritual as well as a bodily evolution starting with seeds, which belonged to the realm of vegetation and which were accompanied by a vegetative soul. The seed grows and develops into an animal shape and finally acquire human characteristics and a human soul. In this theory, embryonic growth was conceived of as a kind of metamorphosis, a transformation which implied that the older form was left behind:

> (T)here are many intermediate forms and generations – and, hence, corruptions, because the generation of one thing is the corruption of another. Thus, the vegetative soul, which is present first (when the embryo lives the life of a plant), perishes, and is succeeded by a more perfect soul, both nutritive and sensitive in character, and then the embryo lives an animal life; and when this passes away it is succeeded by the rational soul introduced from without, while the preceding souls existed in virtue of the semen.
>
> *(Aquinas,* Summa contra gentiles, *2, 89)*

It is worth noting that Aquinas placed a lot of importance on the idea that human beings, both male and female, were endowed with intellectual faculties and a free will and that it was these faculties that distinguished humans from animals. Accordingly, the foetus could not be categorized as a human being before it had passed through the first stages of development. When the foetus moved, it was interpreted as an exercise of free will and taken as a sign of its humanity. This movement, which is usually referred to as 'quickening', was subsequently used as a means to indicate the difference between a growing seed and a human foetus. Since only human beings can have a human soul, Aquinas believed that the soul "is infused at that point when the foetus is sufficiently developed, in its brain and sensory system, to support the soul's intellectual operations" (Pasnau 2002: 111). Aquinas' theory provided a pragmatic basis for differentiating between the first stages of a human life, a theologically legitimate model which allowed legal authorities to decide whether or not an abortion was murder – or not.

The three metamorphoses that the human seed undergoes, according to Aquinas' theory, is reflected in contemporary medical distinctions between the *zygote* (fertilized egg), the *embryo* between week 2 and week 8, and the *foetus* between week 12 and week 40 (to the birth of a fully developed baby). Aquinas' theory of the three stages of development of the human foetus is based on the principle that form corresponds to content. Hence, Aquinas refers to the seed in the earliest stage as a vegetative soul (cf. what we today refer to as 'zygote'). In the second stage, the soul has the shape and qualities of animal's soul (cf. embryo), and in the final stage the foetus develops a human form and is given a human soul. All three forms of the soul are necessary: the vegetative soul provides life and growth; the animal soul provides motion and emotions; and finally the human soul provides rationality and faith.[4]

As mentioned earlier, the idea of human generation as a process involving metamorphosis was already a part of ancient Greek thought. According to Aristotle, it takes 40 days for a male foetus and 90 days for a female foetus to become a human being.[5] The timing evidently reflected a common view which probably stemmed from the celebrated 'founding father' of medicine, Hippocrates (died ca. 370 BCE). In his treatise *On seeds*, he explains that the (male) foetus' body starts to take shape after 30 days. When Aquinas adopted Aristotle's theory, his time frame for foetal development also became a part of official Church teaching. Setting aside its male-centered basis, the theory of 'delayed ensoulment' had far-reaching consequences for medieval society and Church law. It allowed for a basic distinction to be made between two stages of foetal development starting with a first stage, where the foetus is comparable to other animal life, and a second stage, where it can move and where it achieves the status of a human-in-the-making.

Predating Aquinas by several hundred years, an Irish legal text from ca. 800 is the earliest example of a practical application of the distinction between a live foetus and a human foetus, i.e. with a human form and a human soul. The text states that a woman who "causes miscarriage" (abortion) should receive three-and-a-half years of penance, but if it was done so late in the pregnancy that "the soul has entered it", the penance was fourteen years (McNeill and Gamer 1974: 166). The legal definition of abortion, namely, "the wilful destruction of the embryo in the mother's womb", was clear enough, but there were serious difficulties attached to the practical application of the distinctions between various stages and between male and female foetuses. Even more importantly, there were deep uncertainties regarding the exact time of conception: whether the semen started to grow at once or whether it needed some time to adjust to the uterus. To make things even more complicated, the fertility cycle of women was unknown, and its association with menstruation was unclear. In the Hippocratic–Galenic tradition, menstruation was seen as necessary purgation and simply referred to as *menstrua*, literally, the monthlies. Galen, the great medical authority, explained it as a consequence of women's bodies being colder: "The effect of this defect of heat – and a defect it was, for heat was the very principle of life, the absence or deficiency a sign of a less perfect life form – was that women were unable to concoct [literally 'cook'] their nutrients as thoroughly as men" (Green 2002: 19–20). The absence of menstruation during pregnancy was because the menstrual blood – this excess matter – went to nourish the child, and after birth it was converted into milk. Medieval legal texts identified the decisive moment of ensoulment at about four or five months into the pregnancy. This was the time of quickening, i.e. when the mother could feel the foetus move, which is also referred to as 'vivification' or 'animation' in legal texts. In the absence of reliable clinical tests, quickening and the size of the womb were the only practicable ways of verifying an alleged pregnancy. Uncertainty about the length of pregnancy may also explain why seventh-century theologians discussed the correct date for celebrating Virgin Mary's conception – unsure of whether it was seven or nine months after the feast of her nativity.[6]

Abortions before quickening were *not* regarded as murder. In the time frame between the loss of menstruation (suspicion of pregnancy) and quickening, a wide range of folk medical practices to some extent made it possible for women to stop unwanted pregnancies. But in this connection, it is worth noting that regardless of when or how it was done, the Church regarded abortion as a sin. The laws of the Catholic Church (Canon law) identified a number of sins and listed the corresponding penalties. In one of the oldest legal texts, the Irish Canons (*Canones Hibernensis*, ca. 675), abortion was punished as a moral sin (akin to fornication or illicit sexual activity). In accordance with Augustine's ban on sexual activity, except within the confines of marriage and for the explicit purpose of procreation, the guilty party, if an unmarried woman, was given a penance of three-and-a-half years "on bread and water" for abortion. Interestingly, adultery was punished much harder than abortion, the guilty party being given a penance of "seven years on bread and water" (*Canones Hibernensis* in McNeill and Gamer 1974: 119). Penance could also mean exclusion from the community, or it could be played off as a fine, which in the case of murder was equivalent to the price of three-and-a-half female slaves or 26 silver *denarii*. McNeill and Gamer point out that the development of secular law went hand in hand with Church law; the two institutions divided the tasks between themselves (McNeill and Gamer 1974). Normally, the sentence was given by the religious court, and the actual corporal punishment was carried out by the civil court.

The Penitential Ascribed by Albers to Bede from the eighth century makes a distinction between good and bad women when penance for abortion is meted out. The court should take into consideration both the nature of the crime and the moral standard of the person: "A mother who kills her child before the fortieth day shall do penance for one year. If it is after the child has become alive, [she shall do penance] as a murderess. But it makes a great difference whether a poor woman does it on account of the difficulty of supporting (the child) or a harlot for the sake of concealing her wickedness" (*The Penitential Ascribed by Albers to Bede* in McNeill and Gamer 1974: 225). Interestingly, the text distinguishes between three types of women: first the mother, who is fully responsible for her actions, second the poor woman, who is in a desperate situation, and finally the harlot (i.e. the prostitute). The distinction which is made between the last two, who are both poor and usually unmarried, shows the medieval Church's preoccupation with moral issues. It condemns the harlot, but is strikingly compassionate towards the poor woman who is unable to take care of her child. Similar provisions were included in the first compilation of Canon law, Gratian's *Decretum* from 1140. Its full title is *Concordia discordantium canonum* (*Concord of*

Discordant Canons). It was compiled by the Italian monk and lawyer Franciscus Gratianus, whose goal was to harmonize contradictory canons and unify Church law by comparing canons from previous centuries and from different provinces. Gratian based his work on established authorities, notably the Bible, conciliar legislation, church fathers (e.g. Augustine), and secular law, with a goal to arrive at a systematic corpus of canons. His compilation was incorporated into the first official corpus of Canon law promulgated by Gregory IX in 1234, *Decretalia Gregorii Noni,* usually referred to as *Liber Extra,* which replaced all local laws and was binding for the entire Church; it remained so up until the revision of 1917. Gratian followed established custom and did not categorize abortion as homicide if it occurred "before the soul is in the body". However, he did not make any suggestions as to when exactly the ensoulment took place. Another distinction with immediate practical importance was between the death of a foetus inside the womb (spontaneous abortion) and the death of the foetus immediately after birth. Taking the life of a newborn child (infanticide) was defined as murder and punished accordingly, whereas abortion "before animation had occurred" was treated as a sexual offence.

In the fourteenth century, Aquinas' work was accepted as orthodox teaching at the Council of Vienne (1312), which thereby confirmed his theory of human conception as official Church teaching. The council formulated the agreement with Aquinas in negative terms, defining any other theory as heresy: "We define that anyone who presumes henceforth to assert, defend or hold stubbornly that the rational or intellectual soul is not the form of the human body of itself and essentially, is to be considered a heretic".[7] This allowed for a certain period between conception and ensoulment to pass, during which abortion was classified as morally wrong but not punished as homicide. Taking into consideration the pre-modern lack of precise knowledge about the functioning of human procreation, uncertainties about women's reproductive system, and the actual duration of pregnancy, the legal time frames stipulated in Canon law were strictly theoretical. Although the Church persistently regarded it as a sin and meted out punishment before and after quickening, for practical reasons we may presume that the majority of abortions went unnoticed and therefore unpunished.

For women, the lack of precise knowledge about the female reproductive system meant that the first stage of pregnancy was a private period – a time when they could make their own decisions. John Riddle calls it a window of opportunity: "There was an indefinite but fairly certain time, a window of opportunity as it were, during which a woman could end what we call pregnancy, and neither she nor her contemporaries regarded the act as an abortion. Taking a drug for delayed menstruation was just that and nothing more" (Riddle 1997: 27–28). As mentioned earlier, menstruation was an uncertain indication of pregnancy since its connection with female fertility was unknown. Since irregular menstruation was not uncommon in a society where malnutrition and infections would affect women's health, a woman who took drugs to "induce menstruation" was seen as just that: a woman looking after herself. In the vast majority of cases it would remain a private affair and remain unknown to ecclesiastical and legal authorities.

Although the annual confession introduced for the laity at the Lateran Council in 1215 provided the local clergy with detailed knowledge of the sins committed by the congregation, few women would see the taking of a remedy to instigate menstruation as a sin and report it in their confessions. According to Galenic medicine, to induce menstruation counted as a health precaution because menstrual blood needed to be expelled in order to maintain the balance of body fluids and avoid illness. Consequently, a woman who took drugs to 'produce menstruation' would do so without moral qualms and without fear of committing a sin. Nobody could know why her menstruation had seized in the first place, and often the herbs that were used were not even categorized as abortive drugs. In other words, abortion was a vague category in pre-modern society. Despite harsh punishments, contraceptive herbs and other devices were well known and widely used as a method to regulate procreation. The Church seemed to have accepted this, since it judged the various methods differently, arranging them according to degrees of sinfulness. Aquinas' teacher, Albertus Magnus (ca. 1200–1280), listed remedies for contraception as well as abortificants in his book about medicinal herbs.[8] This explains the widespread use of abortive herbs like birthwort. The widespread use of folk remedies is documented by the large amount of books on medicinal plants that have survived from the period before the printing press. For instance, the widely popular *De secretis mulierum* (*On the Secrets of Women*) by Pseudo-Albertus, which was published in the late thirteenth century, has come down to us in 83 manuscripts. In the fifteenth century, it appeared in over 50 printed editions, and in the sixteenth century in over 70 printed editions (Riddle 1997: 59).

Medieval Europe was an agricultural society, where knowledge of the processes of procreation and pregnancy in cattle was commonplace. People knew that a premature calf or kitten had a limited chance of surviving outside its mother's womb – even after it appeared to be 'fully formed'. Therefore, for all practical purposes the important distinction was not before and after ensoulment – as Aquinas had maintained – but before and after birth. And it was birth rather than ensoulment that occupied most people's minds. Additional factors which also contributed to the uncertainty surrounding pregnancy and early abortion was the physical impossibility of distinguishing between an induced abortion and a spontaneous abortion or miscarriage. Riddle refers to statistics based on midwife accounts in Lancashire County (England) in the seventeenth century which show that of 1,000 deliveries, 1 to 3 per cent ended in abortions (i.e. miscarriages). He goes on to note: "These figures certainly are low, but we must remember that an abortion was recorded only when the act was declared" (Riddle 1997: 179). In the end, most accusations hinged on the credibility of the two main persons involved – the accused and the accuser – and their respective status, moral authority, and social standing. In addition, there were two other ways of deciding the matter: if an eye witness to the abortion gave testimony, or if a pregnant woman failed to produce a child after a given amount of time. The latter case would naturally lead to suspicion if there was no witness who could state for a fact that a stillbirth had taken place. In order to avoid such accusations, it was customary to have at least two witnesses present at delivery: the midwife and the husband.

When an accusation of abortion was brought to the attention of the authorities, it had to be in regard to a pregnancy which was visible to others: Accusations of abortion had to be substantiated by witnesses; they would simply be impossible to sustain before the belly showed, i.e. when pregnancy had become a social fact. Before the belly swelled, pregnancy was, if anything, a private affair. Taking these practical difficulties into consideration, we may presume that the number of abortion cases that were tried in court was low and that they for the most part consisted of late-term abortions (after 4 to 5 months). Since there was also considerable physical risk to the mother in the abortion process – and since abortions after 4 months were extremely risky – few women would have survived long enough to stand trial. Therefore, the majority of abortion cases were never tried in court. Another problem was the relative lack of knowledge about human anatomy. One of the first places where anatomy was put to practical use was in the legal system of the papal state in Rome (Pastore and Rossi 2008). In 1621, Roman physician Paolo Zacchia published a book which has been called the first forensic manual: *Quaestiones Medico-Legales* (Duffin 2011). It provides unique insight into the anatomical knowledge of his day. His description of a foetus shows that knowledge about pregnancy and procreation was scarce. Zacchia was a highly respected member of his profession and was frequently used as an expert witness in court.

One of Zacchia's cases concerned an alleged abortion and involved a widow who was accused of fornication.[9] His task was to help the court to settle whether the widow had given birth to a stillborn child or a mole. Zacchia's medical term is *mola*, which means 'a shapeless mass'. In contemporary medical usage, the term 'mole' refers to abnormal tissue in the uterus. Meanwhile, the doctor was also required to answer whether it was possible, as the woman in the case herself insisted, that she had been made pregnant by her late husband, who died two years before the unhappy delivery took place. Zacchia's analysis reveals a lot about seventeenth-century medical knowledge. What may astonish present-day readers is that Zacchia confirmed that the child was indeed the husband's. His reasoning went as follows: The widow had given birth to a stillborn child and not a mole, although it looked like one. But since it had caused her belly to swell, had been delivered in pain, and was furnished with an umbilical cord, it proved that the pregnancy was indeed caused by the husband before he died. Zacchia went on to explain how he had arrived at this conclusion: Since it was a well-established fact that the husband had been impotent, his seed would have been sick and therefore engendered a sick child which resembled a mole.

The dead husband of two years was therefore the father, and the inheritance should fall to the widow and not to the monastery which had accused her of fornication.

It is worth noting that the proof presented in court consisted entirely of witness statements. Empirical proof in the case of abortion was excluded on principle because it was impossible to conserve biological matter long enough to allow for its examination in court. The law spoke of women who "intentionally bring about abortion", "commit abortion", or "take a potion", but the case of the mole shows that the court lacked medical knowledge and would be unable to determine the age of an aborted foetus or distinguish between miscarriage and abortion. As illustrated by the widow's case stated above, economic interests, not moral concerns, would often decide whether a rumour about an abortion would be brought before the court. Thus, the most important distinction in law as well as in folk tradition remained – for all practical purposes – that between pregnancy and birth; foetus and child.

Although Zacchia does not mention it, the midwife traditionally played the crucial role of expert witness in court. After all, she had the firsthand experience which was required in order to identify the age of an aborted foetus; she also had knowledge of female anatomy. It was also the midwife who investigated the damage done in rape cases. The midwife was a medical expert with a profession that was recognized all over medieval Europe. Paris, for example, had an official midwife, a 'sworn matron' from the fourteenth century onwards. Similar positions existed in German towns as well as in Switzerland and Italy (Ackerknecht 1976). In addition to assisting at birth and appearing in court as an expert witness, the midwife gave testimony in divorce proceedings in cases where the wife asked for a divorce. The midwife would examine the wife, and if she determined that the latter was a virgin, she would give testimony of the husband's impotence, which was the only grounds for divorce recognized by the Church.

The midwife combined several functions. In addition to her main task of assisting in childbirth, she also had a religious function; she performed emergency baptism if the child was weak and in danger of dying before the priest arrived or before it could be brought to the church for baptism. In seventeenth-century Spain, part of the regular obligations of the parish priest was to give spiritual guidance to the midwife (Pardo-Tomás and Martinez-Vidal 2007: 52). Included in this instruction was the correct procedure to follow in connection with a caesarean section. It should be noted that at the time surgery was not a part of standard medical procedures; rather, it was a specialized task performed by barbers or even butchers. Thus, the midwife would more often than not perform the caesarean section herself, but only when the mother had already died in childbirth. Instead of protecting the pregnant woman, the law protected the rights of the father because the child belonged to him. The midwife would cut open the mother's belly, retract the child, and perform the baptism in haste – in most cases – before the child died. The reason for this was religious: Without baptism, the child would not be saved, but now it could be buried alongside its mother. Caesarean sections, however, were highly unusual, and in the few cases in which they were performed, the mother seldom survived.[10] Due to the lack of anaesthetics, few surgeries could be successfully performed, and (as mentioned above) caesarean sections were usually done after the mother had died. Catholic formalism dictated this macabre practice. It was made a rule by Pope Benedict XIV in 1768, when he ordered that a caesarean should be performed on all women who died during pregnancy. The procedure is described in a book published in 1745 (*Abrégé de l'embryologie sacreé – A Summary of Sacred Embryology*) which explains how to keep the foetus alive after the mother's death: The room should be kept warm, and hot towels should be placed on the belly until the caesarean could be performed and baptism could take place (Darmon 1977: 213).

Apart from the fact that midwives were sometimes made city matrons (as mentioned above), midwifery was not a profession in the modern sense, but a competence. In the absence of a qualified midwife – which often happened in the countryside – the mother-in-law or the neighbour's wife would act as a midwife. In patriarchal Italy, it was in fact a rule that the mother-in-law witness the birth of her grandchild in order to grant that it indeed 'belonged' to the family (Filippini 1990: 296). This does not mean that midwifery was an exclusively female occupation. In fact, the first manual for midwives in the vernacular, Der Swangern Frauwen und Hebammen Rosegarten, was written by apothecary and physician Eucarius Rösslin (1470–1526) and published in Strasbourg in 1513. Rösslin practiced as a (male) midwife, but the vast majority of midwives were women. In 1671, the British midwife Jane Sharp published a medical manual, which would later become famous for being the first book on medicine written by a female author. The book shows that she was well versed in the dominant medical theories of her day. She frequently refers to ancient authorities like Hippocrates and Galen, as well as Avicenna and Ptolemy, and does not shy away from expressing her own opinions, explaining that "I answer that the beginning of conception is not so soon as the Seed is cast into the womb, for then the woman would conceive every time she receives it" (Sharp 1999: 58). In the same vein, she refers to Galen's medical theories when trying to explain why not every act of sexual intercourse resulted in pregnancy. According to Galen, the foetus fails to emerge for two reasons: either the semen lacked heat and vivacity, or the temperature conditions in the mother's womb were deficient.

John Riddle argues convincingly that in medieval Europe it was the woman herself who had the ultimate authority when it came to birth, since "pregnancy was not thought to have occurred until the woman so declared it or her pregnancy was so visibly evident that it could not be denied" (Riddle 1997: 26). The way that a society identifies problems and makes provisions to handle them relies entirely on the knowledge at hand. Medieval Europe was an agricultural society, and the distinctions between life and death and between humans and animals were important. Therefore, a lot of attention and theological speculation went into explaining exceptional cases which challenged established distinctions, e.g. the pregnant woman who does not give birth, or the foetus that is born two years after the death of its supposed father.

Notes

1 There were also a few female theologians, e.g. Hildegard of Bingen, Catherine of Siena, and Teresa of Ávila, but their impact on Christian theological discourse is of recent date (Schüssler Fiorenza 1992, Børresen 2002).
2 Among the 30 Doctors of the Church, there are three women: Catherine of Siena, Teresa of Ávila, and Thérèse de Lisieux; all of them were added to this exclusive list after 1970. The last female theologian and mystic, Hildegard of Bingen, was declared a saint as late as 2012.
3 Contemporary Church teaching relies on another theory often referred to as "immediate ensoulment". This theory is the basis for the official Catholic absolute ban on abortion which became part of its teaching in the 1917 revision of Canon law.
4 Information about foetal development is available at the US Library of Medicine (http://www.nlm.nih.gov/medlineplus/ency/article/002398.htm).
5 Aristotle, *History of Animals*, VII, 3, 583b.
6 The reference stems from Noonan (1970: 19–20), who doubts its accuracy.
7 Council of Vienne, Decree 1.
8 Albertus Magnus, *De Vegetabilibus, Libri VII*, cited in Riddle (1997: 30).
9 *Quaestiones Medico-Legales, Consilium 39*, translated by Ada Lapp, available at http://meds.queensu.ca/medicine/histm/zacchia%20latin%20list.htm (accessed December 19, 2011).
10 The historical origin of the caesarean section is uncertain, but the name is linked to the myth of Julius Caesar's birth. Roman law provided that a caesarean should be attempted in order to save the child when the mother died in childbirth. The caesarean section was not performed as a measure to save the mother's life until the improvements in surgical techniques in the nineteenth century made it possible to do so. See the US National Library of Medicine entry on the caesarean at http://www.nlm.nih.gov/exhibition/cesarean/part1.html.

5

EXCEPTIONAL BODIES

Saints, relics, and dissection

Christian ideas about the human body are complex and ambiguous. At the core of these ideas is Jesus Christ, the son of God incarnated in the body of a man. The body is celebrated, recreated, and consumed in the Eucharist (communion rite), where the priest transforms bread into the body of Christ. The Corpus Christi rite was introduced in the thirteenth century and soon thereafter became enormously popular. This was a celebration of Christ's body in abstract form. In huge public processions, the communion bread or wafer was paraded through town in a decorated frame, often of pure gold, which the priest held high above the crowd. Thomas Aquinas formulated the doctrine of transubstantiation, which states that there was continuity between the communion bread (host) and Christ in heaven (Rubin 1991: 30). The medieval period saw the rise of a more emotionally charged religiosity. Images of the son of God adorned church walls, depicting Christ suffering on the cross in visible pain and with blood pouring down from his wounds as he silently calls for the laity's attention (Derbes 1996). But Virgin Mary and the saints were more important in the daily lives of ordinary people. They called on the Virgin to secure healthy children and to help with childbirth. Pregnancy was one of the most frequent reasons for women's visiting the shrines of saints, where they prayed for fertility; gave thanks for a safe delivery; made promises; and pleaded for good fortune and health.

Christian teachings and dogma concerning the human body, gender relations, and procreation were expressed in various ways. Only a few people ever managed to live up to Christian moral standards, and those were the saints. After death, the saint's merits were recollected in stories (*vitae*), while the body was venerated at the grave (often in a side chapel). Like other human beings, saints were tainted by Original Sin, but they were made different by God's mercy when he blessed them and made them a part of his sacred order. This exceptionalism was at the heart of the medieval fascination with saints' bodies, a fascination which also inspired the first dissections. Saints' bodies are an interesting exception to the rules that govern human bodies. They are holy, they are dead, and they are venerated. Therefore, they constitute a fascinating intermingling of religious, medical, and moral ideas that in some indirect ways have influenced Western ideas about the human body.

Historically, the first saints were made into martyrs as a result of the Roman persecutions of Christians. Their dead bodies were mutilated and dismembered, and their body parts were gathered by other Christians and, in time, dispersed to different churches around the Empire. The religious value of martyrdom was linked to idea that suffering and self-sacrifice turned the body into a sacred object, a logic based on martyrdom being seen as parallel with Christ's suffering and therefore also associated with his resurrection. Martyrs were already saved because they had sacrificed themselves for the faith – just like Christ had done. The mutilated cadaver was a sign of divine presence and proof that it was possible for a human being to become a worthy host for the spirit of God (Brown 1988: 68–69). After the persecutions were over (fourth century), the number of martyrs dwindled, and the martyr's suffering was spiritualized and redefined as a moral category. Now sainthood was associated with a moral life and exceptional devotion. While the bodies of martyr-saints were purged through torture, the bodies of these new saints were sacred because they had been able to withstand temptation. The saint's body was usually placed inside a church, where its presence was marked by a grave plaque, sarcophagus, or sculpture and adorned with telltale signs of folk devotion: candles, flowers, and replicas of healed body parts. It made no difference whether the saint was present in his or her corporal entirety or by a bone from a finger (relic). In medieval Europe, people believed that proximity to the saint's body (touching with one's eyes or hands) had restorative powers and would regenerate their bodies to good health.

Belief in the healing capacities of saints relied on a combination of Christian dogma and magical practice. While the souls of ordinary people await their reunion with their bodies at the Resurrection (Catholic theology held that after death the souls of ordinary people must suffer for their sins in purgatory), the souls of saints are taken directly to heaven when they die. There, they have a foretaste of Paradise as they spend their waiting time in close proximity to God. In pious literature, the saint's death is referred to as his or her birth in heaven – an understanding which is expressed in the saint's feast, which is usually celebrated on the day of his or her death. Thus, the saint's death is a birth in reverse, a new beginning with a new ability to heal and save the lives of others. The logic goes something like this: Although the saint's body (form) remains on earth, and the saint's holy essence (soul) resides in close proximity to God in heaven, the body has a holy quality because it retains its association with the soul.

A relic, which literally means 'remaining object', refers to a body part of Christ, the Virgin Mary, or saints, as well as any other object that can be associated with them. For example, the holy shroud (*Sacra Sindone*) in Turin, Italy, which purports to contain the image of Christ imprinted on the sheet of cloth he was buried in. It holds the image of a male face which is believed to be an imprint of that of Jesus Christ (Tessiore 1994). Regardless of shape or size, the relics "were the saints themselves, living already with God in the incorrupt and glorified bodies mere ordinary mortals would attain only at the end of time" (Bynum 1992: 183). The most valuable relics belonged to Jesus and his mother. But since they had both been taken directly, body and soul, to heaven, only physical objects remained, such as the cross and some of the Virgin's hair and milk (Warner 1990: 294). One of the most important relics was a part of the holy cross which Saint Helen, the mother of emperor Constantine, allegedly brought to Rome from Jerusalem in 330. However, relics of the holy cross were so numerous that Jean Calvin ironically claimed that if all the relics of the Saviour's cross were assembled, they would be enough to build an entire ship (*Traité des Reliques*). The excessive number of relics of the holy cross reflects a pervasive naivety as well as a lack of effective ecclesiastical control with the trade of relics. In fact, Calvin's criticism points to a problem of supply and demand, since Church laws prescribed that each church should have at least one relic – a prerequisite for the ceremony that consecrated the church and transformed it into a sacred space (Jungmann 1986). Most common among ordinary people were relics so small that they could be worn as jewellery. In fact, the demand for relics was so great that the sale of saints' bodies was a blossoming trade (Geary 1978). This increase in relic trade corresponded to the new supply of cadavers from Christian soldiers who died in the Crusades during the eleventh, twelfth, and thirteenth centuries. Since they had died while fighting the unfaithful (Muslims), these soldiers were automatically regarded as martyr-saints. Thus the supply of saintly bodies augmented at a time when Christianity expanded and new churches and chapels were built.

By the twelfth century, most churches had at least one beautiful casket containing a saint's body part, and reliquaries that mimicked the shape of the body part were put on display in churches and chapels for public veneration. Caroline Walker Bynum confirms this when she notes that "by the fourteenth century, however, holy bones were owned and worn by the pious as private devotional objects" (Bynum 1992: 271). High demand and limited availability caused the value of relics to soar to such an extent that only the richest churches could afford to keep a saint's body in its entirety. This was the reason why saints would be cut up and distributed in parts: The left arm would be sold to a church in Holland; the heart would go to Naples; and two ribs would be sent to a village in Austria (and so on).

The cult of saints also included the saints' personal objects. One such relic was the saint's belt. Saint Anselm was a popular saint among women, who would borrow his belt to help with the delivery of their babies. Pregnant women fearing "the dangers of childbirth" would "ask for the belt with pious intention and in the sure hope that they will regain their health if only they can have the use of it for the time-being" (Powell 2012: 798).[1] A similar practice is noted in connection with Saint Thomas of Becket. A woman had been labouring for three days but "once encircled with a stole blessed by St Thomas, she quickly gave birth" (Powell 2012: 800). However, there are relatively few stories about miraculous births at saints' graves when compared with the number of stories that provide other reasons for why women sought their help. Hilary Powell claims that the low number of reported miraculous births before the twelfth century may be due to the selection criteria used by the clerics who collected these stories (Powell 2012). In the twelfth century, she claims, the number of miraculous birth stories augmented as the laity gained a stronger presence in many clerical texts. Other historians have explained this fact as being due to practical obstacles, notably the difficulty of timing the moment of parturition and problems of travelling in such a compromised state. André Vauchez points out that we hear more about saintly intervention and miraculous births from the twelfth century onwards because the idea of invocation from afar, introduced towards the end of the twelfth century, made travelling to the saint's grave redundant (Vauchez 1987). According to Powell, however, the new focus on Virgin Mary as a mother had more of an impact in this regard, raising the profile of childbirth in medieval culture. This argument is supported by Norwegian collections of oral material consisting of prayers, rhymes, and songs which invoke the Virgin's help in childbirth (Grambo 1979).

Pregnancy and birth involve blood in different ways: Blood served as building material for the foetus during the birth process, and the blood and the placenta were both considered to be sacred and unclean. Since blood is one of the central symbols of Christ and his suffering, birth created an associative link between the pain of labour and religious purification and atonement for (sexual) sin. These religious meanings aside, blood was also intimately linked with life and good health, and in medieval medicine blood-letting was a common practice believed to rejuvenate the body. The reasons behind this practice stemmed from traditional Hippocratic–Galenic medicine which held that blood was produced in excess by the liver. Without knowledge of the circulatory system, the ancient teaching recommended the practice of blood-letting, especially when fever produced an imbalance and the body needed cooling. Blood was associated with life, and life spirits would nurture all parts of the body (Høystad 2007). The blood of Christ symbolized this idea, since it was his death through a bloody sacrifice that gave man the possibility of eternal life. Central to the meaning of blood in Christianity is the blood that Christ shed when he was nailed to the cross. We find it again in the Eucharistic rite (communion). In this ritual, wine is used, but the ritual turns it into the blood of Christ.[2] This wine-blood is sacred because it is associated with Christ's sacrifice and the subsequent salvation of humanity. By association, blood that is given up voluntarily was sacred. The blood of the innocent martyrs is one example, and the practice of flagellation (until blood was drawn) in medieval folk practice is another.[3] Nuns in medieval monasteries also fit this model – they were virgins who had sacrificed their ordinary lives and lived in seclusion. Their menstrual blood was a sign of the holy life they were living, and it could therefore be compared to Christ's sacrificial blood. For married women, however, menstrual blood was a sign of failure to conceive, and it was associated with bodily weakness and shame. In this connection, it should also be noted that it was considered "most shameful" to have intercourse with a menstruating woman (Lee 1996: 46). Another superstition held that intercourse with a woman who suffers "a flow of menstrual blood" would produce leprous offspring.

Medieval nuns valued the monthly shedding of blood as a female privilege. Blood was associated with Christ's suffering and brought them closer to Him – a belief which also found expression in blood-letting (Bynum 1992: 100). A more widespread view linked menstruation with impurity. However, this negative association did not mean that this blood was not sacred. In a careful analysis of the concept of purity, Mary Douglas maintains that the sacred is typically both pure and impure – often at the same time (Douglas 1986: 113).

Italian monasteries played a central role in the relic trade, and the majority of dissections of saints' bodies in medieval Europe took place in them. The main reason for this is likely a practical one: An overwhelming majority of saints in the high middle ages were Italians: popes and priests, monks, and some nuns (Weinstein and Bell 1982). An obvious explanation for this preferential treatment of Italian nationals is the geographical proximity to Rome and the fact that the papal bureaucracy, not the various local church authorities, had the final say in the official recognition of saints. Evidently, the monks and nuns who cut up the bodies of dead saints for the relic trade were not primarily interested in human anatomy. If they studied the saint's body at all, they were looking for signs of divine intervention. By the turn of the first millennium, an entire science of holy signs had developed. Among the most reliable signs of sainthood was the absence of decay and the pleasant smell of the cadaver which was known as the 'perfume of sainthood' (Albert 1990). But, as Erwin Ackerknecht rightly observes, dissection does not necessarily result in anatomic knowledge. Drawing a parallel to autopsy practices in primitive cultures, where organs from the dead were used as a form of divination, he claims that "anatomic knowledge is as poor as among those who perform no such autopsies" (Ackerknecht 1982: 14). However, this does not imply that there was no knowledge of anatomy in medieval monasteries. In fact, the practice of mummification, which Italian archaeologists have traced back to the thirteenth century (Fornaciari et al. 2008), requires technical as well as anatomical knowledge. Such knowledge was available in central Italy in the thirteenth century, and Church authorities clearly had no reservations regarding dissection and other manipulations of saints' cadavers.

Medical and theological competence overlapped, as monks would often work as surgeons and physicians. But this was not welcomed by Church authorities, a fact well illustrated by the decision at the Council of Tours in 1163 to prohibit monks and priests from studying medicine. In connection with her work on the origins of the *Trotula* manuscripts – a medieval compilation of women's medical texts from southern Italy which combines indigenous practices and medical techniques from the Arab world – Monica Green notes that in Salerno "the traditional association of clerics and physicians started to break down already in the eleventh century" (Green 2002: 13). Nancy Sairisi argues convincingly that the prohibition was not primarily motivated by moral concerns and that it was in fact an attempt to protect the Church from the growing impact of the medical profession (Siraisi 1990: 44). According to her, the prohibition fell short of its goal and effectively restrained anatomic activities in monasteries instead (Siraisi 1990: 89). What is clear, then, is that the Church's decision to distance itself from anatomical investigations coincided with the emergence of the professionalization of Western medicine. The first historical documentation which bans dissection on moral or religious grounds is *De sepolturis* (*On burial*), a bull issued by Pope Boniface IIX in 1299. The bull condemns the mutilation of dead bodies that occurred in monasteries. What the bull refers to is the practice of boiling the body of deceased saints so that the bones could be separated from the flesh. According to Elizabeth Brown, the bull was motivated by the Pope's private concerns for his own bodily resurrection, as many popes did indeed become saints (Brown 1990: 828). The bull was ignored, however, because the Pope had failed to argue convincingly for his concerns. The demand for relics continued.

Another monastic practice which required some knowledge of anatomy was embalming. The first examples stem from thirteenth-century Italy and show that they already had a firm knowledge of anatomy (Fornaciari et al. 2008). The first embalmed saint was a female, Margherita of Cortona, who died around 1297. She was an unusual saint, one of a very few who were neither virgins, nor proper nuns. From the age of 20 to the age of 29, she had been the concubine of a nobleman and had given birth to an illegitimate child. When her lover died, she went to live in a monastery and went on to found a hospital. Her son grew up to become a Franciscan monk. One may speculate whether the special treatment of Margherita's body was accidental or somehow linked to her motherhood. A female saint who was not a virgin was unusual, to say the least. However, one can only speculate as to whether her mummification and subsequent preservation was due to purely religious reasons or whether it was due to some sort of fascination with such an extremely sinful body. At the time, the majority of saints were cut into pieces and sold, so in this sense too Margherita was an unusual case. Perhaps the nuns anticipated low demands for her body parts, or perhaps they simply wanted to try out a new technique. In any case, there is ample proof of Margherita's local popularity. She was venerated as a converted sinner and remained a popular local saint. Interestingly, the cult of Saint Margherita of Cortona was not officially recognized by Church authorities until 1728, when she was canonized by Pope Benedict XIII, an act which served as proof of her popularity more than 400 years after her death.[4]

A report of a dissection taking place in 1308 shows how monasteries served as centres of knowledge of human anatomy in the pre-scientific era. This dissection involved the body of a deceased nun, Chiara da Montefalco, and took place in the Santa Croce monastery in Umbria. The reason for the detailed report was not the nuns' interest in human anatomy as such, but their search after decisive signs of Chiara's sainthood. The immediate reason for the dissection was that Chiara had claimed that she had "Christ in her heart". Her body was opened up, and her internal organs were described in detail. The nuns who performed the intervention reported that they detected "formations inside Chiara's heart that they took to be symbols of the passion" (Siraisi 1990: 40).

If saints gave rise to a fascination with bodily signs of moral perfection, a similar case can be made for Renaissance art, which valued realistic, true-to-life images and which required that artists have some knowledge of anatomy. In 1435, the artist and architect Leon Battista Alberti (1404–1472) published his influential *De pictura* (*On Painting*), in which he stresses the importance of anatomical knowledge: "Just as for a clothed figure we first have to draw the naked body beneath the clothes, so in painting a nude the bones and muscles must be arranged first, and then covered with appropriate flesh and skin in such a way that it is not difficult to perceive the positions of the muscles" (*De pictura* II, no. 36, Alberti 2004: 72). Alberti advised the painter to make close observation of arms and legs and to start with a sketch of the bones before adding the muscles. With Renaissance art, then, came a need to peek under the skin. Some decades after Alberti's book, Leonardo da Vinci followed his advice and performed dissections on human bodies and made detailed anatomic drawings. These drawings were not published in da Vinci's lifetime, and remained unknown until 1632 (*Treatise on Painting*), and had no impact on the development of the scientific study of anatomy. But, in our context, it is interesting to notice how scientific knowledge of the human body gradually sifted into the cultural matrix of European society and eventually created a new concept of anatomical knowledge as something associated with normal human bodies.

A decisive step towards the scientific study of anatomy is associated with Andreas Vesalius from Brussels (1514–1564). His fame stems from a book published in 1543, *De corporis humani fabrica* (*On the Structure of the Human Body*). The book, which was based on Vesalius' work at the University of Padua, Italy, contained detailed illustrations of the body's inner organs and was based on dissections of human corpses which he obtained from the city's prisons. Contrary to popular belief, Vesalius was not the first physician who performed dissections on human corpses. The first dissections performed for medical reasons in the medieval period took place in the town of Salerno in southern Italy in the twelfth century (Green 2002). These dissections followed the tradition from antiquity of using animals rather than human corpses – as did those performed by Galen (129–200). Legal documents show that dissections were performed for legal purposes already in the thirteenth century in Bologna, where the first handbook on dissection, Mondino de' Luzzi's *Anatomy*, was published in 1316. His book came as a response to this new demand for anatomical knowledge and shows that dissection

FIGURE 5.1 Saint Clare (Chiara) of Montefalco depicted with a heart in her hand. Mural painting on the pilaster of the Nativity chapel in Santa Maria Incoronata, Milan, Italy. Clare of Montefalco had a vision of Christ, who told her that he had placed his cross in her heart. After her death in 1308, nuns in her monastery dissected her heart in order to find evidence, and they found a cross formation. The heart is now kept in a reliquary in the monastery chapel of Santa Croce in Montefalco, Umbria, Italy. Photo © Giovanni Dall'Orto.

on human cadavers was already a part of the university education of physicians, at least in Italy. However, the systematic, scientific study of anatomy was initiated by Vesalius more than two hundred years later.

Knowledge of anatomy was *not* regarded as an important part of medical education. Surgery had a low status in the medieval period, when the dominance of

Galenic medicine made anatomical knowledge largely irrelevant: Why study the anatomy of internal organs when you believed that the balance of body fluids (i.e. the humours) was central to determining a person's health? In European universities, anatomy was taught as a theoretical framework based on Galen's *Institutiones anatomicae*. However, Vesalius questioned some of Galen's descriptions of human organs and concluded that the latter's descriptive mistakes could be ascribed to the difference between human and animal organs (Kusukawa 2004b). Galen had in fact not performed dissections on human cadavers, but on those of apes. In 1538, Vesalius published his first alternative to Galen's *Institutiones anatomicae*, namely, the *Tabulae anatomicae sex* (*Six Anatomical Tables*) at the University of Padua. The drawings were intended to be used in the education of physicians and were introduced in connection with a whole new educational method based on demonstration. Vesalius' most influential book *De corporis humani fabrica* (*On the Structure of the Human Body*) was published in 1543 and replaced Galen's work. Used in combination with dissections, this was a significant improvement in pedagogical method. *De corporis humani fabrica* described detailed drawings in words, and, in an attempt to establish a common medical terminology, Vesalius gave bones, muscles, and blood vessels names in Latin, Greek, Hebrew, and Arabic and placed them on the margins.

Vesalius' famous book was published in 1543, which was in the middle of the Reformation, and this was no coincidence. According to Andrew Cunningham, Vesalius embodies the breakthrough of all that was new: a professor at a Catholic university, but a Lutheran; a doctor trained in traditional medicine, but the inventor of a new science (Cunningham 1997). Cunningham interprets it all as a result of Vesalius' Lutheran ideals and compares his anatomical research to Luther's approach to the Bible. For Vesalius, Luther's motto, *ad fontes,* back to the sources, was an invitation to look beyond taken-for-granted truths. In support of this claim, Ole Grell points out that dissection was rapidly introduced in Lutheran universities (Grell 2004). Although there is no documentation of Vesalius' alleged conversion to Protestantism, he "acted like a Lutheran" (Grell 2004: 88). At least we can say that there were similarities in Vesalius' and Luther's approaches: Both placed the individual at the centre. It was the human faculties (seeing, hearing, reasoning) which were needed in order to arrive at true knowledge. Science was a new paradigm, a new way of being in a world where truth does not reveal itself, but must be discovered. The development of anatomy as a field of knowledge in its own right had far-reaching consequences. As noted above, it is possible to see it as part of the cultural and religious revolution usually referred to as the Reformation. In this connection, it should be noted that these cultural changes cannot be isolated to Protestant countries; rather, they should be seen as a more general cultural change which also affected Catholicism in a profound manner – as expressed in the Counter-Reformation movement which was initiated by the Council of Trent (1545 – 1563). Viewed from this perspective, anatomy may be defined as a true child of the Reformation era.

The story of Christianity in medieval Europe is a story of tension between a religious elite (theologians and clergy), trying to recreate society according to its own ideals, and ordinary people, dealing with their own daily concerns. Important aspects of this encounter between elite and folk; old and new were played out in religious rituals and practices which centred on the human body: the cult of saints and relics; taboos concerning blood or the purification of women; and various traditions related to sexuality and procreation. One reason for this interest may be the inherent discrepancy between a religion which valued chastity and a rural society which valued fertility. Sometimes, this tension produced an open paradox, as when the Catholic Church idealized a celibate religious elite and a virgin mother. Although the cult of saints' bodies does not address pregnancy directly, the religious practices associated with the bodies of saints constituted a cultural basis for the rationale which subsequently informed Enlightenment ideas about the human body and modern medicine.

Notes

1 Powell cites the 1979 edition of *The Life of St Anselm of Canterbury* by Eadmer (translated by R.W. Southern, Oxford: Clarendon Press).
2 According to Catholic teaching, an actual transformation is taking place (transubstantiation) in the Eucharist, whereas Protestants regard the ritual as a symbolic act.
3 There are several excellent studies of flagellation. Norman Cohn's study of millennial sects (Cohn 1970) treats the phenomenon using a broad historical analysis. Franco Ferlaino's work is an example of the anthropological study of the continuation of the tradition in modern Italy (Ferlaino 1990).
4 For a summary of her legend, see *Dizionario dei santi* 1989.

PART II

The Enlightenment

From the Reformation to modernity
(1400–1700)

6

THE REFORMATION

Protestantism, life, and marriage

In the medieval period, the Catholic Church had a monopoly on defining values, norms, and ideas. It also placed a higher value on the clergy and those who dedicated their lives to the Church (i.e. monks and nuns). Since these religious elites were considered to be closer to God than ordinary men and women, a two-track road to salvation was established. This is how Protestant texts usually describe Catholicism in order to legitimize its split. They go on to explain how sixteenth-century Protestantism (Lutheranism and Calvinism) emerged as folk reactions to inauthentic religious ideas and practices. The Reformation can roughly be described as the breaking away of entire nations from the authority of the pope and the institutional framework of the Catholic Church (Chadwick 1990). It was a long process, which started during the late Renaissance (fifteenth century) and reached a peak in the mid-sixteenth century, when Protestants broke legal ties with the pope in Rome (e.g. Henry VIII in England).

Geographically, the Reformation split Europe in two. The new Protestant churches that emerged in the process encompassed most of north-western Europe: the Anglican church (England), Calvinist churches (Scotland, the Netherlands, Switzerland), and the Lutheran churches (Germany, Scandinavia). Historically, the Reformation resulted in what have commonly been referred to as 'wars of religion', which were a series of violent conflicts that ended with the Peace of Westphalia in 1648, which effectively established the sovereignty of the king to decide the religion of his subjects and which laid down the principle of secularism in international politics (Haynes 2009). The king's religious monopoly was a major factor behind religiously motivated emigration to the Americas – a haven of religious freedom unknown in Europe. In the seventeenth century, this religious exodus picked up as Wesleyan Methodist and various Baptist groups emerged and sought a new life in what would later become the United States.

For ordinary people, the transition from Catholicism to Protestantism may be described as a revolution: All the monasteries in Protestant territories were dissolved, the cults of saints – both local and universally acclaimed holy men and women – was abolished, and shrines to the Virgin Mary were either removed or destroyed. At the same time, Protestantism abolished celibacy for the clergy and introduced work and family life as the ideal for everyone, including the clergy. The Reformation had massive political consequences (i.e. wars), but what were the consequences for gender roles and for the prevailing views on pregnancy and birth? The short answer is: not much, and this is because the Protestants ironically adopted the Catholic teachings on man, woman, sin, and procreation.

When the British physician William Harvey described the heart as a pump in 1628 (*De motu cordis, On the Motions of the Heart*), it made theological speculations seem oddly out of place. The heart was neither the seat of the life-soul (Aristotle) nor the body's source of heat (Galen) – nor even the organ of faith as Catholic theology would have it. Science put a stop to a discussion which had occupied natural philosophers since antiquity. It did so not by answering the questions that generated this discussion, but by making them irrelevant. Galen believed (wrongly) that the heart's main function was to produce heat; that the blood was produced in the liver; and that the lungs' main function was to cool the blood. The heart was also the seat of life, and the arteries transported life and heat to every part of the body. When William Harvey (1578–1657) presented his theory of blood circulation and described how the heart functioned as a pump, he had put an end to a discussion about the function of the heart (Siraisi 1990: 82). Unlike the followers of Galen and Aristotle, Harvey based his theory on observation and performed dissections on live animals in order to test his theories (Wright 2013).

The Hippocratic–Galenic understanding of the body had dominated the medical profession from antiquity and defined the body as an intricate system of fluids and temperatures. In many respects, it shared several features with classical Chinese medicine with its focus on yin and yang and the life-force which permeates the entire body for as long as it lives.[1] A radically different body model replaced the Galenic one during the Enlightenment. This seemingly dramatic development caused Shigehisa Kuriyama to ask why the new scientific approach to man was so easily accepted (Kuriyama 1999) and how it came to replace the traditional model of Western medicine. He addresses these two questions in a comparative study of classical Greek and Chinese medicine, which have certain superficial similarities: For example, both emphasize circulation and the importance of balance. He looks at the wider Greek context and finds a preliminary answer to these questions in the practice of dissection. Chinese medicine never used dissection as a method, and to Kuriyama this signals a crucial difference: the need to go beyond the skin and look inside for explanations. He traces the same idea to Greek art, which focused on the beauty of the human body in motion and which thereby created "a particular way of peering into the body" (Kuriyama 1999: 134). Because the Greek notion of beauty gave importance to light and shadows, and found particular delight in examining the way that muscles create "rippling contours" on the skin, Greek artists needed to learn how the muscles worked and how they gave shape to the body. From this interest in muscles and joints, they developed the need to "peek inside".

Even more relevant to our study is Kuriyama's persuasive account of the Greek distinction between form and essence, which provided the underlying logic of medical practice. Kuriyama argues that "anatomy shaped what the fingers felt" and goes on to describe how the need to explain muscle functions inspired anatomical investigations and the search for hidden meanings under the skin (Kuriyama 1999: 32). This interpretative framework allowed the Greeks to identify virtue with certain forms, as when they discerned virtue in "well-jointed and sinewy legs", while inarticulate, fat, and female bodies were of lesser value. Thus, the dualism of form and content gave sense to the idea of bodily beauty and created an associative link between form, function, and moral virtue. Unfortunately, Kuriyama does not consider the influence that Christian ideas and practices had on subsequent developments in medical thinking. But he does bring to the fore the cultural embeddedness of our ideas and points out the delicate and complex interactions between different modes of understanding.

A negative attitude towards sexuality and the idealization of asceticism were, as we have seen, at the core of the Catholic moral system. The world was full of temptations, and man's will was weak; therefore, the ideal life was spent in the secluded environments of a monastery, where evil – and the passions – could be held at bay. In Catholic monasteries, asceticism went hand in hand with the inversion of bodily pleasure; that is to say, asceticism turned into self-inflicted pain (Bynum 1992). The purpose of life was salvation, and a good relation to God required strict obedience, which above all else meant keeping (bodily) desire under control. An entirely passive attitude towards sexual desire was recommended for women as well as men. In marriage, both husband and wife should let nature take its course, but keep sexual desire under control and only give in to it for the expressed purpose of creating offspring. Although the Protestants closed the monasteries and embraced marriage even for the clergy, the traditional Catholic view on the human being essentially remained unchanged.

Christian attitudes towards marriage were, as we have seen, closely tied to sexuality and procreation. These attitudes were instrumental in how marriage was viewed and bore the stamp of having been elaborated among clergy who lived in celibacy. In a religious system which valued sexual abstinence and asceticism, the married life was simply less desirable than the monastic life, or, for men, life as a member of the clergy. Writing about Catholic views on marriage, John Witte nevertheless points to an overall positive valuation of marriage in medieval society:

> Marriage was viewed (1) as a created, natural institution, subject to the laws of nature; (2) as a sacrament of faith, subject to the laws of Scripture; and (3) as a contract, subject to the general canon laws of contract formation,

maintenance, and dissolution. These three perspectives were, in an important sense, complementary, each emphasizing one aspect of marriage: its divine origin, its symbolic function, and its legal form respectively.

(Witte 1986: 300)

Although the Protestant churches broke with Catholicism's ascetic ideals and monastic traditions, the social function of marriage remained fundamentally unchanged. Of course, marriage had for all practical purposes functioned as the basic social unit in Catholicism as well. In fact, only a very small percentage of the Catholic population consisted of clergymen, monks, and nuns, who spent their lives in celibacy. A life spent as an ascetic having made a vow to practice sexual abstinence was the exception, not the rule; it was only available for a select few. This exclusivity was also a precondition for the religious value of monks, nuns, and clergy, who constituted a religious elite and expressed their exclusivity by distinguishing themselves from the (ordinary) married masses. When the Protestants closed this avenue and emphasized the equality of all Christians, marriage became the only option for a Christian life. However, the main intention behind the Protestants' dissolution of monasticism was not to advance marriage, but to hasten the demise of religious elitism, which lacked a biblical basis.

Although there were strong theological grounds for the Protestant critique of monasticism, the theological reasons for elevating marriage were not equally strong. The Protestants could condemn monasticism and criticize extreme asceticism as unbiblical, but they were theologically barred from turning the opposite – sexual desire – into a virtue. The pervasive authority of Augustine would not allow it. So the Protestant rhetoric would place more emphasis on criticizing the power and privileges of monastic orders and place less emphasis on attacking celibacy and asceticism. Martin Luther, himself a former Augustinian monk, married a former Cistercian nun in 1525. The couple had six children and lived a 'normal' life. Together with other members of the former religious elite, they exemplified the Protestant ideal of a Christian life: married men and women who dedicated themselves to a life with God in this world, an ideal which sociologist Max Weber referred to as "inner-worldly asceticism". How this inner-worldly asceticism tallies with married life is perhaps best illustrated by Protestantism's emphasis on restraint, temperance, and a pronounced awareness of the sinful nature of man.

For Luther, marriage was a religious duty and sexual intercourse between two spouses was not just a way of complying with God's command and making children ("be fruitful and multiply", Genesis 1:28); rather, it was a way of paying tribute to God. Luther was known as a sensuous man who praised the intimacy – body and soul – of the married couple (Carlson 2007), but he was more subtle in his writings, praising instead the Christian family for its social role in the upbringing of children. And because of the Lutheran awareness of God, the ideal marriage should also include God in daily life, an example of this being the making of everyday chores into a way of relating to God. Luther did not propose an alternative to Catholic views on the body, and he did not challenge traditional gender roles and the subordination of women. Protestantism conformed to Catholic tradition and maintained that the harmony of a marriage relied on a sexual hierarchy with the man as the head of the household and the woman as his helpmate. The main purpose of the Protestant marriage remained as Augustine had defined it: an arrangement which ensured the continuation of the human species. Although Protestantism raised the status of marriage, the rules of conduct remained the same. These similarities between the old and new forms of Christianity were also expressed in the legal systems of Protestant countries, where the provisions of Canon law, except for the laws for the clergy, had been maintained.

After the Reformation, at the end of the sixteenth century, Catholic abortion laws were for a brief time made more severe. The change was short-lived because it was found to have broken with the authority of Augustine and Aquinas. The Protestant churches were in a radically different situation: Having broken with Catholicism, they could disregard Canon law. But although Protestant countries broke away from papal dominance, they did not – in practice – break with Christian norms as they were traditionally expressed in Canon law. Civil and criminal laws were largely reintegrated into the legal systems of Protestant countries. Among other things, the punishment for abortion essentially remained the same. Where pregnancy and abortion were concerned, the new Protestant countries modelled their own policies on Canon law, which had remained unchanged since 1140. But in 1588, Pope Sixtus V (1585–1590) made a change in Catholic abortion laws when he issued a bull, *Effraenatam* (*Without Restraint*), in which he condemned "those who knowingly seek and succeed at procuring or aiding in procuring an abortion (via medicines, poisons, violence, overbearing physical stress or labour)".[2] This law was part of Pope Sixtus V's moral purge and must therefore be seen in conjunction with the death penalty he had instituted for clergy who broke their vows of chastity.[3] To illustrate the horrors of this pope's rule, Eamon Duffy relates a saying that in the first year of the reign of Pope Sixtus V there were more criminal heads on spikes than there were melons for sale in Rome's markets (Duffy 1997: 219).

The new abortion law introduced by Sixtus V discarded the traditional differentiation between the formed and unformed foetus, and introduced one kind of punishment for all abortions: the death penalty. Regardless of the foetus' age, the would-be mother was to be excommunicated and then executed. This was the same punishment meted out to 'ordinary' murderers, the only difference being that everyone associated with the abortion was also subject to excommunication and execution. However, the new penalty had little practical consequences outside the Papal States (most of Italy). In Catholic countries, the pope only had jurisdiction within the Catholic Church and his bailiwick was limited to Church matters (e.g. excommunication). In these states, it was up to the secular authorities (the king) to implement the penalty – from collecting a fine to performing an official hanging or beheading. Hence, the king had a choice whether or not to follow the pope's provisions. In fact, the change introduced by Sixtus V was never ultimately effectuated in these states because it lasted for only three years before being revoked by the next pope (Gregory XIV, 1590–1591), who found the punishment to be too harsh.

In a papal bull issued on 31 May 1591, Pope Gregory XIV reinstated the previous law on abortion, which distinguished between the different levels of foetal development and which varied the penalty accordingly (Lopez 2012). In Gregory XIV's version of this law, the main distinction was between the foetus before and after ensoulment as defined by Aquinas, and only the latter should be punished with excommunication. This newer version also recommended the 'quickening test' in order to establish whether or not ensoulment had taken place. This important distinction was based on a combined theological–biological model, based on the works of Aquinas, which correlated ensoulment with the foetus' ability to move. Like in other court cases, witness statements were the principal means of establishing facts and of ensuring that the same procedures were followed in all criminal cases.

In countries that broke with the Catholic Church, Canon law automatically lost its legitimacy and was set aside, but for practical purposes it was largely maintained. With the exception of laws concerning the clergy and monastic rules and regulations, Canon law was translated into the new laws of Protestant kingdoms. Marriage and abortion laws remained mostly the same in Protestant and Catholic countries alike. By the end of the seventeenth century, the impact of traditional Canon law began to wane. Ironically, the first effect of this change was the development of a decisively more negative attitude towards women. In her study of Norwegian marriage laws, Kari Telste points out that the legal reform that had been implemented in 1734 evinced a much stricter approach to sexual morals than its predecessor. While older laws described the man as the responsible party in cases of sexual promiscuity, the new laws described the man as the seduced party (Telste 1999: 246). Based on a statistical analysis of court cases, Telste argues that the new law did not in fact reflect a change in the sexual conduct of Norwegian women, but instead reflected a popular culture rife with stories about 'lewd' and 'dangerous' women. In short, instead of introducing a misogynist attitude towards women, the new Protestant law simply reflected dominant social ideas. Women had always carried the burden of sexual sin. For example, while sexually active women were often referred to as 'loose women', there was no similarly derogative name for sexually active men. It seems ironic, then, that Protestantism did not raise the social status of women after Luther had raised the status of marriage and praised family life. Men had concubines and visited prostitutes, while unmarried mothers faced society's scorn.

Although the Reformation banned the cult of saints and the Virgin Mary, the mother of Christ retained an important place in folk culture. She was, after all, a kind of semi-goddess and a moral ideal for all Christian women. Ordinary and sinful women alike could not emulate the Virgin Mary, but pregnant women came fairly close. However, the ritual of purification after delivery was a reminder of the difference between them and the Virgin. The ritual of purification after delivery, usually referred to as the 'Churching of women', was an obligatory rite of passage for women who had given birth – regardless of whether the child was healthy or stillborn, or whether the mother was married or unmarried. The ritual is first mentioned in the sixth century in a letter from Archbishop Augustine of Canterbury to Pope Gregory the Great in the Venerable Bede's *Ecclesiastical History of England*. The ritual is then described in liturgical books from the eleventh century, while in the twelfth century, there are references that show that the resumption of marital relations before the performance of this ritual was considered to be a mortal sin (Lee 1996: 44). Finally, by the end of the nineteenth century, the ritual was optional, and only performed on demand. From the fourteenth century onwards, however, it had been obligatory. It served as a symbol of women's re-entry into normal life after a period of rest after delivery. Its scriptural basis was a passage in Leviticus which states that the mother is unclean for 40 days if she gives birth to a male child and 80 days if she gives birth to a female child:

> Speak to the people of Israel, saying: If a woman conceives and bears a male child, she shall be ceremonially unclean for seven days; as at the time of her menstruation, she shall be unclean. On the eighth day, the flesh of his foreskin shall be circumcised. Her time of blood purification shall be thirty-three days; she shall not touch any holy thing, or come into the sanctuary, until the days of her purification are completed. If she bears a female child, she shall be unclean for two weeks, as in her menstruation; her time of blood purification shall be sixty-six days.
>
> *(Leviticus 12:2–5)*

The ritual would be performed shortly after the period of uncleanliness had passed. It echoed Jewish practices of ritual purification, but, more importantly, it also tied in with popular ideas about sexuality. Christian dogma defined the body as sinful, and this applied especially to its sexual function, which was tainted by Original Sin, an idea which also found support in another passage in Leviticus, which states that both man and woman are unclean for one day after intercourse:

> If a man has an emission of semen, he shall bathe his whole body in water, and be unclean until the evening. Everything made of cloth or of skin on which the semen falls shall be washed with water, and be unclean until the evening. If a man lies with a woman and has an emission of semen, both of them shall bathe in water, and be unclean until the evening.
>
> *(Leviticus 15:16–18)*

Mary Douglas' theory of religious purity and impurity is illustrative of the logic behind this attitude to bodily emissions (Douglas 1966, 1970). In her account, bodily orifices are associated with impurity because they open the body to the environment and break the bodily borders. Both intercourse and giving birth involve the transgression of the female body, the symbolic breaking of its integrity: when the man 'enters' her body and when the newborn emerges from her body. On this logic, giving birth is a transgression which needs to be followed by a ritual cleansing in order for the woman to be restored to her former state. The ritual was sustained by strong taboos: For example, it was believed that intercourse with a woman before her Churching could harm the child and cause leprosy (Lee 1996: 46). When the ritual was made obligatory in the fourteenth century, the prescribed period of 40 days from delivery to ritual was abandoned, and instead the ritual was to be performed as soon as possible. This was not necessarily a good thing, since the woman's period of impurity gave her a respite from daily duties. During this time (the laying-in), she was surrounded by female company, which started with the midwife's presence at birth (Lee 1996: 48).

Since the ritual was obligatory, even if the child was stillborn or died shortly after birth, it is quite clear that its traditional meaning was as a ritual of purification and that it was modelled on the ritual of Mary's purification: "When the time came for their purification according to the law of Moses, they brought him up to Jerusalem to present him to the Lord" (Luke 2:22). The ritual concerned the mother alone. The child was usually brought to church by the father or midwife to witness the occasion, but the child had no part in the ritual itself. It was adopted by the Protestant churches after the Reformation, its structure remaining almost unchanged (Knödel 1997). It contained the following elements:[4]

> When the congregation is seated, the mother waits at the church entrance. Her head covered, she is kneeling. The priest arrives, saying prayers from the Psalms over her head, followed by Gloria, Kyrie and Our Father. He then sprinkles her with holy water, the same as used in baptism (i.e. water blessed by the priest) before she is led into the church by the priest. In the Catholic rite, the priest does not lead her by the arm, but offers her the left extremity of the stole and leads her into the church, saying: 'Enter thou into the temple of God, adore the Son of the Blessed Virgin Mary who has given thee fruitfulness of offspring'.[5]

In the Protestant churches, the ritual was renamed "Thanksgiving of Women after Childbirth" (in the Anglican Church this new name was introduced in 1552), but it retained its former structure. The message of the Psalms that were used give a good impression of the serenity of the rite: "The Lord is my shepherd, I shall not want. He makes me lie down in green pastures; he leads me beside still waters; he restores my soul. He leads me in right paths for his name's sake" (Psalm 23:1–3). Clearly, the benevolent Father who cares for the living is the focal point here: "The Lord will keep you from all evil; he will keep your life. The Lord will keep your going out and your coming in from this time on and forevermore" (Psalm

121:7–8). And in rich metaphorical language, the Garden of Eden is evoked: "Happy is everyone who fears the Lord, who walks in his ways. You shall eat the fruit of the labour of your hands; you shall be happy, and it shall go well with you. Your wife will be like a fruitful vine within your house; your children will be like olive shoots around your table. Thus shall the man be blessed who fears the Lord" (Psalm 128:1–4).

Interestingly, the ritual is absent from the first manual for the post-Reformation Lutheran Church of Norway (*Kirkeordinansen* 1539). Instead, women were advised "to keep away from church for the traditional period in order not to cause offence" (§11). But the tradition had lingered on, and the ritual was reintroduced in 1607. But in 1754 it was made optional, and over the next century it gradually disappeared. Similar developments are found in the Anglican Church as well as the Catholic Church. One possible explanation for the ritual's demise is the redefinition of the body which had started during the Enlightenment. Another explanation is sociological in nature and points to the transition from close-knit rural communities to industrial urban communities, a process which started in the nineteenth century and which was accompanied by a decline in religious affiliation. In addition to external factors, the religious meanings of pregnancy and birth also changed. To what extent the ritual of Churching was perceived as a necessary act of cleansing, and hence associated with some kind of public humiliation of the 'sinful woman', would probably depend on the way the priest conducted the act – as well as on the circumstances surrounding the birth (e.g. conception out of wedlock). Becky Lee mentions that unmarried women would seek to have the ritual performed outside their own parish (Lee 1996). Nevertheless, the gradual disappearance of the ritual was probably not due to women's protests; instead, it was likely part of a more general change in religiosity. In the eighteenth century, Pietism introduced an individualistic and inner turn into Protestantism, and this resulted, among other things, in a de-emphasis on ritual and a new focus on experience:

> The need for, and the possibility of, an authentic and vitally significant experience of God on the part of individual Christians; the religious life as a life of love for God and man, which is marked by social sensitivity and ethical concern; utter confidence, with respect to the issues of both life and death.
>
> *(Stoeffler 1973: IX)*

Under the influence of Pietism, religion lost much of its communal basis, as personal faith started to become emphasized. A similar change, albeit on a smaller scale, can be traced in Catholicism, which saw a rise in individual religious practices (e.g. pilgrimage) and private prayer (Eriksen and Stensvold 2002). With the onset of modernity, the ritual of Churching became optional and gradually fell out of use.

Obviously, these changes also reflected a change in the Christian approach to the female body as well as to childbirth. They may also be a result of the strengthening of the medical profession. As historian Thomas Laqueur observes, new ways of interpreting the body reflect new social realities (Laqueur 1987: 4). Put differently, the ritual lost its former importance as the female body ceased to be defined religiously and came to be redefined as a biological object.

The Reformation was a catalyst which set things into motion. Graphically speaking, we may say that science emerged in the gulf that separated Catholicism from Protestantism. The monopoly of the Catholic Church had been broken. With two competing versions of the same God, the idea of absolute truth was impossible to maintain and the quest for truth – by means of scientific investigation – could begin. Historically, we may say that science developed within a Christian context. But by no means did it emerge because of the latter. Put differently, "when Catholics and Protestants started competing for the same God, relativism was introduced into European thought". This observation was first formulated by Peter Berger in *The Sacred Canopy* (1967) and elaborated further in *Between Relativism and Fundamentalism* (2010). Berger writes about the historical importance of the Reformation and the forced acknowledgement of religious diversity which it entailed. "Pluralism relativizes. It does so both institutionally and in the consciousness of individuals" (Berger 2010: 5). Arguing that pluralism, not secularism, was the most important feature of religion in the contemporary world, Berger sees religion as a civilizing factor.

The Reformation created new (religious) authorities and opened up new avenues of reflection. One of these was the individual's own responsibility towards God. Charles Taylor describes this as a shift in background which may be described as a move from transcendence to immanence, from God to Nature, "from a world in which the place of fullness was understood as unproblematically outside or 'beyond' human life, to a conflicting age in which this construal is challenged by others which place it 'within' human life" (Taylor 2007: 15). Although Protestantism was the prime mover, the Catholic Church followed up with its own measures. The Counter-Reformation is often described as having been a strategy designed to counteract the onslaught against papal power; however, as David Luebke argues, the Counter-Reformation was part of the same historical processes and responded to the same challenges that resulted in the Reformation (Luebke 1999).

Notes

1 Kuriyama emphasizes the difference between Greek and Chinese medicine (Kuriyama 1999), but the distance between Galen and modern medicine is probably even greater.
2 Citation in Brind'Amour 2007. This law has received a new importance in contemporary abortion debates, notably in the rhetoric of anti-abortion activists.

3 I am not aware of similar attempts to enact radical changes to abortion legislation in any Protestant countries at the time.
4 See Natalie Knödel's analysis of the rite available at http://users.ox.ac.uk/~mikef/church2.html.
5 Citation from *The Catholic Encyclopedia* available at http://www.newadvent.org/cathen/03761a.htm.

7

THEORIES OF PROCREATION

The period of 200 years between the seventeenth and nineteenth centuries is usually referred to as the Enlightenment. It is often described as a sudden awakening or depicted as a revolution where old religious 'truths' were replaced with scientific knowledge. Among the historical reasons for the radical changes that Europe underwent in the sixteenth and seventeenth centuries must be counted the discovery of America in 1492 and the opening of maritime trade routes to the East in the sixteenth century, both of which fundamentally changed the European view of the world. The emergence of modern science was a part of these developments. It was a slow process, and it took more than two centuries of uneasy cohabitation before science emerged as a competing secular world view. Still, it should not be forgotten that science began as a quest for knowledge about God's creation. Medical science is a case in point. Spurred on by the big discoveries mentioned above, scientists set out to gain new insights into God's creation on a micro level.

The Reformation created a split within Christianity (Protestantism emerged as an alternative to Catholicism). By the middle of the seventeenth century, the scientific study of human procreation and pregnancy started to change. Up to that point, Aristotle's theory had informed elite conceptions of the human body, while the tradition from Galen dominated medical practice. In the scientific quest of the Enlightenment, both resurfaced in a new setting and gave rise to two competing theories of human procreation: *epigenesis* and *preformation* (De Renzi 2004: 213). Interestingly, there was no split between Protestant and Catholic scientists. Religion may have provided them with different habits and traditions, but it did not determine their scientific research. Enlightenment science was a secular arena, but nevertheless, Christianity continued to exert strong but indirect influence on it. Christian ideas about the human being – our moral weaknesses and propensity to sin – continued long after Enlightenment science had launched competing theories of human procreation.

The origins of new theories must be sought in the undercurrent of practical medicine. Since antiquity, the theories of Hippocrates and Galen had defined the man's semen as seed and had compared the mother's womb to the soil. But Galen made an additional claim, namely, that women also produced seed, which, like male seed, was emitted during orgasm. Consequently, Galen not only envisaged conception as a sign of male creativity, but approached it as "the result of the reception, mixing, heating and stimulation of the male and female seeds in the uterus" (De Renzi 2004: 208). This was a well-known theory in medieval Europe, and it inspired research on human reproduction among Enlightenment scientists. This does not, however, mean that Galen broke with a patriarchal framework of understanding. The female seed was less important and weaker than the male variety, and only the male seed could bring life – if this were not the case, women would have been able to conceive singlehandedly without male assistance, and men would therefore be superfluous. To the contemporary reader, this may seem strange, but at the time it received enough scientific interest to warrant its own term: 'spontaneous generation'. However, the majority of Enlightenment scientists subscribed to one of the two dominant theories at the time, namely, epigenesis and preformation.

As the term suggests, epigenesis held that the foetus developed gradually from a simple form to a complex body. This progressive understanding was based on the notion that growth came about through an inherent capacity or inner force in the semen – a force which ensured that the offspring would start to develop and eventually grow into the same shape as the father (De Renzi 2004: 209). Once the seed was in the right environment (the womb), it would start to grow according to the pattern of its species. Thus, the seed would develop, if temperature and humidity allowed it, into a human, a dog, a potato – all according to its own prototype. The process was complex as well as delicate, and any change in external conditions could infringe on the foetus' growth; for example, insufficient nutrition would result in a female child. According to the competing preformation theory, however, every new human being was fully formed from the start. The father's semen contained a ready-formed miniature, a preformed individual. Thus, Adam's seed would, according to this theory, contain all successive individuals, one inside the other in increasingly smaller versions. It is not hard to see how this theory went hand-in-hand with Augustine's theory of Original Sin. But for various reasons, this correspondence did not give preformation many supporters among theologians. Instead, preformation was the preferred theory among scientists for the next 200 years. However, there were two opposing theories within the preformationist camp: *animalculism* and *ovism*. The scientists who were known as animalculists maintained that the father's semen contained a miniature version of the would-be individual. Obviously, this theory fitted almost seamlessly with Augustine's rendering of Original Sin, with Adam serving as the master copy for all subsequent generations. The competing theory, ovism, held that a preformed individual was already present in the mother's egg (*ovum*) – usually referred to as female seed – which provided a kind of frame on which the male seed could work in order to initiate growth (De Renzi 2004: 208).

Discussions between the followers of epigenesis and preformation theory lasted for more than 200 years – from the middle of the seventeenth to the late eighteenth century. What made the disagreement so profound and what brought the debates to a virtual standstill was twofold: Not only did scientists disagree about the interpretation of empirical data, but they referred to different facts altogether. The latter problem was mainly due to the poor quality of their handmade microscopes. And because the quality of the instruments varied, the results of one experiment could seldom be repeated by another scientist with a different microscope. Nevertheless, the microscope did for medical science what the telescope did for astronomy: It allowed scientists to develop more detailed and systematic knowledge and laid the foundation for modern scientific disciplines. The microscope was invented in the Netherlands in the 1590s (lenses), and Galileo's microscope from around 1630 added a focusing device. It was supposed to reveal the true nature of the physical world, but when the instrument came into general use in the second half of the seventeenth century, it did not give rise to scientific agreement. Instead, it enhanced the inherent bias of all research methods, allowing scientists to see the evidence they wanted to see – which naturally supported the theory that they wanted to endorse. Thus, the discussions went on with no 'winner' until the advent of better technical equipment allowed nineteenth-century scientists to arrive at an agreement in favour of epigenesis.

The foundation of The Royal Society in London in 1660 was an important step towards cooperation among scientists. Scientists from all over Europe communicated their findings to the Royal Society (in Latin), and thereby participated in the same scientific debates. It served as a truly international body for the "improvement of natural knowledge", to quote from its official name. It monitored scientific debates and created the basis for an independent scientific community far removed from the control of religious authorities.

Anatomical research during the Enlightenment was of varying quality. With hindsight, it is possible to say that the discovery of ovaries (named female testicles) and the subsequent studies that revealed how the ovaries contained seed (*vesicules* in Latin) – or eggs as we now call them (*ova* in Latin) – were particularly important. From the 1670s onwards, similar observations of female eggs were made independently by several anatomists – although it took more than two centuries before the matter was finally settled.[1] Ovaries in egg-laying animals had been known for some time when the discovery of a similar organ in humans challenged the Christian distinction between humans and animals. For when ovists claimed that humans developed from eggs, they implicitly compared humans to egg-laying animals and disrupted the distinction between the species as expressed in Genesis. But in the seventeenth and eighteenth centuries, neither the

Catholic Church nor any of the Protestant churches took these new theories seriously enough to engage in the scientific debate; instead, they held on to Aquinas'
theory of procreation. But, among the few Christian theologians who participated
in these debates, animalculism was clearly the theory that was in favour. Almost
like an illustration of theological dogma, the theory envisaged the miniscule individual inside the father's (Adam) sperm. One can only wonder why the Church
authorities let this possibility of having dogma be supported by science pass. But
taking the unequal power of science and theology into consideration, it becomes
obvious that Christian leaders were not looking to science for confirmation of
religious truth; if anything, they expected it to be the other way around.

But even if animalculism could have served as a model for Christian ideas
about procreation, it was epigenesis which was best suited to Aquinas' theology
and which formed the basis for abortion in Canon law. In accordance with the
epigenesis theory, the law took for a fact that the foetus developed from the
father's sperm in the mother's womb and passed through distinctive stages until it
was fully formed. Ovism was the theory most clearly at odds with Christian
theology. If we transpose this theory to religion, it would mean that Eve had eggs
embedded somewhere in her inner reproductive organs when she emerged from
Adam's rib and that the eggs inside the Virgin Mary contained the form of Christ
even before his conception. This was hardly compatible with Christian dogma.
However, the latent conflict between science and religion was not open at this
time. Most scientists omitted it and refrained from open confrontation with religious truths. If they were aware of a (latent) conflict, they would pay lip service
to religious authority and attend church rituals like the rest of the population. In
the few instances in which scientists did admit to a conflict, the outcome could be
dramatic, as in the famous case of Galileo, who barely avoided excommunication
(Finocchiaro 1997). The facts and frameworks that were set in motion during the
Enlightenment eventually resulted in the separation of science and religion. Some
of the main contributors to the study of (human) procreation elaborated their
theories through the dissection of both human corpses and various kinds of animal
carcasses. Since dissection was allowed only on corpses of convicted criminals,
female corpses were few and knowledge of female anatomy lagged behind.
Therefore, studies of pregnancy and how the foetus develops in the mother's
womb were generally not derived from dissections performed on human bodies.
The emerging theories on pregnancy and foetal development, then, varied and
were to some extent dependent on the animal carcass that was used.

Among the pioneer anatomists who contributed to more detailed knowledge
about the female reproductive organs was a former student of Vesalius, Gabriele
Falloppio (1523–1562). In a book he published in 1561, Observationes anatomicae (*Anatomical Observations*), he described the female reproductive organs in a
strikingly poetic fashion as follows: "That slender and narrow seminal passage
arises from the horn of the uterus very white and sinewy but after it has passed
outward a little way it becomes gradually broader and curls like the tendrils of a

vine until it comes near the end".[2] As suggested by its name, he discovered the Fallopian tubes, i.e. the tubes that connect the ovaries with the uterus. But without access to a microscope, which was invented almost 100 years later, Falloppio described the tubes (incorrectly) as being attached to the ovaries, thus repeating Galen's old interpretation (Elmer 2004). Taking into account that Falloppio was a Catholic priest having served as a canon at the Cathedral of Modena for two years before he studied medicine, he shows a surprising degree of intellectual independence. He studied the female reproductive organs, including the clitoris; named the vagina; and asserted the existence of the hymen in virgins – a knowledge which traditionally belonged to midwives. Falloppio is also celebrated as the inventor of the condom, a linen sheath "soaked in medication", i.e. abortive herbs (Jütte 2008: 96). However, he did not intend it to serve as a contraceptive device, but as protection against syphilis.

Although Falloppio's links with the Church were severed when he started to study medicine at the age of 23, he did not make an official break with it. Since the Catholic Church conceived of the priesthood as a status, and not as a profession, Falloppio remained a part of the clergy and lived in celibacy throughout his life. Nevertheless, his scientific studies were evidently not controlled in any way by the religious authorities. The main reason for his intellectual freedom, however, was the protection he had as a professor of anatomy at the University of Padua, an institution which was under the protection of Venice, a city-state that was so powerful that its universities were independent of the Church. Falloppio's life story illustrates the uneasy relationship between the religious and the scientific realms: an ordained priest who spent his life on science and could do so because he lived under the protection of the Venetian city-state.

For scientists living in Protestant countries, the relationship with religious authorities was different. Luther emphasized the two separate realms of church and state, religion and the secular world, thereby creating a space in between for the pursuit of science. Since it belonged to the realm of human endeavour, science was under the protection of kings rather than bishops. Nevertheless, Luther himself saw God as the ultimate source of healing. The physician was acting on God's behalf – applying the knowledge acquired through diligent study of the natural world (Grell 2004: 88). During the political instability and upheaval of the seventeenth century, the free pursuit of science flourished in Britain. William Harvey (1578–1657) was one of the most prominent anatomists of his day. He studied in Padova (at the time Galileo was there) and revolutionized medicine with his discovery that the heart functioned like a pump. Furthermore, Harvey was among the first supporters of Descartes' body model (Wright 2013). Indeed, his definition of the heart as a pump marked the start of the mechanistic body model, which eventually suppressed the traditional humerological approach with its focus on body temperature and fluid balance.

Famous for his discovery of the circulatory system, Harvey also made his mark in embryology. He was convinced that all life has its origin in eggs – "*ex ovo omnia"* – and reportedly performed elaborate investigations on live animals – which he undertook in his own home to avoid criticism. Harvey had a brilliant career, and in 1618 he received the title 'Physician Extraordinary' from James I, a king with Catholic leanings, who was nominally an Anglican and who had taken on the role as head of the Anglican Church. Interestingly, King James regarded his royal position as divinely ordained and held aspirations to be an absolute monarch, which also affected his role as ultimate authority of the Church. His reign ended in 1649, when he was executed by Oliver Cromwell (1649–1660). But Harvey seems to have emerged untainted by his association with the monarch. The last years of his life Harvey dedicated to comparative studies of the reproductive organs of various animals. The last three chapters of *Exercitationes de generatione animalum* (*Studies in Animal Generation*), which was published in 1651, were dedicated to human generation. Here, Harvey argued that human beings stem from eggs. He also refuted the dominant view of menstrual blood as the building material of the body. In this connection, he made an explicit argument for epigenesis by illustrating how the gradual formation of limbs took place, and he supported his claims by detailed descriptions of dissections that he had performed on live animals.

Enlightenment science was an international affair; it was an Italian scientist, Marcello Malpighi (1628–1694), who further developed Harvey's studies of the exchange between arteries and veins in the capillary system and who wrote a thesis of how blood and air are mixed in the lungs (Lawrence 2008). Like Harvey, Malpighi was an ovist. In 1673, he published his theory on procreation, which was based on a detailed study of chickens' development. His book was called *De formatione de pulli in ovo* (*On the Formation of the Chick in the Egg*). Like other anatomists at the time, Malpighi conducted extensive comparative studies of organs in different types of animals. Himself a Christian, he was convinced that the human body was a part of nature and that fruitful comparisons could be made between chicken and frogs, silk worms and human embryos – since they were all a part of God's creation. A good microscope allowed Malpighi to study the chicken embryos in great detail. He reportedly detected a twelve-hour-old chicken embryo and described how the preformed structures gradually became visible.

Malpighi was appointed chief physician to Pope Innocent XII (r. 1691–1700) and spent his last years in the Quirinale Palace in Rome. Innocent XII was a pope of the Enlightenment, a modern man who valued knowledge and rationality. Among other things, he abolished the papal right to bestow Church properties on family members – a radical measure undertaken in order to stem corruption within the Church. This pope's choice of Malpighi as his physician was clearly an appointment based on the latter's merits as a scientist and reflected Innocent XII's positive attitude towards science. Malpighi's most important contribution to the study of procreation was methodological. He was among the first scientists to use the microscope, and he enthusiastically embraced Descartes' dictum of approaching the body as a machine. However, he did not replace Galen's theory of the balance of humours with Descartes' theory, but combined the two. He used Descartes as a frame of reference, but it was Galen who inspired his research questions. Malpighi's dissections and microscopic investigations were in fact attempts to find the origins of bodily fluids. This led him to the discovery of the glands, which he regarded as the fundamental structures of the body and he referred to as the "workshop" of nature (De Renzi 2004: 176). When viewed through the microscope, most organs, according to Malpighi, have a granular structure that produces excretions by extracting elements from the blood. Malpighi understood this to be a rule; therefore, the liver emitted bile, the kidneys urine, and the testes semen. Malpighi was also among the first to describe the development of the silk worm from a caterpillar into a silk moth. According to him, the development was initiated by a pre-existing moth structure within the caterpillar.

Malpighi's work on the silk worm gained him admission into the Royal Society of London in 1669, and he was thereby able to get in touch with other scientists across Europe, including Protestants such as the Dutch anatomist Jan Swammerdam with whom he corresponded directly. The fact that Malpighi was a Catholic and Swammerdam a member of the Dutch Reformed Church did not factor into their relationship. Matthew Cobb argues convincingly that their scientific communications continued even after Swammerdam became a mystic and withdrew from science, but he admits that their relationship changed: "After 1675 the 'debate' took on a strange form – the protagonists were unaware of each other's work – nevertheless it did continue, indicating that both scientists thought it important" (Cobb 2002: 136). This episode illustrates the importance of the Royal Society of London, which monitored the debate. Although their correspondence criss-crossed and answers were furnished after one of the parties was dead, the fact that a papal physician in Rome and a religious mystic Protestant in the Netherlands held each other in mutual respect, and the fact that both were recognized as important scientists by the Royal Society, is evidence of science developing into an increasingly autonomous and secular enterprise.

The most influential among the Dutch anatomists was probably Regnier de Graaf (1641–1673), who was a strong proponent of ovism, a theory which held, as we have seen, that the individual existed in miniature inside the egg. According to de Graaf, the female egg contained a miniature human that started to grow as soon as it was infused with the life force of the father's sperm. De Graaf defined the male's sperm as "nothing other than the vehicle of an extremely volatile animal spirit, which imprints a vital contact onto the matter of the embryo that is the female egg" (Roger 1997: 238). Together with his teacher and two fellow students, Jan Swammerdam and Niels Stensen, de Graaf dissected several female cadavers in Leiden in the winter of 1667. In accordance with Dutch law, these cadavers were donated to science by the prison authorities (Dupont 2008). Since most of them were former prostitutes and had given birth, the three students conducted detailed studies of female reproductive organs, studies which resulted in the redefinition of an organ formerly known as the female testicles. According to de

Graaf and his fellow students, these were in fact ovaries, a small organ which other anatomists had already identified in egg-laying animals.

The discovery of the human ovaries was an important contribution to embryology, but de Graaf's own commitment to ovism implied that he understood (wrongly) that the growth of the foetus was merely an increase of size. Meanwhile, de Graaf did not actually discover the female egg, but instead inferred its existence from the existence of the ovaries. What de Graaf and his fellow students discovered was an organ that is now known as the Graafian follicles, i.e. the structures that contain the immature eggs. The eggs were extremely difficult to detect; transparent and hidden by layers of tissue, they were in fact invisible before improved microscopes made it possible to detect them.

Although de Graaf did not hold any official teaching position, he was an influential scientist with important contacts in the European scientific community. At the time of his premature death (he was only 32 years old), he had received official recognition for his contribution and was already a member of the Royal Society of London. One of his associates, Antonie van Leeuwenhoek (1632–1723), was among the most prominent exponents of animalculism, the theory which held that the human individual existed preformed inside the sperm (Pinto-Correia 1997). He was a lens maker by profession and a self-taught anatomist. Regnier de Graaf introduced Leeuwenhoek to the Royal Society of London and helped translate his works to Latin; in 1678, Leeuwenhoek's *Philosophical Transactions* was published by the Royal Society. During the previous year, he wrote a letter to inform the Royal Society of his discovery, explaining his observations with enthusiasm: "I have often observed the sperm of a healthy man without waiting for it to become corrupt or fluid/watery, five or six minutes after ejaculation. I have noticed that a large number of small animals, I think it must be more than a thousand, on an area no larger than a grain of sand".[3] Although Leeuwenhoek was convinced that the sperm contained the germ of the new individual, he accepted de Graaf's discovery of the egg; he maintained, however, that it only served as nourishment for the growing seed.

Leeuwenhoek was a devoted member of the Dutch Reformed Church and had a profoundly religious attitude towards nature. He regarded scientific research as a religious task aimed at uncovering "the wonders God designed in making creatures small and great" (Graves 1996: 71). Since he was an expert lens maker and had access to the best technical equipment, he was also in a favourable position to make discoveries. Leeuwenhoek's most acclaimed contribution to science was his discovery (through observation) of *spermatozoa*, which he referred to as 'animalcules'. Their small size had made them impossible to see with less precise microscopes. And because he observed movement in live sperm, and since movement was the main characteristic of life, his discovery proved that male seed was indeed 'life-giving'. Interestingly, he received support from de Graaf although the latter was an ovist and held a different view regarding procreation.

Jan Swammerdam (1637–1680) was another Dutch anatomist and a former colleague of de Graaf's who also participated in the dissection of female cadavers in the winter of 1667; he made an important contribution to the description of female reproductive organs (Pinto-Correia 1997). However, Swammerdam had a falling out with de Graaf: He accused the latter of taking sole credit for the discovery of female ovaries. The allegations were not entirely without merit, since de Graaf had in fact published his findings without attributing them to his collaborators who worked with him during the winter of 1667 (Pinto-Correia 1997: 45). Swammerdam was an ovist like de Graaf, and he held that all creatures developed from miniscule individuals inside the egg. And like him, Swammerdam also rejected self-generation (spontaneous generation) on the grounds that it would be unnatural: It would allow chance and accident to rule rather than natural law (Cobb 2000). Swammerdam also discussed the role of the male seed, which he regarded as life-giving. His critique of epigenesis theory was published in 1669 in *Historia Insectorum Generalis* (*The General History of Insects*). It was based on his meticulous study of the development of the silk worm from a caterpillar to a moth; but unlike Malpighi, who had been unable to prove his theory, Swammerdam managed to describe some minute structures inside the caterpillar which he held to be the beginnings of wings. He took this as proof that the epigenesis theory was wrong when it described growth as metamorphosis, and he argued that the moth wings proved the existence of a preformed individual.

Although Swammerdam's study of the silk worm was later shown to be incorrect, it nevertheless paved the way for comparative anatomy and, more specifically, the theory that higher organisms share parallel patterns of development with lower organisms. Swammerdam was unmarried and a pious Protestant, but unlike his co-religionist Leeuwenhoek, he gave up science for religious reasons. In 1675, he became a religious mystic and joined a quietist sect in search of spiritual perfection. One year prior to this transition (1674), his friend and colleague Niels Stensen visited him in Amsterdam only to find him suffering from malaria and severe depression (Kermit 1998: 65). One year later, Swammerdam was to join Antoinette Bourignon's radical religious sect. This was quite literally a destructive choice, since the sect denounced science as the work of Satan. Consequently, Swammerdam burned all of his scientific papers – the result of years of research.

Antoinette Bourignon (1616–1680) was a laywoman and a visionary who preached in northern Europe in the 1660 and 1670s.[4] Hers was a Protestant sect, and she preached that it was possible to live a perfect life 'inside the world', i.e. outside any monastic system or ecclesiastical authority. Bourignon was born in France to a rich family with extensive properties, including an island (Nordstrand) just off the coast of Germany. It is here that Antoinette Bourignon wanted to bring her devotees and make a utopian society. Calling herself the new Eve and referring to Revelations 7, "the woman clothed with the sun", she attracted the hostility of Catholic as well as Protestant clergy. In Germany, she was stopped by Lutheran clergy and thereafter fled to the Netherlands, where she settled for a while until she was expelled. She then moved to Paris at approximately the same time that Swammerdam joined the sect. The sect had strict ascetic ideals of a life in silence, meditation, and renunciation of physical and material pleasures. Swammerdam was part of the inner circle for about two years. His religious devotion cooled, however, and during the remaining two-to-three years of his life he reportedly returned to science and took up his correspondence with Malpighi (Cobb 2000).

The third participant in the winter dissections of 1668–69 was Danish anatomist Niels Stensen (1638–1686). He was Swammerdam's friend and de Graaf's colleague, and he was known in scientific circles as Nicolas Steno and Niccolo Stenone. He was a truly international scientist, who studied in the Netherlands and France, was a member of the Royal Society of London, and held a position as an anatomist in Florence, having been granted that appointment by Leopold Medici, Galileo's former student, in 1666. Apart from his international career, his life story has several points in common with that of Swammerdam, for at the peak of his career he too left science for religion. While still an active scientist, Stensen made several anatomical discoveries. In 1675, he published a scientific article in which he described the female reproductive organs, including the eggs in the ovaries. This was three years after Swammerdam, and five years after de Graaf, had published their results. Like other anatomists before him, he did comparative studies of human and animal anatomy, and while in Florence he reportedly dissected a gigantic whale in a city square (Kermit 1998: 47). The last years of his scientific career Stensen dedicated to the study of the human heart. He was the first person to conceive of the heart as a muscle, an explanation which filled the gap in William Harvey's famous discovery that the heart functioned as a pump in the circulatory system.

Stensen also made comparative studies of the brain in various animals, searching for Descartes' *glandula pinealis* (pineal gland), which he had declared to be the seat of the human soul and which could only be found in the human brain. According to Descartes, the *glandula pinealis* served as a link between the body and the mind; Stensen was interested in this connection, so he devised a theory based on axiomatic Christian teachings on the uniqueness of mankind over and against animals. Since animals have no mind, no rationality, and no higher faculties, he reasoned, their brains must lack the pineal gland. Stensen referred to this idea as "a well formulated and promising hypothesis" (Grell 2007: 210). But his anatomical studies did not reveal any structural differences between human and animal brains, and he concluded that Descartes' theory of the pineal gland as seat of the rational soul was wrong, since it also existed in animals. In the same vein, Stensen dismissed the idea of the heart as the organ of the soul. In Christian thought, it was regarded as the most prestigious organ, "that more spirituall part of man, which is, as it were, the heart of that heart, that is, the soule", as stated in a seventeenth-century sermon to cure the hard-hearted (Slights 2008: 141). After having dissected a number of hearts, Stensen concluded that "there is nothing in the heart which is not also present in the muscle" (Kermit 1998: 35). There is good reason to believe that these results were decisive for Stensen's religious conversion. In a letter, Stensen attributed his rejection of Descartes to God's Providence, "implying that God had directed his anatomical undertakings" (Grell 2007: 210).

In 1667, while still in Florence, Stensen converted to Catholicism. A possible reason for his conversion, and ultimately for his change of careers, may be what he himself described as disappointment with the explicatory limitations of science. As an anatomist, he had also dissected hearts and had discovered that it was no different from other muscles in the body. Stensen's departure from research and subsequent pursuit of a career as a priest may also have had something to do with the fact that he had lost an appointment to a professorship in his native town of Copenhagen (1670) because he had refused to declare himself a Lutheran. He left Copenhagen in 1673 and returned to Florence, where he started studying theology and where he was ordained a priest (1674). Eventually, he was appointed bishop in northern Germany (Osnabrück), where he became widely known for his asceticism. Somewhat paradoxically, Pope John Paul II declared him a patron of science in 1988.

What most Enlightenment scientists resolved to do pragmatically, namely, going to church on Sunday and performing dissections on Monday, Swammerdam and Stensen were unwilling or unable to do. One may speculate whether in fact Stensen's religious crisis had something to do with his extensive research on the heart. As a matter of fact, in a letter to the German philosopher Gottfried Wilhelm von Leibniz (published in Naldini 1986) he gives some indication that this was indeed the case, as he expresses relief at having been saved from "the Cartesian philosophy". It was not the machine theory he objected to, however, but the lack of humility and excessive pride he found in Descartes. In Stensen's view, God was omnipotent: "It is impossible that he has given me the ability to think, without him foreseeing all my thoughts".[5]

Like ancient Greece, seventeenth-century Europe was an agricultural society. People were well aware of the practical aspects of animal breeding, and the causal link between intercourse and pregnancy was well known. The questions that inspired research on human procreation were not interested in how procreation took place, but why it took place: Why did women become pregnant on certain occasions and not on other occasions? In the Greek model, it was framed as a question: Why does seed start to grow? This question inspired the theories of epigenesis and preformation, which have been discussed in some detail above. These were modern theories based on empirical studies, but their bases and inspirations were traditional. If Augustine's theory of Original Sin informed animalculism, it would be fair to say that Galen's idea about female seed inspired ovism and that the epigenesis theory resembled Aquinas' theological explanations of procreation, which provided the theological underpinning of abortion in Canon law for more than 500 years. From this perspective, it is possible to argue that the popularity of the competing theory, preformation, among Enlightenment scientists points to a latent split between science and religion.

Another issue that had to do with answering the questions that surrounded human fertility, but which in fact did *not* occupy the early Enlightenment scientists treated above, was the role of menstruation. They took it for a fact that women, unlike animals, did not have periods of heat when they were fertile and eager to copulate. Consequently, they assumed (wrongly) that menstruation was the human version of animal heat: "menstruation in a woman came to be interpreted as the precise equivalent of the heat in animals, marking the only period during which women are normally fertile" (the French physician Achille Chéreau cited in Laqueur 1987: 27). These problems continued to occupy scientists, but they required entirely new approaches in order to be solved.

Notes

1 A definitive discovery of eggs in human females was not made until 1827, when a decisive study – *Epistola de ovi mammalium et hominis genesi* (*On the Origin of the Mammalian and Human Egg*) – was published by the German zoologist Karl Ernst von Baer.
2 Citation from Ankum, Houtzager and Bleker 1996: 365.
3 Letter from Leeuwenhoek to Pieter Rabus dated 30 November 1694, which can be found in Leeuwenhoek's *Vifde Vervolg der Brieven* (*Fifth Volume of Letters,* published in 1696). Here, it is cited from Gilbert 2013.
4 Unfortunately, there are no published studies in English or French of Antoinette Bourignon and her sect – although many scientific articles and books mention her. Matthew Cobb, who has written extensively on Swammerdam, refers (in a footnote) to a French book from 1912 by H. Bouquet (*Le mysticisme d'un anatomist*) (Cobb 2006), and Clara Pinto-Correia, in her chapter on Swammerdam, gives just a brief account of Bourignon in a footnote (Pinto-Correia 1997: 316, n.19) without reference to sources. The information I present here is based on the "Antoinette Bourignon" entry in *Encyclopaedia Britannica Online*, which is available at http://www.britannica.com/EBchecked/topic/75874/Antoinette-Bourignon.
5 For the letter, see Naldini 1986: 23 (my translation).

8

VARIETIES OF SCIENTIFIC TRUTH
Descartes, Deism, and relativism

Enlightenment science's conception of the human body as an assemblage of organs and functions was hardly compatible with the Christian view of the body as a 'temple of the soul'. The main proponent of this new understanding was the French philosopher René Descartes (1596–1650). Indirectly, however, Christianity provided a framework (world view) and a vocabulary which allowed a new approach to nature to emerge. Deism, a philosophical world view which emerged among intellectual elites in the sixteenth and seventeenth centuries, made the transition easier. Central to Deism was the notion of "the world as designed by God". It served as an intermediary stage between the Christian and the scientific world view, where man, not God, was at the centre of the universe (Taylor 2007).

To investigate human organs and provide scientific descriptions of sperm and eggs was one thing, but to explain complex processes such as pregnancy and foetal growth was quite another. For Enlightenment scientists, pregnancy and birth were natural functions of the female body. Therefore, they made detailed studies of procreation, but left the mother's body, so to speak, untouched. In their view, pregnancy and birth were practical matters which required certain technical skills, not theoretical explanations. These were concerns for women and midwives, not physicians. Speaking of midwifery, it would also be influenced – in its own way – by the changes in medical science brought about during the Enlightenment.

The seventeenth century saw a marked increase in the growth of specialized knowledge and the subsequent professionalization of medical expertise (Schiebinger 1987: 70). A decisive sign of this change was the marginalization of midwives, a process that peaked in 1760 when they were no longer recognized as expert witnesses in abortion cases under British law. Abortion was to be treated like other crimes, and the courts were instructed to prosecute this crime "according to the common-law standards of proof that were applied to most other crimes"

(Clark and Crawford 1994: 7). The expert witness in these cases was to be a physician. As a direct outcome of research activities carried out during the Enlightenment, the medical profession changed from a field of mixed practices to a defined field of knowledge with the university-educated physician on top and midwife and barber–surgeon below. In other words, the medical profession was developing into an exclusive (male) enterprise. At the same time, the field of medicine was becoming smaller as a range of practices were excluded after having been defined as unscientific (and therefore unserious). Although midwifery still counted as one of a few specialized disciplines, female midwives were unable to find a place in the system, since university education was for men only (Siraisi 1990). In Europe and America, women were admitted to secondary schools and universities starting from the last part of the nineteenth century.

The professionalization of medicine started in the sixteenth century with improvements in university education. An increase in the number of educational facilities resulted in a significant rise in the number of university-educated physicians who set up their practices in large towns, where they catered to the wealthy. Although midwifery was excluded from these developments, it too underwent some modernization as 'midwife knowledge' was systematized and published in written manuals such as Jane Sharp's from 1671 that we mentioned earlier in Chapter 4. But unlike other areas of medicine, midwifery was not developed further; no standard curriculum emerged, and no university education either. Midwifery was practiced mainly by women, and midwives had a low social standing compared to (male) physicians. Writing about British midwifery, Sheena Sommers claims that by the eighteenth century "male physicians had replaced female midwives as the preferred birthing attendants among the aristocracy and wealthy middle class" (Sommers 2011: 89). The midwives lagged behind because they had no formal education and did not know Latin; they merely had practical skills and a basic knowledge of surgery. But unlike male barber–surgeons, they missed out on the competition: During the seventeenth and eighteenth centuries, barber–surgeons underwent a transformation as they formed their own guilds and initiated a process whereby their education became increasingly standardized. In the nineteenth century surgeons were recognized as fully fledged members of the medical community with obligatory university education and official certification. The driving force behind this transformation was the surgeons' need for official recognition, and the way they did it was by emulating the far more prestigious physicians with their university education and their exclusive guild. In the process, the barber–surgeons also took over much of the midwives' functions – the most notable of which was being the expert witness in court. The female midwives were gradually reduced to being mere helpers in the process (Ackerknecht 1976). Important to note here is that these 'male midwives' helped redefine pregnancy as something which could be understood and managed through science rather than through experience. Like other bodily functions, pregnancy and birth were objectified and increasingly moved further away from the female sphere of influence.

Ackerknecht's critical analysis of the emergence of the medical profession begs the question of whether it would have been possible for the midwives to have followed a similar trajectory and to have emerged from the Enlightenment as medical experts like the barber–surgeons. The simple answer is 'no'. Women were in a socially subordinate position and barred from acting independently: They were not allowed to organize guilds and were unable to start their own scientific educational facilities. The midwife's loss of social prestige is ironically the reverse of the barber–surgeon's gain of prestige. But even though pregnancy and birth were included in the (male) physicians' field of expertise, the man-midwifes did not replace women from performing midwifery outside the hospitals. In the countryside, where women continued to give birth at home, midwifery continued much as it had before.

Although physicians studied at universities and were respected among the social elites, it took a long time before new medical theories translated into more effective medical treatments. In medical practice, the treatments prescribed by the Hippocratic–Galenic tradition continued much as before and continued to shape the experiences and expectations of ordinary people. In one area, however, this folk knowledge was closer to the facts than the new, Enlightenment medical theories: the notion that women could experience orgasm. It stemmed originally from Hippocrates, who, in *On Generation*, explained how the semen was an extract from all body parts, particularly from the brain, and that this was the reason behind the intensity of the pleasure which resulted in orgasm (Darmon 1977: 38). Galen – who agreed with this last argument – compared male and female orgasm, and claimed that they served the same function: Just as the male orgasm was necessary in order for the man to emit his seed, so too women experienced orgasm and emitted seed during sexual intercourse. The theory was a part of folk medicine from antiquity to modernity. It never influenced Church doctrine and was ignored by official knowledge regimes, and this can partly be explained by its close association with a vice; in short, it encouraged sexual pleasure in women. The midwife Jane Sharp's manual from 1671, however, takes Galen's theory for granted when it describes the anatomy of the clitoris as follows: "being nervous, and of pure feeling, when it is rubbed and stirred it causeth lustful thoughts, which being communicated to these ligaments [that fasten the womb] is passed to the vessels that carry seed" (Sharp 1999: 56). Here, Sharp refers implicitly to Galen's theory of female orgasm and how the orgasm was indeed a prerequisite for procreation.

The discrepancy between folk knowledge and official Church teaching points to a persistent conflict between official religion and folk culture, between laypeople and religious elites. The two converged, however, in the view on woman's role in society: Both assigned her a subordinate position as assistant to her husband in everything, including his procreative project. As the passage from Sharp's manual shows, Galen's theory on female orgasm was part of folk culture, but was ignored by theology. It was simply incompatible with Church doctrine after Augustine, who in a logical tour de force had linked Original Sin with sexuality. Since Enlightenment scientists were uninterested in women's experience and valued rationality more than they did Galenic medicine, insights like Jane Sharp's were ignored.

When Enlightenment scientists studied pregnancy, the most interesting question was not the function of the uterus before, during, and after pregnancy, but why a woman would become pregnant in the first place and – in conjunction with this – why some women would become pregnant almost regularly while others would be barren. For centuries, this problem was approached not in terms of fertility but as a question of foetal growth and the nutritive conditions in the womb. Modelled on their foreknowledge of the reproduction of animals and plants, scientists approached it as a question of growth. Normally, seeds (sperm) would start to grow when they reach the soil (womb). However, experience showed that sometimes seeds would not grow. Christianity explained it fatalistically, viewing the entire process of life maintenance and reproduction as God's domain, "so neither the one who plants nor the one who waters is anything, but only God who gives the growth" (1 Corinthians 3:7).

During the Enlightenment, research on human reproduction focused on the male seed rather than on female body functions or conditions in the womb. What intrigued scientists the most was the seed's capacity to grow, a process which they explained by referring to a 'life-force' – an almost mystical quality inherent in the semen. Regardless of which theory they followed, Enlightenment scientists believed that the man's seeds carried the life-force, soul, or form depending on which term they used. It was the semen that had the capacity to allow something that at first did not exist to come into being.[1] Christian theology relied on Augustine, who identified God as the ultimate source of life and "the form which operates internally" in the seed (*City of God* XII, 26). Augustine's use of the word 'form' in this connection is instructive. It shows evidence of Aristotelian influence. In fact, he redefined Aristotle's concept of faculty in Christian terms as an internal force which belonged to God. Aristotle's concept of faculty, on the other hand, was an inherent part of all living creatures. As growth is the other side of decay, procreation is not just the opposite of death, but is intrinsically linked to it. God had created each species with its own characteristics, and he had furnished each one with the unique capacity to evolve into its own form or shape. This form resides in the semen and ensures that a pea grows into a pea, a kitten becomes a cat, a human foetus becomes a child, and so on. Growth was monitored from the inside of each living creature, and theologians as well as scientists agreed that the crucial event – the beginning of life – was when the seed started to grow, be it in the earth, or in the womb of a woman. This was a mystery that Enlightenment science tried to understand.

Like the theological experts who took traditional ideas about women and female bodies for granted, Enlightenment scientists did not question established gender relations, but allowed traditional assumptions to influence their research questions. Thus, they took for granted the idea that the father was the source of life and restricted the mother's role in procreation to the provision of building and nutritive (menstrual blood) material. But since the menstrual cycle was unknown, Enlightenment theories about pregnancy and the foetal growth process remained speculative. Methodological obstacles added to the problem, since it was ethically impossible to anatomize pregnant women. Instead, they studied other species. One would study rabbits, and another would study dogs, while a third would extrapolate his findings from hens and they would all disagree deeply about the growth mechanism in humans. Two main positions can be discerned which coincide roughly with the two main theories of procreation. The supporters of the epigenesis theory understood growth as metamorphosis – for example, the change from a larva to a butterfly. They envisaged foetal development in the womb as a gradual evolution from formless matter to an animal shape to a human form. The competing theory, preformation, held that a pre-existing human individual existed in male sperm (animalculists) or in the female egg (ovists). Its proponents understood growth as a simple increase in size. As we have seen, the two theories could also combine, as when William Harvey and Regnier de Graaf combined epigenesis with a modified form of ovism. These differences aside, Enlightenment scientists agreed that the male seed initiated and maintained the process of growth.

A point of disagreement, however, among scientists concerned timing: When exactly did the foetus become a human being? Was it a sudden vivification of preformed individuals as the preformationists claimed, or was it a matter of slow development (metamorphosis) through a prescribed number of stages as the proponents of epigenesis maintained? This was a question of vast importance far beyond scientific circles: It was the basis for legal proceedings in connection with abortion, and it had a direct impact on people's lives. Before the question could be settled, the scientists had to arrive at a shared understanding of *what* started the process and *how* it was sustained. Was it a quality in the semen, in the egg, or in the menstrual blood?

As we have seen above, the question of growth intrigued and preoccupied Enlightenment scientists. But it only did so for a time until it was eventually abandoned. The interest in growth illustrates the close connection between religion and science at this point in time. This was not a question which derived from empirical studies, but which stemmed from Aquinas (who relied on Aristotle for his biology) and distinguished between three forms of the soul, identifying one of them – the vegetative soul – as being responsible for growth. As a theologian Aquinas was interested in the difference between the three forms of the soul and what it is that sets humans apart from animals. The question for him was the superiority of the godlike soul over the vegetative and sensuous souls. When Enlightenment scientists failed to identify either of these souls under the microscope, the problem was eventually left unanswered. Put differently, since there was no room for the soul in the mechanical conception of the body, the soul eventually became an exclusively religious category.

The French philosopher René Descartes (1596–1650) approached the human body in a way which epitomized the scientific breach with traditional thinking when he described it as if it were a mechanical object – a thing. Although Descartes made no attempt to openly criticize the Christian conception of man, his mechanical body model did in fact serve as an implicit critique of Christian anthropology, the latter emphasizing a moral approach to the body. In the words of Steven Shapin, "to do mechanical philosophy was therefore to be seen to be doing something radically different from attributing purpose, intention or sentience to natural entities" (Shapin 1996: 37). Similarly, Descartes made a categorical distinction between body and mind (*cogito*) which went against the grain of Christianity's idea of the human being as a unity of body-and-soul and godlikeness (*imago dei*). Although Descartes' relationship to religion was unclear, Shapin argues that Descartes did in fact make a conscious breach with old ways of thinking (Shapin 1996). In practice, however, Enlightenment science did not break away from theological dominance, since the study of nature was (in principle) subordinated to theology in the Church-dominated universities. Here, a practical division of work, as it were, between them allowed the natural philosophers to pursue the systematic investigation of nature quite independently of theology. This work division was logically based on a particular understanding of the Christian world view, which saw the entire world as a hierarchical system (a great chain of being) with man at the top. The entire world was God's creation, and man's superiority, which was based on his godlikeness (*imago dei*), gave him responsibility for the rest of the world and thereby allowed him to investigate and analyze it to the best of his ability. Moreover, what distinguished human beings from other living creatures was not (only) the soul, but the rational mind and the human capacity for self-reflection – as expressed in Descartes' famous dictum *cogito ergo sum* ('I think therefore I am'). On this view, the human body was a physical object among other objects, something which could be studied in a similar manner as the rest of the world. It was a generalized human body, with its individual characteristics being totally irrelevant, including gender differences. Thus, Descartes did not actively exclude women from his theory, but he also did not write about women specifically, because to him sexual difference was a physical reality and he considered men and women to be equals when it came to their mental capacity (Witt 2012).

When Descartes published his theory of the mechanical body in 1664 (*Treatise on Man*), the model provided a new theoretical basis for the medical sciences. But it had no evident practical advantages. In fact, the Hippocratic–Galenic model of the body survived in medical practice for centuries before new scientific methods yielded new treatments in the nineteenth century. For centuries, medical research was strictly theoretical and existed as a parallel corpus of ideas to the one that ruled the practical treatments prescribed by folk medicine.[2] The main cultural categories also remained the same: body and soul, matter and spirit. But Descartes made the split between body and mind deeper. He replaced 'soul' and called it

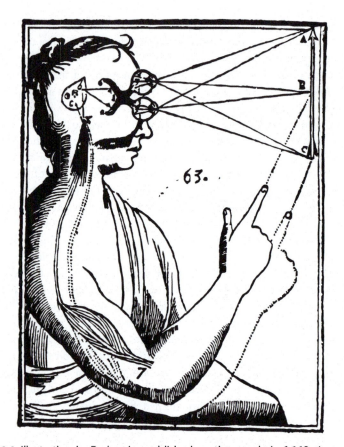

FIGURE 8.1 Illustration in *De homine* published posthumously in 1662. According to Descartes, the soul was situated in the pineal gland, here shown behind the eyes. The pineal gland served as a centre of translation, so to speak, transmitting messages via the nerves automatically from the eyes to the muscles as well as between man and God. Self-published work by Giovanni Dall'Orto/Wikimedia Commons.

'the cognitive mind'. The mind was a strictly abstract phenomenon, and the body was a (living) mechanical object. Body and mind were not mere opposites, but each belonged to its own realm: res extensa and res cogitans, respectively (Hattab 2001, Hatfield 2014). Descartes' approach to the human body was grounded in the notion that all objects, including the human body, consisted of a passive substance which possessed geometrical attributes and certain forms; his was a theory which in many respects foreshadowed the theory of molecules and atoms, but which was incompatible with the traditional model of the four basic elements: earth, air, fire, and water. Instead of continuity between the human body and the elements of nature, Descartes proposed an entirely new way of viewing the human body as an assemblage of organs. While the traditional model emphasized continuity and focused on the balance and the relationship between the body and its environment, Descartes' body was a composite structure consisting of smaller parts. The most significant relationship was not that between the body and its environment, but that between the body and the scientist and his expert gaze. What happened to the conception of the human body during the Enlightenment can be described as a total reorientation: Christian anthropology, which approached the body with a moral gaze and which looked for signs of sin and grace was replaced by the Cartesian model of the body as a machine. The body should be studied in the same manner as the world, that is, with a detached, rational gaze. Everything could and should be studied as objects in and of themselves, including the self. A more radical change can hardly be imagined. How was it possible to leave God's moral gaze behind and replace it with one's own?

Although Descartes' theory was to some extent compatible with the Christian understanding of nature, the human body implicitly remaining a part of God's creation, the Christian soul had no obvious function. For Descartes, what distinguished human beings from all other living creatures – the rational mind and the human capacity for self-reflection – was expressed in his famous dictum *cogito ergo sum*, which made rationality and self-reflection the most distinctive characteristics of the human being. The Christian (and Greek) idea of the soul had no role to play in this system. However, Descartes did in fact present an intermediary solution by locating the soul in a tiny structure in the interior of the brain, the pineal gland (Descartes 1649). But this was not the human organ of faith but of consciousness. Descartes' soul served merely as a seat of control, linking the will to bodily functions. Thus, Descartes replaced the soul with the mind or consciousness, and he placed it in the brain, or, as Roy Porter puts it, the soul was translated into the self or mind (Porter 2003: 372). Interestingly, 'consciousness' was used interchangeably with the Christian concept of 'conscience', or the ability to pass moral judgement on the self, for quite some time. In Christian anthropology, however, moral conscience was a function situated in the heart and associated with our ability to perceive the good or the divine (Stevens 1997: 271).

Descartes' concept of the mind was not so far removed from Christian thought as it may seem, since the traditional tripartite division of the Christian soul identified the rational soul as the highest and most important component (it was usually placed in the brain); the emotional soul was associated with the heart, and the life-soul was associated with the blood. Although the bodily location of the soul was a contested issue among medieval theologians, the New Testament and patristic writings combined to give the heart pride of place (Stevens 1997: 266). The theological interest, in this regard, was not bodily functions, however, but the hierarchical order of bodily organs. Descartes regarded the brain with the pineal gland as the most important organ (Stevens 1997). It was not man's capacity for rational thought, then, which marked the difference between the two conceptions, but Descartes' emphasis on the self-reflecting 'I'. This was a new image of man, which relegated faith to a secondary position. While the

Christian concept of the soul included both rationality and emotions (*psyche*) as well as a life-force, Descartes' mind (*cogito*) did not. For him, the soul was the thinking capacity: "I consider the mind not as a part of the soul, but as the whole soul that thinks".[3] When seen from this perspective, Descartes' concept of the mind can be said to have bridged the gap between medieval and modern man. His 'I' was a thinking mind–soul which relates to everything else, including the body, as something external or other than itself. The body is like everything else in the world – something to be studied, dissected, taken apart, and put back together again. Over the next few centuries, questions concerning the location of the soul and the life-force receded into the background. Abandoned by medical science, the nature and function of the human soul was left to religious authorities to decide.

After the Reformation, religion became a problematic and increasingly controversial issue. In Protestant countries, where the Reformation struck deep into the lives of ordinary people, and even in Catholic countries, the upsurge in religious fervour led to innovations in religious life and more lay engagement (oratories, lay orders). Among scientists, there were, as we have seen, mixed reactions. Even though most of them conformed to the dominant religious practice, the influence of institutional Christianity remained strong and criticism was not tolerated. The well-known trial of Galileo Galilei (1633) is emblematic of this. It set religion and science as incompatible entities, where one (religion) demanded control over the other (science). What the famous dispute was about was Galileo's astrological theory, which was incompatible with the Church's conception of the earth as the centre of the universe: The Earth was the fixed, stable ground and a perfect and eternal sign of God himself. Church authorities demanded that he withdraw his theory and accept revealed Truth. Galileo submitted to the pressure, but as he left the court a free man he reportedly muttered: '*eppure si muove*' ('but it moves anyway'). According to Maurice Finocchiaro, the pope's main concern in the Galileo trial was to ensure the integrity of the principle of God's omnipotence and have Galileo admit that God's creation could not be completely known to man (Finocchiaro 1997: 307–08). This would amount to accepting pre-established limits to science, and it required the scientist to show humility (a Christian virtue). In other words, the pope demanded a demonstration of remorse from Galileo as an outward sign of the great scientist's acceptance of the pope's supreme authority. The problem was, of course, that such an acceptance was impossible because scientific enquiry cannot thrive under such externally imposed limitations. The legal case against Galileo therefore marked the start of a slow process – a process whereby science was gradually released from the cognitive restraints of theology (and therefore the control of the Church). Eventually, it became impossible to ignore the fact that religion and science were in fact not just two different paths to the truth, as the Deists maintained, but that they led to different truths. Deism, a religious and philosophical world view, as Charles Taylor observes, emerged among intellectuals across Europe in the seventeenth century (Taylor 2007). During the Enlightenment, it offered an alternative to Christian dogma; it approached nature as a divine creation, but it replaced Christian theology and moral philosophy with a vague and open-ended philosophy.

Deism attracted intellectuals from Catholic as well as Protestant backgrounds. It can be explained as a world view particularly well suited to scientists (Preus 1987). It relied on the conception of God as *deus otiosus*, a passive and distant God who leaves the world to fend for itself. He was an unengaged, neutral God and very different from the morally engaged God of Christianity. Deism's passive God was only knowledgeable through his creation. Hence, Deism provided science with a religious legitimation and made scientific practice comparable with religious devotion. Nature was a source of truth, the 'book of nature' being either a supplement or an alternative to the Bible. With this redefinition of nature – as a sign of God – came the idea that God is accessible through the study of nature and a belief in 'natural religion', that is, an inherent capacity in humans to appreciate God independently of established religion and holy scripture (Taylor 2007: 221).

Deism had strong proponents among Enlightenment elites and played a fundamental role in providing science with a world view that endorsed scientific pursuits as honourable and important efforts to reveal the truth. Although critical of established religion, Deism did not present itself as an alternative. There was no organization, no leadership, and no canon, and it therefore posed no obvious challenge to established religion. To the Deists, the world was God's creation, but unlike Christianity they saw it as a completely rational and benign world with no room for Satan, sin, or retribution: "The prevailing doctrines of majority damnation and divine grace were calculated to make God look like an arbitrary tyrant, playing favourites in a capricious manner, and more concerned with arcane points of honour than with the good of his creatures" (Taylor 2007: 274). To those who saw established religion like this, Deism came across as a viable alternative. Deists saw man as a part of nature and believed that human reason should be used for the common good and help realize nature's potential. As part of nature, humans too could better themselves, become less greedy and more generous, less egotistical and more tolerant. Deism subtracted moral principles from nature and derived its positive view of man from this connectedness with the rest of creation; man was a part of the great chain of being. When Deists regarded natural science as a search for God's laws, this was not a particularly Christian God. But since Deism did not propose any alternative to organized religion, religious authorities left the Deists alone. For all practical purposes, the hierarchical order between science and religion remained in place throughout the Enlightenment and beyond. The Church or, more correctly, the different varieties of Christian churches continued to claim privileged access to the truth, and as long as scientists kept silent on the subject and did not openly challenge revealed truth, a work division (as we saw above) was put into place which helped sustain the idea that science was in fact compatible with religion.

Enlightenment anatomists investigated all parts of the human body and described each organ in minute detail. From a strictly anatomical point of view, gender difference – in humans as well as in animals – was restricted to the reproductive organs. Scientifically the female body was equal to the male body except that its genitals remained inside the body, whereas the male body's reproductive organs were on the outside. A good example of this is de Graaf's drawing (1692) of the genitals of a girl with the clitoris looking like a penis, which was entitled, quite tellingly, *De mulierum organis generationi inservientibus* (*On Unusable Female Reproductive Organs*). According to Clara Pinto-Correia, illustrations like these were common and "fueled the enduring popular belief in correspondence between the clitoris and the penis, and inspired later tales often protruding two inches outside the vagina" (Pinto-Correia 1997: 258). Stereotypical ideas of male perfection and female imperfection informed scientific investigations and in turn strengthened the idea of the female body as a biological deviance that was due to unfavourable conditions in the womb. A similar notion informed Galenic theories, which claimed that the biological difference between man and woman was due to a temperature deficiency in the female foetus: The higher body temperature of the male foetus allowed the genitals to propel to the outside of its body, whereas the colder body temperature of the female foetus meant that it would remain inside and be weaker than its male counterpart. Women's menstruation was also a sign of the fact that the female body was colder. In a similar vein, pregnancy was regarded as a favourable condition for women's health, since the menstrual blood was used as nourishment for the child and had no time to accumulate and cause ill health. The qualitative difference in body temperature between man and woman was also reflected in the quality of their respective seed. Thus, men and women were fundamentally the same, except that the female body was a less perfect body than the male body. Such misogynist views were part of the scientific world view and implicitly conditioned scientific interpretations. When anatomical research revealed more details about the reproductive organs, it was initially made to accommodate traditional gender models (Schiebinger 1987). Therefore, precise anatomical descriptions of the female reproductive organs were slow to emerge. It was Descartes' new model that provided the rational framework for the pursuit of exact anatomical knowledge. When modern science replaced folk medicine in the course of the nineteenth century, the medical practices based on Galen's pre-scientific theories gradually disappeared from view.[4]

What is a human being? Scientists cut, discussed, and scrutinized what they observed around them, while the theologians prayed to God and directed their gaze towards eternity. What is construed as knowledge varies according to taken-for-granted horizons or world views – even where the meaning of physical phenomena and biological processes are concerned. By focusing uniquely on bodily functions, natural science effectively cut the human being in half. Scientists dissected cadavers and studied the miniature processes of each and every organ in the human body and willingly left the soul to the theologians. The legacy of the Enlightenment was therefore a revaluation of the Greek split between body and soul. From being a philosophical and theological distinction, it became a reality when

Enlightenment science thrived on the professional and practical distinction between body and mind, the tangible and the ephemeral, reality and fantasy, and science and religion.

As long as the power and authority of the Christian churches were not seriously threatened, science had a functional relationship with institutional Christianity, which largely ignored scientific theories. Before the nineteenth century, scientific medicine was excessively expensive, its cures were largely ineffective, and medical doctors were available only in large urban centres. Folk medical practices were based on the Hippocratic-Galenic tradition and provided tried and tested cures. They were not exclusive, but a part of folk traditions and integrated into the Christian world view. For a long time, science remained within the horizon of the same Christian world view. But with hindsight, we can say that the potential for conflict was obvious. It surfaced in the nineteenth century, when more effective scientific solutions were put in place.

Notes

1 *De anima* 413 b1, here cited from Aristotle 1993: 24.
2 Interestingly, several aspects of medical treatments in the Hippocratic–Galenic tradition were reintroduced by so-called 'alternative' medical practitioners in the second half of the twentieth century, when a 'holistic' approach to the body became popular. On the role of alternative medicine within the so-called 'new religious movement' (NRM) or New Age, see Hunt 2003.
3 Cited in Pasnau 2007: 3.
4 Female orgasm reappeared – albeit without any direct function for procreation – in the field of feminist studies and mainstream culture in the twentieth century. A key event was the publication of a scientific study of female sexuality (the *Hite Report on Female Sexuality*) in 1976. Shere Hite's groundbreaking report, with her scientific description of female orgasm, tallied well with the feminist movement of the 1970s. By describing the female orgasm as a natural physical reaction of the clitoris, the report effectively removed ages of moral stigma and suppression of female sexuality.

PART III

Modernity
1800–1900

9

THE FEMALE EGG AND MEDICAL INVENTIONS

The emergence of what we associate today with medical science was a gradual process, which started during the Enlightenment and had a decisive breakthrough in the nineteenth century. This was a century that was marked by radical change. Following industrialization, urbanization, and the introduction of public education, Western society was restructured as people moved to the cities from the countryside and made a transition from farm labour to wage-earning industrial labour. Parallel to these developments, the social status of women remained unchanged. Clearly, it was a complex process which involved the passage from an agricultural world overlooked by God and religion to a mechanical universe open to exploitation and a detached scientific gaze. Viewed from a Christian angle, these developments meant the loss of Christian hegemony – except in the private sphere, where gender relations and family life remained imbued with Christian norms and values. New social conditions changed the lives of everyone, but for the vast majority of women the transition from the open countryside and agricultural work to crammed flats and factory work put their roles as mothers and housewives under strain. Although the change in living conditions was equally dramatic for working-class men, childcare was women's domain, and frequent births and large families became increasingly problematic. Quite unrelated to such social matters, scientists developed radically new insights into female anatomy and embryonic development, which paved the way for the gradual emergence of a new status for women's bodies and the mother's role in procreation. We may say that a decisive shift in patriarchal logic was (unintentionally) instigated by scientific research. The nineteenth century saw the removal of the biological basis that so far had underscored the suppression of women. This was not a planned development. Following their own agenda, scientists more or less accidentally produced a number of insights into female fertility and reproductive organs that had decisively positive effects on women's lives. Thus, medical research in the nineteenth century provided an empirical basis for subsequent feminist emancipation.

Standard textbooks on embryology start with Karl Ernst von Baer (1792–1876), who discovered women's eggs in 1827 (Buettner 2007b). He published the find in a celebrated work entitled *Epistola de ovi mammalium et hominis genesi* (*On the Origin of the Mammalian and Human Egg*), where he described a yellowish spot within the follicle as an egg, a structure which was only visible with a good microscope. Von Baer is also known for having coined the term 'spermatozoa' for what earlier scientists referred to as animalcules (cf. Leeuwenhoek), and having identified the nucleus of the male seed, which he believed (wrongly) to be a parasite. As we have seen above, several anatomists have made claims to the discovery, notably de Graaf and the other ovists of the seventeenth and eighteenth centuries. But when they believed they had observed eggs, they had in fact only identified the follicles in which the eggs reside. This misidentification, which came as a result of primitive microscopes and not a faulty theory, is nevertheless the reason why the history of science does not credit them with the find. But the reason why Karl Ernst von Baer gets the honour is perhaps harder to understand, since the egg that he discovered was in fact not a human egg at all, but that of a dog. The rationale behind it was the notion that the human body was like any other body and that comparison between the species had been practiced since the times of Aristotle and Galen, whose anatomical knowledge derived from animal dissection. When von Baer's description of the process of foetal development in mammals (embryology) was immediately recognized as being relevant to humans, it was because comparative anatomy had – ever since the Enlightenment – systematically analyzed body organs across species, including the human species. The uniqueness of human beings, their godlikeness, was defined as a hidden quality in the human soul and did not concern them; although humans were the highest creatures in God's creation, enjoying a privileged position in relation to creator, they were still a part of nature.

Within the framework of comparative anatomy, von Baer's discovery was readily accepted as proof – beyond any doubt – that procreation in humans involved an egg. But the exact mechanisms of procreation were still unknown. This was the subject of another study, which von Baer published between 1828 and 1837: *Über die Entwicklungsgeschichte der Thiere* (*On the Development of Animals*). Here, von Baer presented his epigenetic theory. He explained how the growth of the fertilized egg proceeds from homogeneous matter to ever more heterogeneous forms. His theory, which is known as the 'germ layer theory', explained how distinct layers within the egg subsequently develop into specific organs. Von Baer also formulated a general law of embryonic development. This law effectively contradicts the populist notion – which had become widespread – that wrongly argued that the individual foetus' development reflects the evolutionary stages of the species (Buettner 2007b). The main points of von Baer's law are as follows: 1. The general features of a large group of animals appear earlier than the special features of the group, to which the embryo belongs; 2. Less general characteristics of the group develop from the most general until finally the most specialized group characteristics appear; 3. Instead of passing through the stages of other animals, each embryo of a given species departs more and more from them; and 4. The embryo of a higher animal is never like the adult of a lower animal, but only like its embryo. However, von Baer's theory of evolution has often wrongly been conflated with the evolutionary theory proposed by Ernst Haeckel (1834–1919) which maintained that the development of each individual recapitulated the entire evolutionary process. Haeckel's evolutionary scheme was a stark oversimplification and became popular outside the scientific community. It was infamously employed by Nazi propaganda to promote racist theories, a misuse which tainted Haeckel's faulty theory and put a moral strain on evolutionary embryology. However, it should be noted that Haeckel's model differs from von Baer's careful description, which emphasized the special characteristics of each species: First, the individual embryo shows the general characteristics of the group to which the individual belongs (e.g. vertebrate animals), and the specific characteristics of the group (e.g. mammals) occur later in the process of development. If transposed to modern embryology, this implies that the foetus' nose is first a human nose and that the child only later develops the kind of nose shape typical of the family traits of one of its parents. Although von Baer's theory departed in most respects from earlier epigenetic theories of foetal development (embryology), it did share the traditional view on growth, claiming that foetal development involved stages of increasing complexity. So when von Baer published his results, he was able to show that they were not totally new, but had several features in common with traditional epigenetic theories. Therefore, the scientific milieu readily accepted von Baer's arguments.[1] In fact, we may see von Baer's discovery of the female egg and its role in procreation as the missing link in a scientific discussion which had gone on since the time of the first Enlightenment scientists: the role of women in procreation. However, it would be wrong to say that von Baer's discovery resulted in the immediate demise of traditional ideas about children as their fathers' offspring.

From von Baer's discovery onwards, science produced a whole range of results that contributed to a new understanding of the mother's role in human reproduction. By the end of the nineteenth century, it was clear that she contributed more than the uterus and the provision of menstrual blood as 'building material'. But the exact mechanism of conception, i.e. the entry of the sperm into the egg cell, remained unknown. The scientists' preconception about women's menstruation was part of the problem. They believed (wrongly) that menstruation was equivalent to heat or brunst in animals and therefore failed in the timing of their experiments. In fact, the menstrual cycle and the woman's fertile period was not described until 1907. Another reason why it took 80 years from the discovery of the egg to a better understanding of human conception was that two other discoveries had to be made first. Before scientists could look for an answer to the riddle of conception, they had to know about cells and chromosomes. Ten years after von Baer's discovery came the first theory of the cell (1838). The term 'cell' (derived from Latin *cellula*, small compartment) had already been coined by Robert Hooke in 1665. Hooke studied tissue from cork and used the word 'cell' to describe the small units in the plant tissue that he had observed with his microscope. However, this was not what we now associate with the word cell, but a honeycomb-like pattern of cells that constitute plant tissue. Thus, Hooke observed and described tissue, but he did not develop a theory of the 'cell' as the building block of living organisms.

One of Hooke's contemporaries, the Dutch anatomist Antonie van Leeuwenhoek, came closer to developing a theory of the cell when he discovered single-celled animals (later identified as bacteria) in a drop of water from a pond. But even though he had the cell before his eyes, he did not have "the mental tools to understand what he was seeing" (Pinto-Correia 1997: 353). In 1683, he sent a drawing of his observation to the Royal Society of London, to which he described it as 'animalcules'. Although he was not aware of it, Leeuwenhoek was the first to observe living cells. But because others were unable to repeat these observations (because their microscopes were less powerful), Leeuwenhoek's discovery did not become the scientific breakthrough it might have been. When a theory of the cell was launched 150 years later, it was based on more precise observations of cells and the cell nucleus. With better microscopes, scientists could observe how life was engendered through cell division. These observations then became the basis for a final break with pre-scientific notions of life-forces as somehow being inherent in male sperm. In 1838, Matthias Schleiden published *Beiträge zur Phytogenesis* (*Contributions to Phytogenesis*), in which he presented a theory that the cell was the building block of all living organisms. He observed that different parts of the plant were composed of cells, and he formulated what was to become an important biological principle: The cell was the primary building block of all living creatures. With hindsight, it would be fair to say that Schleiden's cell theory realized the full potential of Descartes' body-as-machine model, since it described how complex structures are in fact built from one type of (living) material. Another German scientist, Theodor Schwann (1810–1882), also contributed to cell theory when he identified the nucleus in animal cells. He was the first to argue that the nucleus played a role in generating new cells (1839), and he formulated the basic stance of modern biology, namely, that the cell is the basic unit of life. He also coined the term 'metabolism' to describe the observable changes in living cells, thereby replacing the age-old notion of the life-force.

However, another discovery was needed before a biological explanation of life could replace the traditional notion that there was a life-force inherent in male seed. In 1855, Rudolf Virchow (1821–1902) published his cell theory, in which he argued that in fact all life derives from cells. According to this theory, then, there is no need for an external life-force or godly intervention to create life. The only thing necessary for a new cell to emerge is a cell (*omnis cellula e cellula*).

When humans procreate, the child develops from existing cells, which come from its parents. In many respects, therefore, Virchow's theory was incompatible with the Christian world view and God's place in it. The theory could have provoked religious criticism, but it went largely unnoticed outside scientific circles. One question which Virchow's research left unanswered, however, was the function of the nucleus of the cell. It raised the rather controversial possibility of self-generation by questioning whether the sperm nucleus was in fact necessary for the fertilization of an egg cell. The development of a general theory of the cell marked another decisive step away from traditional medical theories of the human body, which were based on the idea of the four humours. It was also a decisive step towards the demise of the 1,000-year-old Hippocratic–Galenic tradition in Western medicine.

With hindsight, it is easy to say that the debates between the supporters of preformationism and the supporters of epigenesis were entirely futile discussions because the participants lacked crucial insight into cell generation and the crucial role of the cell nucleus as the carrier of genetic information. The first systematic study of hereditary processes was conducted by the Augustinian friar and biologist Gregor Mendel (1822–1884), who studied heredity in plants. He applied statistics to demonstrate that heredity followed certain patterns (Mendel's Law), and refuted the commonly held notion that traits would pass from one generation to the next through simple blending. However, his work went unnoticed and did not enter into the scientific discourse until several decades after his death. Living in an abbey from 1843 onwards, Mendel stood with one foot in science and the other in religion, and he found himself at the periphery of the scientific community. His research was evidently a part of his religious calling, and although he followed lectures at the University of Vienna for ten years, it would seem that he consciously avoided participating in scientific debates. He served as a physics teacher at the abbey gymnasium for several years and conducted research on heredity by studying peas which he grew himself. This study resulted in his first and only scientific article, "Versuche über Pflanzenhybriden" ("Experiments on Plant Hybridization"), which today is generally acclaimed as being the first ever work in genetics. It was published in a scientific journal in Brno (in today's Czech Republic) in 1866, but it went unnoticed. Two years later, Mendel was made abbot of his monastery, and although he continued his research, he did not publish. Mendel's present-day notoriety stems from the rediscovery of his 1866 article by American scientists after the turn of the century.

Unaware of Mendel's research, Charles Darwin (1809–1882) followed another track in his studies of heredity. His theory, known as pangenesis, was published in *The Variation of Animals and Plants under Domestication* in 1868, nine years after his groundbreaking *On the Origin of Species by Means of Natural Selection* (1859). Because of Darwin's status, pangenesis had some (unmerited) success. It should be noted, however, that unlike his previous study Darwin's pangenesis theory was not grounded in empirical evidence. Obviously Darwin was aware of this, since he referred to it as a provisional hypothesis: The likeness between parents and off-spring was caused by tiny hereditary particles, *gemmules*, which were transmitted from parent to offspring. Starting from Virchow's dictum that only cells can generate cells (*omnis cellula e cellula*), Darwin described the gemmules as a kind of secretion from the parental cells which diffused and aggregated in the reproductive organ.

Darwin's pangenesis theory approached heredity in terms of a form-giving principle in the semen of the father, and it can perhaps be described as a materialistic version of traditional Augustinian ideas about the transmission of Original Sin, except that Darwin included the mother in his equation. The gemmules stemmed from both parents and were so tiny that they were transmitted through the sperm cells. But because it lacked empirical evidence, Darwin's pangenesis theory disappeared after two decades, and the mechanism of heredity remained unknown throughout Darwin's career. But in 1884, two German scientists, Eduard Strasburger and Oscar Hertwig, described the fusion of the male and the female *pronuclei* (nuclei of the cell) (Lopata 2009). Thus, it was established that conception does indeed involve the union of egg and sperm nuclei. This model led to a total replacement of the age-old vegetative 'mother-earth-and-father-life' model, as it were, and it assigned to women the central role in the making of the human child. Twenty years later, around 1900, other scientists confirmed Mendel's theory of heredity. The *chromosome*, a small structure that could be observed in the cell nucleus through the microscope, was readily accepted. However, Darwin's pangenesis theory lingered on until 1903, when it was finally refuted by two scientists, who, independently of each other, described the chromosome as a unit which transmitted hereditary material from the parents to the fertilized egg. The discovery of the chromosome eventually paved the way for research into metabolism and together with it the discovery of hormones during the 1930s and beyond. Developments in this field of knowledge had huge practical consequences, especially for women, since they made possible the development of chemical contraception (contraceptive pill) and artificial fertilization techniques (IVF).

In the nineteenth century, the scientific community was strictly male, and female matters as well as feminist perspectives were not automatically on the scientific horizon. Science followed its own agenda and more or less accidentally produced a number of insights that changed – if not the basic conception of women's bodies – the overall quality of women's lives. One of these insights was a chemical pain-relief agent known as *chloroform*, which was first referred to as *chloric ether*. The formula was invented in the 1830s, and the first patient was successfully placed under full narcosis in 1847. In the 1850s, hospitals started to use chloroform during delivery, and Queen Victoria contributed largely to its acceptance when she gave birth – without pain – to Prince Leopold in 1853 under chloroform sedation. Chloroform was soon adopted by surgeons, and it contributed vastly to the scope of surgical procedures. Another discovery which affected women in a positive way was *nitrous oxide* ('laughing gas'), which was first used as a pain-relief agent by an American dentist in 1844. The nineteenth century was a period of intense medical research and saw an almost total remodelling of medical practices. Hospitals were built on a massive scale in cities across Europe as part of the industrialization and urbanization processes (mentioned above). For women, however, these changes were not always positive. Pregnancy and birth had always been a perilous affair, but the introduction of hospital births did not improve the situation. On the contrary, during the first half of the nineteenth century there was a 10–15 per cent mortality rate for women during labour, most of them having died from *puerperal fever*. But without the use of comparative statistics, these high mortality rates went largely unnoticed or were explained by unfavourable local environmental conditions in the ground or in the sky, the weather, or magnetism.

In many hospitals, the survival rate for women giving birth was nine out of ten at the end of the nineteenth century. A comparative study of statistics for hospitals in Norway shows that the death rate for women in childbirth was as high as 12 per cent in some hospitals at the turn of the century (Lund 2006: 1779). However, in the second half of the century, when hospital hygiene improved, the number of deaths caused by puerperal fever was significantly reduced, amounting to just 1 per cent. In this connection, the story about Ignaz Semmelweis is instructive. At the time, the mechanism of bacterial infection was unknown. While Semmelweis found a way to avoid puerperal fever, he failed to explain its source (bacteria). Working in a Viennese hospital in 1847, he observed that his department had much higher mortality rates for women after childbirth (114 in 1000) than other departments (27 in 1000). He linked this to the fact that the doctors in his department performed autopsies and went directly to the delivery room. Therefore, he concluded that fragments from the cadavers stuck to the physicians' fingers and caused the fever. But since the fever was found everywhere, not only in hospitals in which autopsies were performed, it obviously had other causes. Therefore, Semmelweis' hygienic measures were ignored. Four decades passed before, in the late nineteenth century, developments in bacteriology made it possible to explain puerperal fever as a general occurrence of bacteriological infection. At the end of the century, improved hygiene and more effective anaesthetics reduced the suffering and perils of childbirth. At the same time, changes in the surgical procedures used in caesarean sections were introduced. Women were now placed under full sedation, and the entire uterus was removed – a technique which dramatically reduced post-caesarean infections and the number of deaths that would ensue. Nevertheless, the fact remains that women in the nineteenth century rightly feared childbirth. In spite of better surgical techniques (e.g. caesarean section) and much improved pain relief medications, childbirth was dangerous.

The transition of birth from the bedchamber to the hospital was a mixed blessing. When the medical profession entered into the female realm of childbirth, the midwife, the mother-in-law, and the female neighbour left. Those women who traditionally helped in childbirth were substituted with male medical professionals and hospitalization. Childbirth was defined as a medical condition. In her study of obstetrics in the Victorian period, Mary Poovey argues that the socio-cultural liberation of modernity somehow left women out. Male dominance continued, and even intensified, she observes, as there was a marked tendency to "infantilize and objectify women as weak and irresponsible" (Poovey 1987: 155). Modern birth practices added to the burden. Hospitalization meant that the would-be mother was isolated from her daily environment and reduced to a passive spectator to her own delivery. Regardless of social background, women of the nineteenth century did not have ownership of their own lives socially, politically, or physically.

Chloroform was first used in 1847 by a Scottish obstetrician, James Simpson (1811–1870), in connection with a delivery. Almost immediately, it was put to use by the medical community as a general pain-relief agent in connection with all kinds of surgery – but not in childbirth. The main objection from medical experts was that pain-relief agents would damage the child. But the strongest objection came from elsewhere; it came from people who protested against such a remedy on religious grounds. The most frequently used argument was based on Genesis and the expulsion of Adam and Eve from Paradise: "To the woman he said, 'I will greatly increase your pangs in childbearing; in pain you shall bring forth children, yet your desire shall be for your husband, and he shall rule over you'" (Genesis 3:16). Here, painful childbirth is directly attributed to God's divine plan and natural law. How could doctors administer a pain-relief agent when God ordered Eve to give birth in pain? Simpson defended his discovery by making another inference from Genesis, arguing that chloroform was comparable to the steam engine: If Adam's work could be made easier, the same could be done for Eve. To deny chloroform to women would be like saying that the steam engine was a sacrilege. He even had an additional argument, quite similar to the first, that pointed out that God himself had used anaesthesia in connection with birth when he caused Adam to fall asleep before he created Eve from the latter's rib (Poovey 1987: 140). Coming from a medical doctor, this line of argumentation, explicitly referring to religion in the nineteenth century, was rather unusual. It proved to be unwise and turned the entire question into a religious matter. But these arguments would become moot after Queen Victoria used chloroform during childbirth (1853) and later spoke freely about the experience. Thus, a queen was needed before male doctors would change their practice to set the mother's needs over religious qualms.

Apart from ineffectual contraception devices such as animal-intestine condoms and herbal infusions, there was not much that could stop unwanted pregnancies. Industrial production of rubber condoms started in 1839 (Goodyear), and the diaphragm started being made in 1880, but they were not available to the majority of women, since legal and moral impediments meant that both remedies – popularly known as 'French letters' – were sold via the mail. Both devices met with relative success among the upper classes, but they did not come into general use before well into the twentieth century. The Church was not the only institution to express moral concerns. In 1873, the US congress passed a law, which listed contraceptives as obscene material and prohibited their sale via the postal service. The law, known as the Comstock Law, marked a new moralistic trend in public attitudes towards sexuality – a trend which can be seen in the full title of the law, which was known as the "Act of the Suppression of Trade in, and Circulation of, Obscene Literature and Articles of Immoral Use". It criminalized both the buying and selling of contraceptives across the US, and it also put a stop to private importation as well as postal sales. This law had no parallel in Europe, where rubber condoms were produced (in Britain from 1870). And also in Catholic countries, religious prohibitions were increasingly ignored.

However, this moralistic reaction was deeply rooted in Christian tradition. The Swiss Reformation theologian Jean Calvin's commentary on Genesis is illustrative of the Christian attitudes that were prevalent at the time. In a passage in which he warns against *coitus interruptus*, a traditional method used as a kind of natural birth control, he remarked: "To retreat on purpose from the woman so that the seed falls on the ground is a double monstrosity because it reduces the hope for further lineage and it kills the infant ... before it is born".[2] To do so was a clear violation of the Old Testament prohibition against spilling seed on the ground:

> Then Judah said to Onan, "Go in to your brother's wife and perform the duty of a brother-in-law to her; raise up offspring for your brother". But since Onan knew that the offspring would not be his, he spilled his semen on the ground whenever he went in to his brother's wife, so that he would not give offspring to his brother. What he did was displeasing in the sight of the Lord, and he put him to death also.
>
> *(Genesis 38:8–10)*

This passage provided the biblical basis not only for banning *coitus interruptus*, but also for Christian prohibitions against masturbation and homosexual activities. Following Augustine's doctrine on sexuality, procreation, and Original Sin, Calvin clearly saw the spilling of seed as a violation of the Christian notion of marriage.

According to Christian tradition, women were weaker, more sensitive, and less rational than men. A specifically female body function like pregnancy meant that a woman had one additional bodily characteristic which made her less mind and more body. These ideas were reflected in anatomy. In 1759, Madame Thiroux d'Arconville, a French intellectual, published *Traité d'ostéologie,* a translation of Alexander Monro's *Anatomy of the Human Bones* of 1726. The book lacked illustrations, but Madame Thiroux d'Arconville added what proved to be the first anatomical drawings of female skeletons and female sculls that were smaller than their male counterparts to show "that women's intellectual capabilities were inferior to men's" (Schiebinger 1987: 43). The medical sciences perpetuated traditional gender norms and lent support to traditional notions of women as being weaker than men and therefore being in need of male protection. Analyzing the first anatomical drawings of female skeletons, Londa Schiebinger observes that female characteristics were understood as deviations from male characteristics and hence defined as abnormal (Schiebinger 1987). The idea of women as faulty men was a taken-for-granted cultural fact which was questioned only by a few. It permeated social arrangements as well as cultural habits, scientific research and the legal system.

Traditional Christian attitudes to pregnant, unmarried women were not respectful. Instead of protecting the rights of the pregnant mother, the law protected the rights of the father because the child belonged to him: It was the fruit of the father's procreative powers. Marriage was the framework within which procreation should take place. It was within this context that the wife took care of her husband and nurtured his offspring, and it was in the father's home that children would remain in the unlikely event of a divorce or marital break-up. Unmarried women or unwanted pregnancies had no place in this ideal. Lacking a man, the unmarried pregnant woman was an icon of sexual promiscuity and faced social scorn. Similar ideas about women and family were embedded in nineteenth-century secular laws. As Kristin Luker observes regarding nineteenth-century American legal practice, it was "quite consistent with preceding Catholic canon law: early abortions were legally ignored and only late abortions could be prosecuted" (Luker 1984: 13–14). A stricter approach to abortion was introduced into British law by the Ellenborough Act of 1803. This law defined abortion as murder and prescribed the death penalty for the mother. However, the law did maintain the traditional Christian distinction with regards to foetal development and only classified abortion after quickening as murder. In 1837, this distinction was removed, however, making British abortion laws stricter than Canon law at the time. The punishment, though, was less severe, since the death penalty was replaced by a life sentence. In the US and other Western countries, stricter laws were introduced from the 1820s onwards. By 1860, all states had laws against abortions except in cases where it was necessary in order to save the mother's life, a category which is usually referred to as 'therapeutic abortion'. Christian churches followed suit; the Presbyterian Church, for instance, defined abortion ("parents who destroy their offspring") as a crime against God and nature in 1869 (Davis 1984: 6).

Another aspect of patriarchal suppression was women's lack of legal status. In 1854, the English feminist Barbara Leigh Smith Bodichon published a pamphlet showing the poor state of legal rights for married women. When a woman was married, she lost the rights she enjoyed as a single woman and the husband became responsible for her acts. He also took over her property, that is, her "personal property before marriage, such as money in hand, money at the bank, jewels, household goods, clothes" (cited in LeGates 2001: 18). In Britain, the Married Women's Property Act (1870) gave married women the legal right to inherit and to dispose of their earnings. Britain was no exception, and from the last part of the nineteenth century onwards, Western countries gradually removed these legal obstacles to gender equality one by one. First, economic autonomy was granted, then access to higher education, which was followed by the recognition of women as political citizens with the right to vote. Finally, modern regulations have mended more subtle forms of injustice related to biology (e.g. legal abortion). Whereas the first laws granted women the same rights as men, the later laws address "the real inequality that women face in law and in life for being pregnant" (Raymond 1993: 68). One discovery with far-reaching consequences was the female egg.

In the nineteenth century, established religion came under an increasing amount of pressure and Christianity lost its former cultural hegemony as traditional society gave way to modernity. The dismantling of Christian cultural dominance also affected scientific research, which became institutionally and culturally independent during this time. As the space between religion and science became wider, and the relationship between the two gradually became more antagonistic, medical science developed more effective but invasive methods when surgery replaced traditional medical cures designed to restore the balance of body fluids. The patient's experience had no place in this new regime. The body was a system of separate organs, and the patient's bodily sensations – pain, cold, heat, or dryness – were subjective experiences and therefore had no scientific value. Scientific research on human procreation fit this model well. Pregnancy and birth, on the other hand, did not. When pregnancy and birth were included in this mechanical–medical outlook, the pregnant woman was reduced to a womb: She was a uterus with a nutritive function providing an environment which was conducive to the growth of the foetus. In this line of thinking, birth implied the termination of the womb's nutritive function. Thus, pregnancy was somehow detached from the woman, and she was functionally reduced to a birth machine.

Notes

1 The reception of von Baer's egg theory is a textbook example of Thomas Kuhn's description of the social preconditions in the scientific community for a paradigm shift (Kuhn 1962).
2 *Calvin's Old Testament Commentaries.* Citation in Pinto-Correia 1997: 321.

10

THE DIVINE CONCEPTION
Religious reactions to modernity

In the mid-nineteenth century, developments in scientific research on human reproduction had reached a stage where it had little in common with Christianity. The unravelling of hereditary substances in the cell (chromosome), for instance, was obviously incompatible with Christian anthropology. In spite of the fact that modern science totally recast the biology that underpinned it and gave women a crucial part in procreation, Christian theology continued to place women in an inferior, nurturing position. Not even the discovery of the female egg, which placed the dogma of the Incarnation in a totally new light, caused a theological reaction. After all, if the offspring is the joint product of mother and father (female egg and male seed), then the Virgin Mary must surely be granted a much more prominent role in the making of Jesus than traditional Christian dogma would allow. It would seem, then, that the split between science and religion was so deep that theologians could regard such questions as irrelevant. But the Catholic Church came close to expressing a reaction when it launched a new Marian dogma.

In 1854, Pope Pius IX (r. 1846–1878) pronounced a dogma of Mary's Immaculate Conception. The dogma stated that the Virgin Mary was born without sin (*immaculata*), meaning that she was miraculously exempted from the consequences of Adam's original sin. The new dogma was the first Marian dogma in more than a 1,000 years and implied a radical step towards declaring Mary as more divine and less human than before. In fact, her conception had been miraculous because, unlike all other humans, she was born without sin. Her father's seed would normally transfer Adam's sin to the foetus (Mary) and contaminate her flesh and subsequently her (rational) soul as soon as it was infused into the foetus after around three months (Børresen 2002: 134). To declare a dogma means simply to state the truth as the Church authorities see it. In this case, the dogma was valid only for Catholicism. Whereas all dogmas prior to the schism between the Orthodox East and Catholic West (1054) are shared by all Christian churches, the dogma of Mary's Immaculate Conception from 1854 was declared after the Reformation. It was refuted by Protestants, not only because it struck them as being politically problematic, but also because it lacked a biblical basis.[1]

A dogma of the Immaculate Conception seems to be a tall order in a century which celebrated rationality and scientific progress. However, the dogma was readily accepted by ordinary Catholics and was even met with considerable enthusiasm. There are several reasons for this response: first, the Cult of the Virgin Mary was generally popular and had been so for centuries. Even more important in the present context was the fact that this cult was already centred on the miraculous, on images with healing capacities, and on fabulous stories of divine intervention at local Marian shrines (Eriksen and Stensvold 2002). The new dogma and the depiction of this 'new' Mary became widely popular, especially after an apparition four years later. In 1858, a young girl, Bernadette Soubirous, claimed that she had seen the Virgin in a grotto outside Lourdes, a small village in the French Pyrenees. She told the parish priest that the Virgin had said: "I am the Immaculate Conception", and asked him what it meant. According to the official story, the priest understood how well this apparition fitted the new dogma and immediately reported it to the bishop, who officially acknowledged the truth of the event in record time (Harris 1999). The standard visual depiction of the Immaculate Conception refers to this event. Often, these sculptures are placed inside some sort of cavity or enclosure inside the church, an allusion to the grotto where Bernadette's vision occurred. The new dogma and the image of Bernadette Soubirous' vision tapped directly into the age-old tradition of Mary's divinity in popular belief. By declaring this new dogma, the pope put his official stamp on popular beliefs which regarded Mary as the (only) perfect woman in history: She was without moral faults, and even her female body was perfect, unharmed, and whole – even after giving birth.

Stories about Mary's miraculous birth as well as the unearthly character of her labour (she remained a virgin also *after* having given birth to Jesus) were part of Christian folklore since antiquity. The most famous account of Mary's perpetual virginity is found in a story about the midwife Salome, who made the necessary investigations after the birth of Jesus to ensure that Mary's hymen remained intact. Other stories tell of Mary's own miraculous birth: She was born to a mother who was 90 years old (like Abraham's wife); her parents were Anna and Joachim (Jesus' grandparents do not figure in the Bible); and she spent her childhood in seclusion in the Temple in Jerusalem. According to the legendary story of Mary's conception, God appeared, like in the case of Jesus' miraculous conception (Luke 1:26–38), in the guise of the Archangel Gabriel. But unlike Mary, her mother was not impregnated by the Holy Spirit, but was miraculously impregnated by her own husband at the age of 90. The stories about the Virgin Mary's childhood are not found in the New Testament, but are a part of the apocryphal literature from the fifth century.[2] Although most of them are just a couple of hundred years younger than the New Testament texts, they were not included in the canon. They were kept alive in popular tradition and they were transmitted by means of Christian art and folk traditions. Lacking a biblical basis, the Immaculate Conception was categorically rejected by Protestant churches.

The belief in Mary's divinity as expressed in the apocryphal texts was effectively transmitted in medieval art, where scenes from Mary's childhood were popular themes and decorated the walls in churches and chapels. The stories themselves were spread together with and indistinguishable from the most popular stories about the saints in the *Legenda Aurea* (*The Golden Legend*), which was first published around 1260. The author (or compiler) of this work was a Dominican priest in northern Italy, Iacopo da Varazze, also known as Jacob of Varagine. His collection of saints' stories was used as a basis for priests' sermons and was more widely disseminated in medieval Europe than the Bible. When the pope declared the dogma of the Immaculate Conception, he placed an official stamp on these folk tales and upgraded their status: They could now be considered as being true. Seen from the point of view of Catholic tradition, the new dogma was hardly controversial, but in the wider nineteenth-century historical context, the new dogma appears as a symbolic demonstration of religious power. It was not only the authority of the pope which was indirectly confirmed by the declaration, but also the supremacy of revelation over rational, evidence-based (scientific) truth. In the nineteenth century, this theory had come under pressure. The pope's solution was to discard one part of Aquinas' teaching, namely, that part which relied on biological arguments. This is all the more telling, since Aquinas' biology largely conformed to the scientific consensus at the time (nineteenth-century discoveries confirmed the epigenesis theory of foetal development) and it endorsed the notion of gradual development. Although he did not explicitly refute the traditional biological underpinning of Christian dogma, the pope implicitly embraced a biological theory of foetal development, which scientists had discarded.

It is hard to see the new dogma of Mary's Immaculate Conception as an isolated and purely religious event. Although the dogma was declared a few years before the details of conception were known and the implications of von Baer's discovery of the female egg was not yet fully understood, the fact that the pope felt the need to make this aspect of Marian tradition part of official teaching can be viewed as a response to the developments in modern science in general and embryology in particular. When the Immaculate Conception stated that Mary was exempted from Original Sin, the logic went like this: Since Jesus was perfect, his mother must have been perfect, that is, not tainted by sin. According to popular legend, Mary's father (Joachim) was singled out by God to produce a child (Mary) by his infertile wife (Anna) through divine intervention. By confirming the legend, as the dogma implicitly did, was to enter into infinite regress, critics maintained, because if Mary was protected from Original Sin (transmitted by her father's seed), her mother too must be free from sin, and so on. Moreover, the dogma was a blatant contradiction of science, notably the discovery of the egg. Viewed like this, the Immaculate Conception dogma may be seen as the pope's refusal of and contempt for modern science. After von Baer's discovery of the female egg in 1827, it became clear that the mother had an equally active role in childbirth. This presented a massive challenge to traditional Christology, since it meant that Mary had in fact contributed more to Jesus than her womb. This was an interpretation that the pope obviously could not allow, since it threatened Christianity's central dogma of the double nature of Jesus: fully man and fully God. The dogma of Jesus' double nature (Council of Chalcedon in 451) is theologically constitutional for Christianity and a prerequisite for inter-denominational recognition of Christian churches and congregations. It was logically based on the Theotokos dogma, which was declared at the Council of Ephesus twenty years earlier. The latter creates a theological basis for the Cult of the Virgin Mary. It stated that the Virgin Mary is the mother of God and condemned Nestorianism for making a wrongful distinction between the incarnated Christ and Christ as Logos. In this sense, the role of Mary's pregnancy logically tied them together. The prevalent theories of human procreation ensured that the incarnated Christ and Christ as Logos were one and the same. Mary's role was strictly passive in spite of its being instrumental for the Incarnation.

According to the dogma of the Incarnation, God manifests himself in his son (Jesus), who is also the son of Mary. This was unproblematic according to the traditional biological model, in which Mary's contribution to the creation of Jesus was limited to her providing a physical milieu for God's seed to grow into its human form (Incarnation). Essentially, Christ was – like any other child – his father's son. Faced with the modern dilemma of the female egg, however, and an increased focus on the mother's role in procreation, the pope chose to ignore science and repeat the traditional view that Christ's humanity was in the flesh, which he received from his mother (Mary), whereas his divinity came from the father (God). Another aspect of the traditional understanding of the mother's role was the idea that she had a certain influence on the foetus (Jesus), since conditions in the womb would influence the child's physical appearance and would also be instrumental in determining its sex. By defining the Virgin Mary as having been conceived without being tainted by Original Sin, Pope Pius IX erased her father (Joachim) from the story and safeguarded Mary's womb from contamination. In this way, the Catholic Church secured Christian dogma from the onslaught of science. The Protestants, however, did not make such bold statements about the superiority of religious truth. This is not because they attached less importance to revealed truth, but because the Cult of the Virgin Mary was a Catholic tradition. By insisting on the miraculous character of Mary's body, however, the new dogma forged a decisive split between science and religion, and forced the faithful to acknowledge the limits of scientific knowledge.

For all Christian churches, the dilemma posed by modern embryology was the same: Were they to accept scientific truths, Jesus would be the son of his mother Mary and be tainted with a sinful human nature like the rest of us. As we have seen, the pope avoided this dilemma by declaring Mary as being free from sin and by defining her conception as a miracle, that is, an event which escapes natural law and the limitations that govern the universe. The new dogma may be seen as an attempt to safeguard Christian teachings from the onslaught of science, which gave the mother an active role in procreation. Science made Christ the product of both mother and father, and hence less divine. By making his mother an exceptional, pure, and perfect woman, however, the Immaculate Conception widened the gap and made the mother of Christ less human.

Apart from the religious paradox of a man who is God and is both his own father and his own son, what is important in the present context is that Jesus' double nature implies that his humanity relies on Mary. By defining Mary as different, less human, and more divine, the dogma of the Immaculate Conception managed to safeguard Christ's divinity from the onslaught of scientific truths. In other words, by pushing his mother further into the realm of the miraculous – and further away from ordinary human beings – Pope Pius IX avoided further discussion. The pope chose to emphasize Mary's uniqueness. But was the new dogma necessary? When seen historically, it seems quite clear that the scientific consensus after the discovery of the female egg in 1827 placed the Church's central dogma in a problematic position. How could Jesus be an equal to God if his mother (Mary) contributed more than the building material for his body? The new dogma addressed the problem and provided a solution by defining Mary as less human. Theologically, this move also made Christ less human, but that is a different problem. The new dogma came at the cost of all of those ordinary men and women who were engaged in the Cult of the Virgin Mary and who were seeking out her image in churches and chapels, lighting candles, and reciting Hail Marys whenever they needed it because she was much closer to ordinary humans and therefore more approachable than her son. The Catholic devotion to Mary was widely popular, especially in connection with childbirth, where rhymes and formulas evoking the name of Mary abound. In many respects, the Cult of the Virgin Mary was characterized by a kind of emotional intimacy which can be compared to the fervent Jesus enthusiasm of Evangelical Protestantism. The modern Marian dogma emphasized another non-motherly and triumphant character of the Virgin at the cost of the more intimate and meeker mother Mary. Images of the Immaculate Mary present her as more distant and more godlike and therefore further removed from the sinful mothers of ordinary children (Eriksen and Stensvold 2002: 129). However, as a strategy to safeguard Christ's human nature from the onslaught of modern biology, the new dogma was a success. It 'saved' Jesus from being tainted by sinful female flesh. It also served to make clear the distinction between religion and science as the pope saw it.

Ten years after the dogma of the Immaculate Conception was announced on the feast for Mary's conception, on 8 December 1864, Pope Pius IX issued an encyclical, *Quanta cura* (*How Much Care*), with a famous appendix usually referred to as the *Syllabus of Errors*.[3] It listed 80 errors which Catholics should avoid, including socialism and democratic elections, and refuted scientific results that were incompatible with Catholic dogma. It is worth noting that the papal critique of modernity coincided with Italian independence (1860) and the dissolution of the pope's territories in Italy. At the time this encyclical was published, Italian troops surrounded Rome. These historical facts aside, more interesting in our context is the pope's attitude towards science: In the encyclical, he declared that science was subordinate to Christian teaching because the latter comes directly from God (revelation), whereas the former searched for truth through the use of human rationality and consequently was imperfect by definition. In this way, Pope Pius IX tried to assert the Church's power as the ultimate authority and augment his status. According to this logic, science and scientific results are true if and only if they are compatible with the Bible and Catholic tradition.

The Church's resistance to science would last far into the next century. This call for scientists to accept religious supremacy was repeated by Pope Pius X (r. 1903–1914) when he introduced an anti-modernist oath for priests and theology professors in 1907. The *Syllabus of Errors* signalled the beginning of a new phase in the Church's attitude towards science. It had been an uneasy cohabitation for decades, but from the middle of the nineteenth century onwards, Catholic theology was explicitly sceptical – not only of scientific inventions but of science's increasing independence as well. It was not the scientific developments, however, that prompted Pope Pius IX to change Church policy, but changing historical circumstances. Nevertheless Pope Pius IX has become a symbol of Catholic resistance to modernity: He stood up to Italian political and military power and therefore projected the image of the self-contained, triumphant Church that faces challenges head on. The dogma of the Immaculate Conception showed the same self-confidence. Alone in a secular world, the pope was not afraid. But as Børresen shows, the new dogma was also problematic in another sense because it purported to replace Church tradition with papal authority (Børresen 2002). Pius IX's boldest move was to have the First Vatican Council (1868) declare the dogma of the pope's infallibility (Duffy 1997), which set aside established theological teachings. The dogma of the Immaculate Conception also raised questions about the Church's theological tradition, which had served as the basis for its authority since antiquity.

For centuries, scientific debates had passed largely unnoticed by religious authorities. But in the nineteenth century, science developed into a formidable rival – since it had its own organizational, economic, and cognitive autonomy – and Christianity came increasingly under attack from freethinkers, atheist elites, and secularists. But the two systems did not enter into a head-on public confrontation until the heated public debates following Darwin's publication of *On the Origin of*

Species in 1859. Just five years later, the Catholic Church took a clear stance against science and declared that, unless it was in accordance with revealed truth, science was false. Without any direct references to Darwin, Pope Pius IX's *Syllabus of Errors* shows that religious authorities were starting to see their contemporary world as a more hostile place. The challenge that Darwin's theory of evolution posed to religion was plain: The theory was clearly incompatible with the story of Adam and Eve, and therefore one of them had to be wrong. Suddenly, science presented itself as an alternative world view, or paradigm, with Darwin as its main proponent.

Although the Catholic Church was alone in issuing new dogmas as a way of countering the changing times, the Protestant churches faced the same challenges and shared its worries. Protests came from all parts of institutional Christianity, although less so from the liberal theologians (Roberts 1988). With hindsight, the rupture between religion and science appears to have been inevitable but unintentional. Darwin actively sought to avoid confrontations with the Anglican Church – and not only out of respect. At the time, the Anglican Church was still a social force to be reckoned with, and Darwin himself was far from indifferent to its power. When Darwin was a student in the 1820s, freethinkers (deists) were given up to six years in jail for blasphemy. According to Darwin's biographers, "blasphemy was a social crime because Christianity was part of the law of the land" (Desmond and Moore 1991: 70). Darwin's colleague, Thomas Huxley, took a clear stand and (vicariously) voiced the need for the autonomy of science, a position Darwin agreed with but never stated in public. His position was clear and uncompromising. In a letter to Darwin, Huxley explained that it was impossible to be "both a true son of the Church and a loyal soldier of Science" (Desmond and Moore 1991: 585).

By the end of the nineteenth century, science had established itself as a separate field of knowledge. It was institutionally autonomous and liberated from Church power, as several universities in Europe as well as the United States were owned privately or by the state. Therefore, the religious criticism of evolution and other scientific theories that went against established biblical truths had little impact on the development of science. Science was autonomous: It developed according to its own logic and its own pace and was impervious to external influences – except for legal restrictions and economic funding. Since the nineteenth century, scientific research on human procreation has developed on its own, independent of religious understandings, except indirectly by laws that reflect politicians' religious values.[4] The critique that Darwin faced from priests and conservative politicians after what they saw as his onslaught against biblical truth (Genesis) illustrates a consistent religious resistance of and scepticism towards modernity. In this connection, it is worth noting that the reactions of religious authorities to democracy were, on the whole, negative. In Europe, the Catholic Church as well as the Protestant churches feared a future in which the power relations between church and king were dissolved in favour of a system where political power was grounded in the people. They doubted the people's capacity to make their own laws without any religious authorities to guide them. For instance, in 1884 the clergy of the Norwegian state church (Lutheran) signed a protest against parliamentarism. In their view, it was against God's will to undermine the power of the monarch and transfer power to a democratically elected parliament (Stensvold 2005a: 357). Political rule was too important to be left to ordinary people. The conflict between political democracy and religious authority was expressed in different ways. In Germany, there was a Kulturkampf (1871–1878) which ended with a concordat, according to which the state gave in to demands for independent Catholic schools. In Protestant countries like Denmark, the king remained – formally – the head of both church and state, while both king and religion were subsumed under the canopy of democratic power, the political running of the state being in the hands of the people.

In the nation-states that emerged in the nineteenth century, democracy was the rule. Even in countries where the king remained the head of state, as in Protestant countries (Britain, Holland, Germany, Scandinavian states), his powers were dramatically reduced. Likewise, in Catholic kingdoms (Italy, Belgium, and Austria) the king was reduced to a symbolic figure. It is possible to argue that the fate of European kings was parallel to that of the dominant religious institutions. Their political influence dwindled as their cultural and symbolic power grew. In all European countries, the traditional alliance of king and church was outmanoeuvred politically, but it was maintained on a symbolic level as the king ensured a symbolic continuity between the old and the new. Parallel to these processes, the concept of 'the people' underwent a complete change. In pre-modern society, 'the people' were formally defined as a collective of subjects belonging to the king. The entire population was divided into status groups which were hierarchically defined by their closeness to the king: nobility, burgers, farmers, and serfs. Modern society was also hierarchical and consisted of distinctive groups (classes) arranged according to economic power and political resources, but unlike pre-modern society there was mobility between them. Each citizen was defined in relation to other citizens – as equals. Democracy recognized the individual as a citizen and understood society as a collective of morally responsible individuals (not families). Thus, the individual was the basic building block of modern, democratic society.

Initially, democratic citizen rights were not universal, however, as women, the poor, and, in the United States, African Americans were excluded. Historically, democratic ideas were first translated into politics in the American Constitution (1775) and the French Declaration of the Rights of Man and of the Citizen (1789). Thomas Laqueur argues that the structural and cultural subordination of women was so ingrained that it surpassed other hierarchies (Laqueur 1987). Although full voting rights for working-class males came at the turn of the century, for women it came decades later. One reason for this was the traditional patriarchal preconceptions about women's role in society, but in addition some influential intellectuals found new reasons to keep women confined to the private sphere. For instance, Jean-Jacques Rousseau, usually associated with democratic values and known as one of the radical thinkers behind the French Revolution, was a traditionalist where women were concerned. In his much celebrated *Emile, ou De l'éducation* from 1762, known for its radical ideas about education, he warned against the detrimental effects that education would have on the female nature. The struggle for equal rights for women was effectively countered by Rousseau and his companions. In fact, women were not allowed into universities until more than a century later. In Europe, as well as in America, the first universities admitted women (to the humanities) in the 1870s, and the natural sciences followed suit soon thereafter. Women obtained voting rights some decades after male labourers – first in the Scandinavian countries between 1913 and 1918, then in Germany in 1919 followed by the United States in 1920, Britain in 1928, and finally the Catholic countries when they were reconstituted after the Second World War (France in 1944 and Italy in 1946). Obviously, voting rights presupposed that women were regarded as equally rational and as deserving the same responsibilities as men. It took some time. And even when women had gained equal rights in society, churches lagged behind; seemingly undisturbed by the revolution in women's lives, they continued on as before.

After Darwin, religion and science emerged as opposite paradigms.[5] From a theological point of view, the 'problem' was that scientific results had to comply with the Christian world view as expressed in the Bible (revelation) or, more precisely, what the respective churches believe it says. Within a century, science had gained the upper hand and religion's claim to truth was effectively relegated to the private sphere. The Catholic Church gathered around the Virgin Mary, while Protestant America adopted strict laws to prohibit contraception and safeguard public morals. But science was in the driver's seat, and religious answers often seemed strangely out of touch – as when Protestant church leaders preferred monarchy to democracy and the pope insisted on the priority of revelation over scientific truth, both parties being critical of women's participation in public life on moral grounds. Church leaders worried: What would society come to when religion was not allowed to teach people the difference between right and wrong, what would the world come to when people no longer had the fear of God in them?

Notes

1 For a short introduction to some of the theological difficulties associated with the dogma of the Immaculate Conception, see Børresen 2002. References to Mary's purity can also be found in the Quran (Sura 3:37).
2 *The Gospel of Pseudo-Matthew* and *The Story of the Birth of Mary* (James 1926).
3 The encyclical with the *Syllabus of Errors* is printed in Carlen 1990. The official Vatican web site has links to all encyclicals from Leo XIII (r. 1878–1903) onwards.

4 Over the past 40 or 50 years, Western governments have established advisory boards on bioethics. For an overview of US biomedical policies, see http://bioethics.gov/history.

5 I use the term 'paradigm', in its broad sense, to mean world view (i.e. a horizon or framework of interpretation). See Kuhn 1962.

11

FERTILITY UNDER DEBATE

Race, reason, and religion at the turn of the century

By the end of the nineteenth century, the gap between science and religion was so wide as to make them into two autonomous spheres which actively ignored each other. At the same time, a dramatic power shift took place as religion was effectively excluded from politics, while science increasingly provided the basis for political decision-making. An illustrative example of this is eugenics, a theory of heredity that provided the scientific basis for mass sterilization programmes. Wanting to create a healthier population, mass sterilization was initiated in all modern states and largely accepted by politicians on both the left and the right, religious authorities, and the general public. With its conception of 'unwanted citizens', eugenics has become a prototypical example of an inhumane policy. To correlate eugenic policies with secularization, however, is a different matter.

The first half of the twentieth century was a particularly dramatic period, with two world wars (1914–1918 and 1939–1945) and the rise of totalitarian regimes: Communism in Russia (1917), fascism in Italy (1924), and Nazism in Germany (1933). When the Catholic Church chose 1917 as the year it would introduce a much stricter policy on abortion, it seemed strangely out of tune with its surroundings: severe punishment for abortion in the middle of the slaughters of the First World War? With hindsight, this change in Church policy proved significant. It signalled a new effort to maintain religious power over at least one part of reality. When political power seemed to be lost for good, the Christian churches turned their attention towards the individual with regard to sexuality and procreation, the most private of private concerns. In view of Christian tradition, this was a logical choice. But as a side effect of this move, the traditional role of women as mothers was emphasized.

A decisive step towards a scientific understanding of female fertility was the discovery of the menstrual cycle at the beginning of the twentieth century.

Following von Baer's discovery of the egg (1827), the connection between ovulation and menstruation received much attention, but misconceptions and prejudices created methodological difficulties (Laqueur 1987: 27). Most scientists maintained the traditional position and compared menstruation to heat in mammals. Menstruating women were associated with lust and were therefore morally offensive to many Victorian scientists, although other scientists maintained that menstruation had the opposite effect and existed in order to prevent the human female from experiencing the sexual excitation (heat) that could be observed in animals. In fact, the relationship between the menstrual cycle and fertility was not correctly described until 1908, when three Scottish doctors explained how ovulation occurred at midterm between two periods of menses.[1] This put a stop to scientific theories based on the age-old notion that menstruation was a particularly fertile period during which women were willing to breed. And more importantly, it prepared the ground for a more practical approach to female fertility, which eventually developed into biomedical methods for assisted fertility and birth control techniques.

For ordinary people, knowledge of the menstrual cycle could be used to control unwanted pregnancies. But the knowledge was effectively kept from the public by ideas about public decency which did not allow such matters to be openly discussed. Needless to say, the self-imposed censorship was most obviously upheld by Christian institutions and leaders. As was the case with another effective method, *coitus interruptus*, where the man ejaculates outside the woman, the Catholic Church effectively refused to even consider it (Genesis 38:9). But as Robert Jütte observes, the very existence of the taboo is proof that this method was in fact used (Jütte 2008: 43). With menstruation properly understood, this could be an effective means of birth control. Nevertheless, the traditional ban on any kind of manipulation of human reproduction meant that it was dismissed on moral grounds by the Catholic Church. The only technique that could be tolerated was permanent sexual abstinence initiated and signed by a religious vow. Augustine had even proposed it as the ideal form of marriage (Clark 1996). It is tempting to suggest that the Catholic Church's view on sexuality and its restrictive attitude towards contraception is somehow connected to the existence of a celibate clergy with unrealistic ideas about human sexuality.

In 1917, the Catholic Church changed its abortion law. It was a part of the first comprehensive revision of Canon law since the twelfth century, and preparations had been going on for several decades. In the new Code of Canon Law of 1917, the traditional distinction – before and after ensoulment – was removed, and everyone who was involved in an abortion, the pregnant woman and her helpers, were to be excommunicated, that is, no longer allowed to participate in the Church. These provisions were repeated in the latest revision (1983), which stated that "a person who procures a completed abortion incurs a *laetae sententiae excommunicatio*" (*Code of Canon law*, Book VI, Part II, Title VI, Canon 1398). Furthermore, all aborted foetuses, if delivered alive, should be baptized; if they were doubtfully alive, then they should be baptized conditionally (Canon 747).

More surprisingly, the revision dictated that baptism should be performed on a child in the mother's womb if it would die during birth (Canon 746). The manner in which such a baptism should be performed, however, was not prescribed. But these laws show that the Church recognized the unborn foetus as a person. Together with the removal of the distinction of the foetus before and after quickening, this new Code has been taken to mean that the foetus should be regarded as a human being from the very moment of its conception.

The new law was not based on medical science or empirical research, but on systematic theological reflection. It set aside Aquinas' date of ensoulment (when God infused the soul into the foetus), which was 40 days for the male foetus and 90 days for the female foetus. In view of developments in embryology, as we have seen, it was easy to brush it aside as a faulty and outdated biological theory. While the old law correlated quickening with ensoulment, and thereby provided a practical way of discriminating between the various stages in foetal development, the new Canon law defined all abortions – regardless of the age of the foetus – as homicide. According to Canon law historian John Noonan, the law was a logical consequence of the Catholic Church's categorical refusal of contraception (Noonan 1970: 39). This seems to be a weak explanation. After all, theologically speaking the law was quite problematic because it broke with an almost 800-year-old tradition which was underpinned by Aquinas' theory of delayed ensoulment. Commenting on this indirectly, Noonan argues that the new law did not imply that Church law prior to 1917 was wrong. While it appears that way, it is because Church tradition evolves with time and must incorporate new insights (Noonan 1970: 20). These theological difficulties aside, it is worth noting that Canon law had no direct effect outside the Church, but it did serve as a normative ideal for Catholic politicians in their work on national laws and international legislation. In countries where the Catholic Church was dominant, this happened quite frequently. However, the severity of the punishment would vary according to how 'excommunication' was translated into secular punishment. The impact of the law was mainly on a personal level, serving as rule of conduct which would make Catholics live morally good lives and avoid sex outside marriage. For practicing Catholics, however, the new law came at a steep cost. Being obliged to confess their sins to a priest, the unlucky woman, and everyone who had assisted her with the abortion were automatically punished with excommunication and banned from participating in the Church. On the local level, attitudes towards women may differ. For instance, Father Patrick, a parish priest in Bruxelles, in a radio interview in connection with the papal election in 2013, praised Pope Francis for his 'tolerance of women'. When the reporter asked what prompted his admiration, Father Patrick explained that as Bishop of Buenos Aires the new pope had advised his parish priests "to baptise the children of unmarried women" (NRK Radio, 12 March 2014). Although Father Patrick's utterance relies on a misinterpretation, it points to a widespread practice of punishing unmarried mothers. Moreover, it is indicative of the Catholic clergy's estrangement from the predicaments of ordinary women – a deficiency which is even more blatantly expressed in the 1917 Canon law on abortion. Discussing the law's theological basis, John Noonan points to the influence of a French Jesuit, Jean-Pierre Gury, who published a book on abortion in 1864 entitled *Compendium on Moral Theology*, in which he argued that the foetus is pre-programmed to become a human and that taking the life of a foetus therefore amounts to taking its life at a later date: "The foetus, although not ensouled, is directed to the forming of man; therefore its ejection is anticipated homicide" (Gury, Compendium theologiae moralis 1864, cited in Noonan 1970: 38–39). According to Noonan, this argument coincided with a growing agreement in moral theology on immediate ensoulment, that is, the belief that the soul enters the egg together with the sperm cell.

Two women played crucial roles in the development of contraceptive methods and women's journey towards receiving equal rights. Their contributions were concrete and practical, and they focused on birth control. The biologist and rich widow Katharine Dexter McCormick (1875–1967) who financed research on chemical birth control from the 1920s onwards, and Margaret Sanger (1879–1966), who was a trained nurse and journalist, shared the simple but basic insight that control over female fertility was the key to improving the quality of life of ordinary women. McCormick and Sanger represented a new type of women: well-educated, well-connected, and politically active feminists who took part – like men – in the public sphere. Sanger was the activist, and McCormick was the facilitator in charge of a vast fortune. The latter invested a great deal of money in medical research on female reproduction. Together, these two women became a driving force behind research which eventually resulted in the contraceptive pill. Although there is general agreement as to their historical importance, the ideologue among the two, Margaret Sanger, still attracts criticism as scholars dispute her intentions. According to Clover Gross, "in many ways the ambiguities surrounding Margaret Sanger's place in history mirror the contemporary confusion around the concepts of birth control, feminism, eugenics, and direct political action" (Gross 2006: iii). McCormick's and Sanger's dedication to birth control as a key to bettering women's lives relied on a number of medical discoveries, such as the function of the *pituitary gland* (1920s) as a remote control system for the fluctuations of hormone production, and the invention of the first pregnancy test (1926). McCormick and Sanger were more dedicated to the cause itself – birth control – than any particular method, but they shared the belief in chemical solutions over mechanical devices such as condoms and diaphragms.

These feminists and their conservative Christian opponents approached birth control from opposite ends of the spectrum. To the former, contraception was helpful because it could prevent unwanted pregnancies and therefore reduce the number of abortions having to be performed. But to the latter, there was no difference between abortion and birth control, a point well illustrated by the Catholic Church, which spoke about contraception as just another form of infanticide (Reagan 1997: 37). Margaret Sanger was perhaps the strongest proponent of the feminist view, and she printed letters from women telling heartbreaking stories about abortion in her journal, the *Birth Control Review*. The journal with the telling subtitle "dedicated to the principle of intelligent and voluntary motherhood" was published by Sanger and financed by her close friends until 1923, when they started the American Birth Control League. In 1916, she opened the first birth control clinic, in Brooklyn, with the expressed purpose of spreading knowledge about birth control techniques, but it was closed down after one month because it was deemed as fostering a criminal activity by the Comstock Law (1873). Sanger's goal was to provide free access to contraceptives, but the Comstock Law, which targeted immoral behaviour prohibited the sale of contraceptives across the United States. A decisive breakthrough in Sanger's campaign occurred in 1936, however, when, in an attempt to circumvent legal obstacles, she ordered a shipment of Japanese diaphragms to be delivered to the medical clinic of a liberal-minded Catholic physician. John Charles Rock subsequently distributed the contraceptives among his patients as a form of medical treatment (Buettner 2007a). This was a clear violation of the Comstock Law; however, after the situation was tried in court, the ruling went in favour of Rock and Sanger: Physicians could receive contraceptive devices via mail and sell them to their patients. This was a decisive step towards legitimizing birth control. In 1938, Sanger started an association for the distribution of contraceptives and information on contraception that was called the American Birth Control League (as mentioned above). In 1942, it gave itself a more 'family-oriented' name: Planned Parenthood Federation of America.[2] Sanger is also credited with the initial idea for the contraceptive pill, which was finally put into industrial production in the 1960s. Margaret Sanger called it 'the magical pill' because it gave women, for the first time in history, complete control over their own fertility.

Among Christian leaders, views on contraception were divided. Conservative Protestants made common cause with the Catholic Church and were strongly critical of birth control. The logic was that the use of contraceptives was a violation of marriage and Christian family values. Liberal Protestants, however, were largely on the feminists' side. An encyclical issued in 1930 by Pope Pius XI (r. 1922–1939) on the last day of the year, when the Church celebrates the circumcision of the Lord, illustrates the conservative position. The encyclical has the telling title *Of Chaste Marriage* (*Casti connubii*) and harshly condemned birth control as sinful and vicious:

> But no reason, however grave, may be put forward by which anything intrinsically against nature may become conformable to nature and morally good. Since, therefore, the conjugal act is destined primarily by nature for the begetting of children, those who in exercising it deliberately frustrate its natural power and purpose sin against nature and commit a deed which is shameful and intrinsically vicious.
>
> (*Casti connubii* §54)[3]

The logical basis for the pope's position was Augustine's view that marriage served to secure human generation. To the pope, the use of contraceptives amounted to a blatant opposition to the Church's moral teaching, hence the vehemence displayed in the pope's choice of words: "those wicked parents who seek to remain childless, and failing in this, are not ashamed to put their offspring to death" (*Casti connubii* §65). In the next section, Pope Pius XI openly condemned contraception because it encouraged people to have sex and introduced a mental and practical gap between sex and procreation.

The non-celibate Protestant clergy had a more practical approach. Some months prior to the pope's declaration, the annual conference of Anglican bishops, the Lambeth Conference, passed a resolution in favour of (limited) birth control. The date of the resolution was 15 August, a symbolic day, namely, a major feast day for the Virgin Mary, on which Catholics celebrate her Assumption. The pope's encyclical was a reaction to the Anglicans' liberal views. Although the Lambeth Conference also rather surprisingly emphasized sexual abstinence as the preferred method over the use of contraception, the Anglican bishops expressed an overall positive view of sexuality. Consequently, they approached contraception not as something immoral, but as something practical:

> The primary and obvious method is complete abstinence from intercourse (as far as may be necessary) in a life of discipline and self-control lived in the power of the Holy Spirit. Nevertheless in those cases where there is such a clearly felt moral obligation to limit or avoid parenthood, and where there is a morally sound reason for avoiding complete abstinence, the Conference agrees that other methods may be used, provided that this is done in the light of the same Christian principles. The Conference records its strong condemnation of the use of any methods of conception control from motives of selfishness, luxury, or mere convenience.[4]

Here spoke the married clergy. As Gloria Albrecht explains, Protestant leaders condoned the use of contraception with their personal experience, which "enabled them to recognise the non-procreative benefits of marital intercourse" (Albrecht 2003: 93). A vast majority of the delegates (193) were in favour of the resolution, while 67 were against it. However, the bishops were not in any way frivolous. They strongly condemned extramarital sex and demanded severe restrictions on the sale of contraceptives, "forbidding the exposure for sale and the unrestricted advertisement of contraceptives, and placing definite restrictions upon their purchase" (Lambeth Conference 1930, §18). The existence of both liberal and conservative attitudes towards sexuality among Christian clergy resulted in radically opposite views on contraception. While Protestant clergy saw contraception in the context of a loving relationship and referred to "the sexual instinct as a holy thing implanted by God" (Lambeth Conference 1930, §13), Catholic clergy and other conservative Christians continued to regard sexuality only in terms of human generation.[5] Pope Pius XI, for example, who wrote about abortion in his encyclical from 1930 (*Casti connubii*), referred to contraception as a mortal sin. Giving birth is women's natural plight, the pope explained. Even if she may die in the process, pregnancy and birth belong to the God-given qualities of being a woman: "We may pity the mother whose health and even life is gravely imperilled in the performance of the duty allotted to her by nature, nevertheless what could ever be a sufficient reason for excusing the direct murder of the innocent?" (*Casti connubii* §64). Although the pope acknowledged the mother's suffering, it was important for him to rise above that and see the process of giving birth in a broader religious perspective. Besides the categorical disregard for women's autonomy and right to make decisions about their own bodies, the pope's defence of the innocent (child) against the sinner (mother) shows the shortcomings of a Church informed by a distant if not dismissive attitude towards the female body. The result had a dramatic consequence: It allowed the pope to see both the foetus and the pregnant woman as objects in total isolation. The pope approached both as abstract creatures that existed in the eyes of God but not within a social context, that is, in the company of fellow human beings.

The pope's rhetoric established the mother–foetus relationship as antagonistic. The mother is a sinner who has the power to make a fatal decision: whether the foetus should live or die. In this manner, he splits the woman in two: on the one side she is a (fertile) female body which is passive and good, and on the other side she is a person with an active mind who makes her own decision (abortion) and is therefore potentially dangerous and evil. This is the modern woman: the woman that secular society increasingly recognized as being equal to man. In the symbolic world of Genesis, this was déjà vu: Women as the daughters of Eve are disobedient by nature and cause disaster (the Fall). The Catholic Church would not allow it. Neither would conservative Protestants, who saw traditional gender relations as God's plan, and the family unit (parents and children) as the ideal context which allowed men and women to live their lives as proper Christians.

The political context in which the Lambeth Conference and the pope made their statements was between the two world wars, in 1930, when various forms of nationalism combined with racist theories to create a rugged political landscape in Europe. Fascism was on the rise everywhere, but the threat of political totalitarianism was not the religious authorities' main preoccupation. Instead, they focused on the individual, on sexual morals, and on family values. In the midst of Nazi Germany, both Catholic and Protestant churches fought for religious freedom and argued for their right to avoid state control over their schools. They voiced complaints against any political decision which placed restrictions on religious activities or infringed on parents' right to decide their children's education. This was the main objection from church leaders, who voiced harsh criticism of obligatory membership in fascist and Nazi youth organizations. But in 1930, the German Nazi state was not yet on the horizon. Instead, it was racism and its translation into political programmes of social engineering which prompted religious concerns. Not only did racism provide a logical basis for nationalist ideologies (and therefore become politically important), it also found support in scientific theories. Ever since the growth of nationalism during the last part of the nineteenth century, research on heredity and folk psychology had been a priority. This type of research had particularly strong political undertones, since it so blatantly served to legitimize nationalist agendas. During the 1920s and 1930s, eugenics emerged as a combination of race theory and biological heredity laws. The term, from the Greek for 'well born', was coined in 1883 by British amateur scientist Francis Galton in his book *Inquiries into Human Faculty and its Development.*

In addition to being a biological theory, eugenics was also a programme for monitoring human breeding. The first international conference on eugenics was held in London in 1912, and the second was held in New York in 1921. The third and last conference was held in 1932, also in New York. In almost every European country, eugenic programmes were put in place to sterilize psychiatric patients, criminals, the mentally ill as well as certain minority groups, notably Gypsies and homeless people without a permanent address. Those who were part of the sterilization programmes were also denied the right to marry and have children.

Eugenics provided a scientific basis for the Nazis' approach to races and nations, which they, using eugenic models, referred to as 'human stock' (Mosse 1964). However, eugenics was not restricted to the Nazis' version of society; it was also eagerly embraced by the entire political spectrum, including the radical left. Christian organizations were critical of eugenics programmes, but they did not openly protest them. One example is the coveted accusation of un-Christian politics voiced in Pope Pius XI's encyclical *Casti connubii* (1930), where the pope argues for the God-given right of all Christians to marry and to procreate:

> For there are some who oversolicitous for the cause of eugenics, not only give salutary counsel for more certainly procuring the strength and health of the future child – which, indeed, is not contrary to right reason – but put eugenics before aims of a higher order, and by public authority wish to prevent from marrying all those whom, even though naturally fit for marriage, they consider, according to the norms and conjectures of their investigations, would, through hereditary transmission, bring forth defective offspring.
>
> *(Casti connubii §68)*

In this text, the pope refers indirectly to racist theories, and he shows a certain amount of tolerance towards them, for example, when he chooses to repeat eugenic concepts like 'defective offspring'. But his conclusion is critical. Interestingly, the pope chooses to use political arguments rather than religious ones, referring to the freedom of individuals and their right to a private sphere outside the reach of state regulations. With hindsight, this emphasis on the individual, on marriage, and on the private sphere seems strangely out of focus when we know that anti-Semitism and eugenics contributed to the advent of the Holocaust. But this was 1930, and what upset Pope Pius XI was that eugenics was incompatible with the Church's view on marriage and procreation. For the pope, marriage belonged to those things which are God-given and lies outside the realm of what humans can decide. The pope was also critical of state programmes for mass sterilization ("medical action despite their unwillingness" refers indirectly to forced sterilization programmes). Although he admits that it may have positive health effects, it is wrong because it sets aside Church regulations which allow people to marry. Such mass sterilization programmes were introduced in most countries at this time. British India was the first and introduced them in 1907; in 1915, they had been adopted by fifteen US states, and in 1933 eugenics programmes were introduced in Scandinavia and Poland (Kevles 1985: 100). Through its scientific prestige, eugenic race theories had a legitimizing effect on racism and added fuel to the anti-Semitism inherent in European culture (Mosse 1964). This goes a long way to explain the lack of political reactions from other countries to the persecution of Jews in pre-war Germany. Sterilization laws in Nazi Germany (1933–1945) were stricter than elsewhere and affected around 220,000 people (Kevles 1985: 117). The regime banned interracial marriages, citing the notion of racial incompatibility – an idea which held that children of mixed races were weaker and had a higher frequency of physical disability and mental illness. According to racist theories, children of mixed races would weaken the quality (mental and physical health) of the entire nation. Needless to say, these theories were just that, unproven theories. And they were part of the rationale behind the Holocaust.

The general acceptance of racist theories was overwhelming, and political support for eugenics before the Second World War was almost unanimous. With hindsight, the silence of Christian churches seems inexplicable, but when seen in its historical context it appears as yet another example of how organized religion is often intertwined with the mainstream ideas and values of the social reality of which they are a part. However, the pope addressed a meek and somehow distorted criticism of eugenics in his 1930 encyclical: "(C)ertainly it is wrong to brand men with the stigma of crime because they contract marriage, on the ground that, despite the fact that they are in every respect capable of matrimony, they will give birth only to defective children" (*Casti connubii* §69). It is worth noting that the pope voiced his protests as a claim to the priority of Church law over state regulations in matters regarding marriage. In his view, marriage was a God-given institution and was therefore outside the jurisdiction of the state. According to the Church's teachings, the only relevant consideration, when people wanted to get married, was the religious affiliation of the bride and groom (they should both be Catholic), not their race.

After the Nazis' ascent to power in Germany in 1933, a vast programme of social engineering was introduced. As mentioned above, the programme was legitimized by eugenics, but it was also based on a crude version of Ernst Haeckel's theory of foetal development. Haeckel had been an important scientist

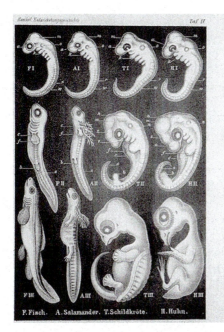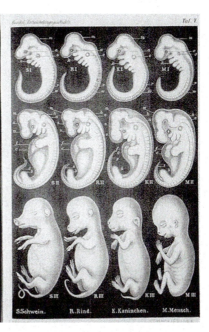

FIGURE 11.1 Drawing from Haeckel's *Anthropogenie* published in 1874 illustrates his theory which states that each foetus undergoes the same stages of development. The drawing, which is read from the top down, shows embryos of fish (F), salamander (A), turtle (T), chick (H), pig (S), cow (R), rabbit (K), and human (M) at 'very early' and later stages. Lithograph by J. G. Bach of Leipzig after drawings by Haeckel from *Anthropogenie* published by George Engelmann/Wikimedia Commons/Public Domain.

in nineteenth-century Germany and was best known as an important proponent of Darwin's theory of evolution. Inspired by Darwin, he developed a theory which held that embryonic development recapitulates the adult stages of their evolutionary ancestors ("ontogeny recapitulates phylogeny").

Because of the Nazis' misuse of his name, Haeckel is strongly associated with anti-Semitism and eugenics. The association is also prominent in contemporary anti-abortion rhetoric, where embryonic research is often presented (wrongly) as building on Haeckel's theory. To create an associative link between contemporary Western abortion practices and the Nazi eugenics programme is obviously an effective strategy to discredit one's opponents (those in favour of legal abortion). Among the many unserious references to Haeckel that confound legal abortion with the horror of the Holocaust, this abstract from an article published by the Institute for Creation Research in Dallas, Texas, is illustrative. The author, one Henry Morris, Ph.D., refers to Haeckel's theory as "the recapitulation theory" and states: "The most recent application of the recapitulation theory has been as a pseudo-scientific justification for the terrible holocaust of abortionism which has been sweeping the world in recent years".[6] Anti-abortion activists have a vested interest in tarnishing Darwin's name by associating him with Nazism and discredited race theories.[7] To a non-expert audience, such arguments may seem plausible, but the attribution relies on superficial similarities. Although a central tenet of Darwin's evolutionary theory was common descent, he did not make the claim that each individual recapitulates the evolution of the species. Haeckel's theory of embryonic development does not in fact correspond to Darwin's thesis. Darwin himself did not perform embryonic research on vertebrate animals, but expressed support for Karl von Baer's law, which in fact states the opposite, namely, that the individuals of each species share the characteristics of their own species.

For Christian anti-abortionists, however, these discussions are merely instrumental. What lies behind their conviction is not another scientific theory, but the belief that conception is sacred and that any kind of impediment to the foetus' development is a sacrilege. As two prominent anti-abortion activists, Donald DeMarco and Benjamin Wiker, would have it, "human beings are indistinguishable from the mother in the womb and from other animals for some time outside the womb" (DeMarco and Wiker 2004: 113). For these authors, each conception requires God's intervention, since each individual is made in his image and is infused with a soul. For conservative Christians, therefore, Haeckel becomes a potent symbol of secular science and a world gone astray.

Notes

1 Thomas Hastie Bryce, John Hammond Teacher, and John Martin Munro Kerr, *Contributions to the Study of the Early Development and the Imbedding of the Human Ovum.* Glasgow: Maclehose, 1908.
2 Today, the organization is a leading abortion provider. View its webpage at http://www.plannedparenthood.org/
3 The encyclical is available from the homepage of the Catholic Church at http://w2.vatican.va/content/pius-xi/en/encyclicals/documents/hf_p-xi_enc_31121930_casti-connubii.html.
4 The conference documents are available at the Lambeth Conference website at http://www.lambethconference.org/index.cfm.
5 The Catholic Church's attitude towards contraception has been repeated almost verbatim in all papal encyclicals until this day – with inhumane consequences, especially after the outbreak of the AIDS epidemic.
6 Available at http://www.icr.org/article/heritage-recapitulation-theory/
7 The fight against Darwin's evolutionary theory is known under two headings: creationism and intelligent design. It falls outside the scope of this book to develop this point further. For an overview of the debate, see the website of an organization which has been engaged in the battle against creationism since 1981: The National Center for Science Education (NCSE) has been defending the teaching of evolution and climate science, http://ncse.com/creationism/analysis/ontongeny-phylogeny.

PART IV

Contemporary debates
The twentieth century to the present

12

WOMEN AND THE VIRGIN IN THE TWENTIETH CENTURY

Feminism and modern attitudes towards pregnancy

Within a few decades of the Second World War (1939–1945), the social status of Western women was redefined, and women participated fully in the public sphere. Among the things that contributed to women's emancipation was political democracy, which had emerged as the winner after six years of war against authoritarian regimes (e.g. those of Germany, Italy, and Japan). Democracy relied on an idea of equality that cut across gender, race, and class hierarchies. In the aftermath of the war, liberal democratic values were high on the political agenda, including feminist issues (Hibbard 2010). In many European countries, women's liberation was a direct consequence of the war effort (Caine and Sluga 2000: 163). Although working women were largely replaced by returning soldiers, the number of women factory workers and functionaries continued to grow. And with access to higher education, the tides were starting to turn.

But beyond social reforms in the postwar years loomed the Cold War, a latent conflict between capitalist and communist regimes, which created a sinister backdrop for Western social and economic achievements in this period. Without trying to account for the political reasons behind the animosity between former allies (the United States and the Soviet Union), suffice it to say that the conflict began soon after the victory over Nazi Germany. From a Christian point of view, the Soviet Union was an illegitimate, immoral, and authoritarian regime and a potent symbol of religion's enemy in the modern world. Christianity was losing ground, and irreligious politics were taking over (secularization). It was not enough to do missionary work and spread the message to the faithful, Christianity also had to fight against irreligious politicians, whose ideas were challenging traditional Christian values.

Starting in the 1920s, a slow but decisive change in attitudes towards female issues was noticeable in all Western countries. One indication of such a change was that a number of countries introduced exceptions to harsh abortion laws, allowing abortion for therapeutic (health) reasons. An important event in this regard was a rape case in Britain in 1938, in which a 14-year-old girl was granted a legal abortion. This was a victory for the public and the press which had supported the girl. The incident established a new principle in legal practice: In questions regarding abortion, the pregnant woman's mental state should be taken into consideration and be regarded as sufficient grounds for abortion. Other countries followed a similar pattern, eventually allowing legal abortion.

A sign of the changing times as well as a catalyst for change towards gender equality was the United Nations Universal Declaration of Human Rights (1948). For various reasons, the Declaration of Human Rights has often been criticized for its alleged Christian bias. This may be true in the sense that the idea of equality of all men is a Christian idea – and a Muslim one for that matter – teaching that salvation is open to everyone and that all men are equals in the eyes of God. The main problem from a religious point of view lies elsewhere, namely, in the definition of man. The monotheistic religions (Christianity, Judaism, and Islam) agree with the Declaration's reference to human dignity, but they find it hard to accept the Declaration's lack of references to divine creation. This was a conscious choice by the committee that had prepared it (Glendon 2001). A premise of the Declaration was equality among humans: "Everyone is entitled to all the rights and freedoms set forth in this Declaration, without distinction of any kind, such as race, colour, sex, language, religion, political or other opinion, nation or social origin, property, birth or other status" (Article 2). The main inspiration was the recent experience of the Holocaust, but in recognizing men and women as equals the Declaration went further than any national laws at the time in acknowledging equality for women. The Declaration was not legally binding, but it aimed to establish international rules that would protect the individual from unfair treatment and undue interference from the state (Glendon 2001). Central to the Declaration was the concept of the human being. By establishing a principle of *equal* rights, age-old privileges of gender, race, and class were delegitimized; however, the concept of the human being was not clearly defined. The question of the status of the foetus was briefly discussed by the Human Rights Commission, which prepared the Declaration for the United Nations in 1948 (Glendon 2001: 146, 175). But the committee suppressed it, since it was considered to be a religious concern and was therefore not an appropriate topic on which to create a consensus. Therefore, the first paragraph grants human status as a birthright:[1] "All humans are born free and equal in dignity and rights". It leaves no doubt that birth, not conception, is the decisive moment when rights set in. As we have seen, conservative Christians disagreed. In their view, the foetus has intrinsic worth because it is a human being created by God – with the help of the father's seed and the mother's womb. The mother's role in procreation is prefigured by Mary: She should be obedient, patient, and accepting. 'Equal rights' has little meaning in this regard.

The Universal Declaration of Human Rights strengthens women's autonomy and their reliance on their own free will. Viewed from this perspective, the pope's declaration of a new Marian dogma in 1950 belongs to a different discourse underlining the distance between the human and the divine. The new Marian dogma known as the Assumption of the Blessed Virgin Mary stated that Mary's body had been taken directly to heaven when she died. In other words, Mary had no bodily remains on earth, but was taken, just like her son, to reside in heaven. Mary's death was not like that of ordinary humans. For ordinary humans, death implies a temporary separation of body and soul, which will be reunited at the Last Judgement. The new dogma ensured that Mary was exempted from human fate and taken body-and-soul after her death. The new Assumption dogma declared that Mary too had been taken directly to heaven. Theologically, the new dogma was a logical consequence of the dogma of the Immaculate Conception (1854), since the latter stated that Mary was without Original Sin; it also implied that she was exempted from its punishment (death).

When the pope declared the new Marian dogma on 1 November 1950, he did so *ex cathedra*, i.e. on his own authority without the expressed consensus of a council of bishops. This procedure relied on the dogma of the pope's infallibility, which was declared by the First Vatican Council in 1871. For the first and – so far – for the last time, the infallibility dogma was put to use in 1950 by Pope Pius XII (r. 1939–58). It was a strong expression of papal authority, by a sovereign leader with absolute powers, and a telling sign of a Church in discord with socio-political developments. This belief that Mary had been taken directly to heaven when she died was not new. An engraving by Pierre Daret of Mary's Assumption used as an illustration in the *Breviarium* (containing texts used in official Catholic rituals) published in Paris in 1647 shows that the belief was already an established tenet of Catholic faith. It was not only a motif in Christian art for centuries, but it was also an integrated part of Catholic practice, as witnessed by the absence of 'normal' relics. Like those related to her son, Jesus, relics related to Mary are objects (ranging from her house in Loreto, Italy, to drops of her milk, found, among other places, in the Santi Apostoli cathedral in Rome). So even if the pope did show his power in such a unilateral manner, he did not issue a controversial dogma, and it would certainly be wrong to claim that the new dogma introduced a change in the religious conception of Mary. On the contrary, the idea that Mary was taken – body and soul – to reside with God in heaven was an old and popular idea. In an attempt to explain its popularity, Caroline Walker Bynum refers to the laity's love and compassion for the Mother of God. In medieval Christianity, the Assumption was something God had done out of his love for Mary, "for without her body, she would be troubled by its lack and therefore unable to enjoy perfect happiness" (Bynum 1992: 229). Since the eighth century, the Assumption had been celebrated with a special church feast on 15 August (Jungmann 1986).

The idea that Mary was taken directly to heaven was also a popular motif in Christian art (Warner 1990), as illustrated by early representations of the Virgin on murals and mosaics in which she is depicted as a queen seated beside her son in heaven. In other words, the new dogma added nothing to prevailing Catholic ideas about Mary. Why Pius XII elevated the Assumption to a dogma in 1950 remains obscure. Perhaps he intended the declaration to result in a new religious focus on Mary, as was the case with the dogma of the Immaculate Conception, but the dogma in 1950 did not even inspire a new way of depicting the Virgin. However, the fact that the pope proclaimed the Assumption dogma in 1950, when capitalism and democracy (United States) competed with communism (USSR) for global dominance in the Cold War, was hardly a coincidence. Historically, a new dogma is an extremely rare occurrence, and when two new Marian dogmas were declared in less than a hundred years (1854 and 1950), and both emphasized the distance between the mother of God and normal, sinful women, we may see it as a critique of modern feminism. Thus, it appears as a particularly political dogma used explicitly to express the Church's understanding of its authority and its role in the world.

When seen from a wider political perspective, the Assumption dogma can also be regarded as a symbolic gesture to underline the Church's commitment to the West. In the context of the Cold War, Western secularism was definitely a preferable alternative to communist atheism. As far-fetched as this may seem, it is logical that the Virgin Mary was evoked as a religio-political symbol in the Church's struggle with its modern enemies, among which communism appeared as the most threatening. The pope's engagement was not motivated by concern for the minute minority of some thousand Catholics trapped inside the Soviet Union, but was rooted in a deep-seated fear of communist expansion (Duffy 1997). Already in the 1920s, the Catholic Church singled out communism (not fascism or Nazism) as the single most urgent threat. But unlike political anti-communism, the Church did not fear communist economics or communist social politics, but communist atheism. It was the latter that made communism a self-declared enemy of the Church. To put things into perspective, it is worth noting that two years earlier the pope had ruled that membership in the Communist Party should be punished with excommunication – the same punishment as for homicide (and abortion). Although the prohibition placed Catholics behind the Iron Curtain in a difficult position, it was an effective tool which made the Church a symbol of anti-communism in Eastern Europe, especially in Poland. In 1950, the Cold War was at its peak with the communist witch hunt in the United States (McCarthyism). To make a long story short, the Virgin Mary had traditionally been an important symbol of faith, and after the Russian Revolution (1917) she was recast as a central figure in the Catholic Church's anti-communist battle (Zimdars-Swartz 1991). The reason why the Church chose Mary as a symbol for its fight against communism was partly because of a miracle that occurred in Fatima (Portugal) in 1917. Three children between seven and ten years of age allegedly met the Virgin on 13 May, who told them that a terrible war would break out unless the Soviet Union was liberated from communism and became a Christian nation.

The apparition in Fatima in 1917 was interpreted by Church authorities as a sign that communism would eventually be conquered by Christianity and that the Virgin Mary was actively engaged in the struggle against atheism. The dogma of Mary's Assumption was part of the Church's strategy to combat atheism and secularism, a strategy which spanned from Marian apparition to militant faith organizations with a strong missionary zeal like the Militia of Mary Immaculate (started in Poland in 1917 by Maximilian Kolbe). But devotion to the Virgin of Fatima became a particularly popular way of combining religious faith and political zeal. The fascist dictators of Portugal and Francisco Franco in Spain were among its devotees (Christian 1984). The Virgin of Fatima also played an important role in the papacy of the Polish pope, John Paul II. Before he became pope, he was Bishop of Krakow during Poland's communist regime and was celebrated as a central figure in that country's religiously based resistance to communism. The apparition of the Virgin of Fatima is commemorated in stories, feasts, and a sculpture which is one of the most popular images of the Virgin in contemporary Catholicism. The sculpture, which is mass-produced and found across the Catholic world, has many traits in common with the standard depiction of the Immaculate Conception, but is distinguishable by its white robe, graceful gesture, and crown. Pope John Paul II donated the bullet that almost killed him in a terrorist attack in Rome in 1980 to this statue. It was intended as a token of gratitude for the Virgin's protection and placed in the centre of the crown of the original statue, which has been placed in the cathedral in Fatima, Portugal.

Theologically, the Virgin Mary is a symbol of the Church. She is the mother of Christ, and by implication she is also the mother of all the faithful. Depictions of her body are therefore symbolic representations of the Church in its aspect as community of the faithful (both living and dead). Nevertheless, this particular interpretation is largely a theological construct and lacks popular support, since the relationship between Mary and the Church remains a highly abstract one: Relying on a concept of the Church as the community of the faithful, on the one hand, and an abstract idea of a mother, on the other, Mary as a symbol of the Church is not a subject of popular devotion. This can be illustrated by Lakoff and Johnson's thesis in *Metaphors We Live By*, where they show how metaphors and symbols, in addition to being particularly heavy with meaning, also have a taken-for-granted quality (Lakoff and Johnson 1980). The cross is such a symbol, pointing simultaneously to suffering, death, and Christ. Mary is clearly not. Despite all papal speeches that evoke Mary as a symbol of the Church, there is no depiction which has the same immediate relation to Mary as the cross and crucifix have to Christ. Depictions of Mary remain depictions of Mary – or in the worst case, simply pictures of a woman. One reason for this may be the discrepancy within Catholic conceptions of Mary. In folk piety, the Cult of the Virgin is first and foremost associated with daily cares and worries. People seek out her images in order to lament their pains, get help with illnesses and everyday concerns, and evoke her name in childbirth

(Eriksen and Stensvold 2002). Viewed like this, we may say that the new dogmas – first the Immaculate Conception and, a hundred years later, the Assumption – added little to the laity's devotion to Mary. On the contrary, instead of deepening her role as a symbol of motherly love, the two new dogmas strengthened Mary in her aspect as a militant fighter for faith in an increasingly faithless world. They emphasized Mary's elevated position and distanced her further from the meek mother of medieval Christianity. We may say that in the battle against communism, Mother Mary, who formerly had assisted at every childbirth in medieval Europe, became a warrior on the political scene.

The Virgin as a queen who is seated beside her son was one of the most important and widespread images in early Christianity. Known as the image of Maria Regina, it shows Mary seated beside her son, the King of Heaven, as "the living embodiment of the Church triumphant" (Warner 1990: 110). During the medieval period, this image became less important as depictions of Mary as a young mother holding a baby Christ became popular (Steinberg 1996). And this meek and suffering mother was a central feature of medieval Franciscan piety (Derbes 1996). Furthermore, many of these images were ascribed with miraculous powers, being able to heal wounds and help with fertility and difficult pregnancies. As mentioned above, the dogma of the Immaculate Conception (1854) gave rise to a pictorial tradition, in which Mary is depicted as a young maiden dressed in white with a light-blue belt around her waist. The modern Mary, who became popular in the nineteenth century, is depicted alone, and, as such, these images refer more clearly to Mary as a symbol of the Church. In this regard, the modern Mary can be taken as a symbolic expression of the Church in modern society: This is Mary after motherhood. It is the Mary of the Apocalypse, a pure, powerful queen who shall lead the faithful and help the clergy in a hostile world.

Although the Assumption dogma of 1950 did not give rise to a new way of depicting Mary's arrival in heaven, it is possible to argue that the dogma added to a popular and highly political story, namely, the apparition of Mary of Fatima, and vested it with theological authority. Dressed in a light-blue gown and with a glory of twelve stars around her, the Fatima Madonna is an illustration of the woman who is described in Revelation and who is usually understood as Mary: "A great portent appeared in heaven: a woman clothed with the sun, with the moon under her feet, and on her head a crown of twelve stars" (Revelation 12:1). More interesting, in the present context, is the next verse, which describes her as being pregnant: "She was pregnant and was crying out in birth pangs, in the agony of giving birth" (Revelation 12:2). But this part of the story has not (as yet) found any pictorial expression. Modern and contemporary depictions of the Virgin Mary present her as a powerful demigod. Stripped of almost everything except a rosary, a crucifix, or 12 stars, she is depicted as a young, strong, and beautiful woman. With a compassionate expression and a welcoming gesture, she symbolizes Christianity all by herself. Gone is the baby Jesus nestling in his mother's arms, and there is no trace either of the suffering mother kneeling in tears at the foot of the cross. The modern Mary stands alone. This change in the conceptualization of Mary – dogmatically and in art – is in itself an interesting development. It may be viewed as a distorted mirror reflection of the modern, independent woman who is not only a wife and a mother, but also a politically active citizen. Viewed like this, we would expect Catholic theology to adjust its views to social reality and grant women equal status to men within the Church. While this is not the case, it may partly be explained by the findings of comparative studies of female goddesses, which show that there is no correlation between religious devotion to goddesses and the social status of ordinary women. As exemplified by the female goddesses in Hinduism, the status of goddesses in the divine hierarchy does not reflect the social position of their female devotees (Young 1987: 7).

While this is not the place to speculate on the resilience of male power in the Catholic Church, suffice it to say that the contrast to developments in established Protestant churches with regard to the status of women is striking. The Protestant national churches in Europe and the liberal denominations in the United States have adapted to the social, political, and economic emancipation of women which took place in Western countries during the twentieth century. While many of the established Protestant churches allow female clergy and have liberal views on contraceptives and abortion, the Catholic Church has taken a leading role in the conservative fight for traditional patriarchal family norms. Thus, it would seem that the Protestant churches keep a closer tap on social developments because of its married clergy. In the Catholic Church, however, the clergy is often closer to Mary than to ordinary women. Since the new Marian dogmas (the Immaculate Conception in 1854 and the Assumption in 1950) made Mary even more holy and more distant from normal women, it is possible to say that Catholic gender relations remain essentially as defined by Augustine. Although the rhetoric has changed somewhat over the last decades, emphasizing the mutual dependence of the married couple, the wife is still essentially a helpmate: "The spouses, in the natural complementarity which exists between man and woman, enjoy the same dignity and equal rights regarding the marriage".[2] Obviously, Catholic theology has its own ideas about the family.

Since medieval times, the Virgin Mary has been a symbol for the Church understood as the community of believers. The theological background for this idea is, among other things, her function as a role model; she is a symbol of the ideal Christian. The story of her immediately accepting her plight as a virgin mother (Luke 2:19) symbolizes faith. And her being a witness to Jesus' death on the cross (John 19:30) signals humility and suffering. The Virgin Mary is a symbol of the collective – clergy and laity, men and women. She is the mother of all the faithful. In Christian art, this 'Mary-as-Church' is represented as a pregnant woman or at least a woman with wide skirts with plenty of room for the faithful to seek refuge. Along these lines, the Catholic Church sees the laity as Mary's body and the clergy as a parallel to Christ at its head. The model preserves the traditional hierarchy of sexual difference which associated Mary (woman) with the body and Jesus (man) with the mind. Although Protestant theology avoids these similar references to the Virgin Mary, conservative Protestants are also devoted to the notion of a divinely ordered gender hierarchy, usually referred to as natural difference and gender complementarity. Transposed to the social sphere, the relationship between husband and wife is another version of the male–female hierarchy. The husband is the head of the household – like Christ – and the wife is the body – like Mary. She is associated with nutritive and caring functions and is – by God – defined by her body, notably her reproductive function. The hierarchical relation inside the traditional marriage is understood by most conservative Christians to be a part of God's design as expressed in Genesis. The subordination of women is sacred, as is the dominance of men. According to this logic, feminism and political struggle for women's liberation and equal rights appear as futile attempts at escaping the natural limits of female biology (pregnancy and contraception) and as unwarranted protests against God's plan. To paraphrase an Italian saying, a woman should always be willing to make a sacrifice because a woman's plight is to suffer.

Between the First and Second World Wars, social scientists tried to explain the radical reduction of religious influence in society and developed the theory of secularization. Taking its name from Latin 'secular' meaning 'of this world', as opposed to eternity and what belongs to God, the theory argued that there was a causal relationship between modernity and the decline of religion (the most influential among these social scientists were two German sociologists, Max Weber and Ernst Troeltsch). The classical secularization thesis claimed that religion was doomed to disappear as scientific explanations would gradually make religious explanations redundant. Scientists predicted the annihilation of religion both as a social institution (church) and as a personal world view (faith). But before it disappeared completely, religion would undergo an intermediary stage in which it would withdraw into the private sphere. Until the 1980s, this was largely accepted as a relevant diagnosis and a convincing future scenario.

Over the last few decades, however, more nuanced theories about religion in modern society have emerged. Based on historical facts, scientists now agree that although the secularization thesis may hold for Europe, there is no causal relation between modernity and secularization (Berger 1999). This claim is supported by empirical research in other parts of the world, which shows that the rise of modernity (understood as social differentiation) is not necessarily accompanied by a fall in church attendance (South America) or religious influence on politics (Middle East). Critics also agree that religion should be studied in its historical context (Davie 1994).

There are also many sociologists who wish to discard secularization theory altogether. José Casanova, a Spanish-American sociologist of religion, points out how the term has become almost void because it is used indiscriminately in three different ways. The first usage Casanova mentions refers to religion's loss of social and political influence. The second usage is understood as decline in the number of people who practice religion and/or report that they have religious beliefs. And the third usage of secularization refers to the marginalization of religion, which Casanova sees as an inevitable effect on religion in a modern, complex society. In order to counter this, religions have the possibility to adapt to society's specialization and refine their religious function (Casanova 1994). As Casanova points out, in Europe the national Protestant churches lost their hegemony during the nineteenth century, and the Catholic Church followed suit. But in the United States, where no church had dominance and religious pluralism was a principle laid down in its Constitution, secularism was held at bay.

According to Austrian-American sociologist Peter Berger, religious pluralism is a social value which fosters relativism and tolerance (Berger 2010). Therefore, a viable democracy requires a strong religious sector. Be that as it may, Berger's main thesis finds support (albeit in a roundabout way) in German sociologist Niklas Luhmann's theory that religion, which has its roots in pre-modern society, has difficulties adapting because, unlike other sectors of contemporary society (educational system, health services, science, banking, bureaucracy, and so on), it once held a hegemonic position (Beyer 1994). In a complex and advanced society, however, no institution can hold a dominant position and claim supremacy over other institutions (Luhmann 1982). Since it is impossible for one institution to achieve hegemony in a complex, differentiated society, religions, which traditionally seek hegemony, are bound to fail to assert themselves and will necessarily be marginalized. Nevertheless, a modern, complex society does not necessarily entail that religions become insignificant with regard to their social, political, and cultural impact. For this fate to be avoided, however, religions must adapt to a differentiated, specialized system and give up their hegemonic aspirations.

The process of secularization in Europe liberated science from religious constraints and relegated religion to one among several specialized institutions. The reasons behind this development are extremely complex, but they cannot be blamed on religion. It was not faith as opposed to rational knowledge which was the problem, as Max Weber and other early theorists claimed – the persistence of religion in contemporary society is a case in point. Instead, secularization was brought on by a complex dynamic of religious pluralism, political ideology (democracy), and the spread of scientifically based knowledge (educational system) to all sectors of society. Politically, the Christian churches still maintained some political power (i.e. as national institutions in Europe). Although Christian churches tried to counter this trend, it was mainly expressed as a critique of society and modernity. Churches reacted with moral indignation to political ideologies, notably fascism and Nazism, but reserved their most vehement criticism for communism (due to its link with atheism, as we have seen). This consistent but often ineffective criticism eventually played a part in the demise of the communist regime in Poland (1989). We may also say that the persistent argument for individual rights (freedom of religion) has been politically successful – associating Christianity with human rights. But in connection with other aspects of individual rights, such as gender equality, Christian discourse is divided.

In the middle of the twentieth century, the pope repeated his predecessor's attempt to take a lead in the fight for religion in an increasingly secularized world and introduced a new dogma concerning the Virgin Mary. It passed unnoticed by feminists and had little effect on Catholic piety. But its underlying logic, the emphasis on the Virgin Mary and motherhood as a means to promote traditional Christian values, has been a tenet of Church policy ever since. Nevertheless, women's position in Western society underwent massive changes. The 1960s and 1970s saw a sharp rise in female participation in politics and economic life. The legalization of abortion reflected the new awareness of female concerns. In connection with the Church reforms announced by the Second Vatican Council (1962–1965), many progressive clerics hoped for a renewal of teachings about gender roles and sexuality. But official teachings on these issues remained unchanged, whereas Protestant churches adjusted to the changing times and the liberalism which characterized Western politics in the decades after the Second World War. They willingly accepted contraception, reluctantly condoned abortion in the first trimester, and some of them even more reluctantly allowed women into the clergy. On the other hand, conservative Protestants – evangelicals and fundamentalists – were in tune with the Catholic Church and started to refine their religio-political tactics.

Notes

1 This argument is persistently repeated by such groups as Family Watch International, Concerned Women for America, and the Catholic Family and Human Rights Institute. See Moe, Stensvold, and Vik 2013.
2 Article 1c, *Charter of the Rights of the Family* issued by Pope John Paul II in 1983. Available at http://www.vatican.va/roman_curia/pontifical_councils/family/documents/rc_pc_family_doc_19831022_family-rights_en.html.

13

LEGAL ABORTION

The rise of liberal-democratic ideas of gender equality

The 1960s and 1970s are often referred to as the heydays of feminism, when access to contraception allowed women, for the first time in history, to control their own fertility and when women were increasingly active in the public sphere, participating in political elections and working outside the home. After women's contributions to the war effort during two world wars, when women performed the work of men, the housewife of the 1950s was a temporary setback. After all, it is difficult to maintain the idea of female inferiority when men and women have the same jobs and women hold political office. When women flocked into the workplace and universities in the 1960s and 1970s, their arrival did not challenge existing power structures, as women repeated the patterns of behaviour associated with their social group (race and class). For working-class women who were already working away from home, the changes of the 'liberating 70s' was hardly noticeable except as a broadening of possibilities.

To conservative Christians, these changes were signs of a society gone wild. They voiced their concerns, but were largely ignored outside their own circles. Most church leaders took a defensive position, however, regarding it as an inevitable historical development (secularization). To many of them, these unfortunate changes were epitomized in the demise of traditional gender roles and a new, hedonistic attitude towards sexuality, which radically detached sex from pregnancy, birth, and marriage. While the majority of Protestant churches (e.g. Anglican, Presbyterian, Lutheran, Methodist) adopted more liberal attitudes, adjusted to changing times, accepted contraception, and (reluctantly) condoned abortion in the first trimester – and while some of them even allowed women into the clergy – the Catholic Church did not. Evangelical[1] and Pentecostal congregations, however, were in tune with the Catholic Church and started to refine their own religio-political tactics to counter the political influence of liberal–democratic, secular, and feminist groups. I use this term 'Evangelical' in a generic fashion to refer to congregations of Protestant origin with cultural and religious roots in the Great Awakenings in the nineteenth century. My usage does not correspond to the list of members of The National Association of Evangelicals (1942), which counts 45,000 local churches representing 40 denominations as members.

When the social role of women changed, female biology became problematic in a new way. An unwanted pregnancy was not necessarily a problem for housewives, but for women with careers and unmarried students, it was a tragedy. As Kristin Luker observes, "to women whose primary role are as wife and mother, control of one's body meant little" (Luker 1984: 118). Women used their political liberty to fight for equality also in matters regarding reproduction, which became acutely problematic once women had 'left the kitchen' and entered the workplace. In the 1960s, a new invention, the contraceptive pill, was introduced which gave women control over their own fertility and revolutionized women's lives. The pill was not only a scientific achievement and commercial success. Since it made pregnancy a matter of choice rather than a biological fate, it had serious political implications, making it possible for women to enter the domain that was previously held by men.

After the discovery of the function of the hormones regulating the menstrual cycle, chemical monitoring of female fertility was a theoretical possibility. The idea emerged sometime in the 1930s, supposedly stemming from the feminist activist Margaret Sanger (1879–1966). But it was only after the Second World War, in 1951, that the idea turned into a project. A rich widow, Katharine Dexter McCormick (1875–1967), agreed to finance research to develop a chemical means of regulating female fertility (the contraceptive pill). The reason for McCormick's engagement was deeply personal. She had lost her husband to hereditary schizophrenia shortly after their marriage. With a master's degree in biology, she had the scientific knowledge to make informed choices about the research projects she supported. Like Sanger, she was also a dedicated feminist, and she became the first president of the League of Women Voters when women's right to vote was introduced in 1920.

From the 1950s, McCormick financed research on female hormones until the research results were translated into the birth control pill and commercial interests took over in 1960. However, there were laws that regulated the distribution and sale of contraceptive devices – for example, the Comstock Law from 1873, which was designed to protect society from obscenity and which effectively denied American women free access to contraception. These prohibitions had to be set aside by political intervention. Feminists like Sanger and McCormick faced massive and often violent resistance from traditionally minded men and people with conservative religious views. Their battle for free access to contraception, which started already before the Second World War and which was partially won in 1936, when the ban on distribution was lifted, was not over until the law against obscenity was reinterpreted and contraception was legitimized. But from the 1960s onwards, the birth control pill was commercially produced and sold on the open market. Within a few years, sales restrictions were lifted so that unmarried women also had access to it and so that all women could – for the first time ever – take control of their own fertility. The condom had done the same for men, but the contraceptive pill was something more than a technical instrument. It changed the function of women's bodies, literally liberated them from biological limitations, and placed gender relations under debate.

John Charles Rock, a medical doctor based in Boston, was Sanger's most devoted collaborator. He was also a practicing Catholic, but unlike his conservative co-religionists he was also a dedicated spokesman for birth control. His main goal was to reduce abortions and unwanted pregnancies, and true to the biblical prohibition against "spilling the seed" (Genesis 38:8–10), he did not regard *coitus interruptus* as an alternative. The method that Rock preferred was the 'rhythm method', which was discovered in the 1920s after the menstrual cycle had been described in detail (1908). The rhythm method could be used as a form of natural birth control, which required nothing else but sexual abstinence during ovulation, a method which in Rock's view was not prohibited in the Bible. In 1936, he started teaching his patients the rhythm method, and in 1949 he published a popular book on the topic. However, he became a controversial figure in the 1960s, when he also started promoting the contraceptive pill, which he regarded as an improved version of the rhythm method. According to his logic, the pill simply created an extension of that part of the menstrual cycle when the woman is infertile ("the safe period"). To Rock's surprise, however, the Catholic Church labelled the contraceptive pill an immoral device and classified it together with condoms and diaphragms as sinful because it separated sexual activity from procreation; therefore, in the Church's view, it was an immoral device which incited promiscuity.

The reason why John Charles Rock believed that the Church would accept the contraceptive pill was not as naïve as it may seem. According to Rock's logic, the contraceptive pill was in accordance with Catholic teaching, since it manipulated the female cycle on the hormonal level and hindered ovulation, thus prolonging a natural period of infertility. Furthermore, Rock's endorsement was theologically legitimized by a pronouncement by Pope Pius XII. In a letter to Catholic midwives in 1951, the pope had, in Rock's interpretation, actually referred to the rhythm method in a favourable manner (Pius XII 1963).[2] To Rock and other liberal Catholics, this letter was a signal that the Church was about to change its teaching and accept natural birth control. However, this was not the case. In fact, the letter did not even mention the 'natural rhythm' of 'birth control', but refers to "days of natural sterility" and states that it was permissible to have intercourse also during such periods, but *not* as a contraceptive method because that would be against the purpose of marriage ("*la validià del matrimonio*"). While the pope in this way was implicitly referring to the female cycle ("period of natural sterility"), he was not implying birth control. On the contrary, when taking into consideration the Catholic view on sex and reproduction, this new knowledge about female ovulation would in fact imply that Catholics should *only* have sex during ovulation, and it was this very restrictive interpretation that the pope addressed.

Rock's mistake was that he believed that the Church wished to help the needy, and in his opinion measures that would prevent unwanted pregnancies would be particularly helpful to one of society's weakest groups, namely, poor, unmarried women. Therefore, he was convinced that the Church would endorse 'natural birth control' as well as the contraceptive pill. However, he cannot have read the entire letter from Pope Pius XII to Catholic midwives in 1951. In the letter, the pope does not show any concern for the well-being of women. In fact, he explicitly rejects therapeutic abortion, that is, abortions made in order to save the life of the mother. Hence, there could be no mistake: Pope Pius XII categorically condemned the use of contraception because it hinders pregnancy – whether the pregnancy was wanted or unwanted was not the Church's concern. In order to avoid misconceptions, subsequent papal encyclicals have avoided the concept of natural rhythm altogether and consistently rejected all kinds of birth control.

In the 1960s, the Catholic Church underwent a reform. Pope John XXIII (r. 1958–1963) was an unconventional pope who adopted a proactive approach to secularization and called a general Church council to re-examine the role of the Church in contemporary society. The Second Vatican Council (1962–1965) had as an explicit goal to bring Catholic faith and practice in line with modernity, a goal which was expressed in Pope John XXIII's motto for the council, *aggiornamento* (modernization). Many Catholics expected the pope to reform ancient rules and explanations, and hoped that priests would be allowed to marry; that clerical ordinations would be open to women, that divorce would be allowed; and that birth control methods would be legalized. None of this happened. The council was radical only on certain formal matters concerning Church organization and ritual practice, but almost no changes involving women or gender relations were passed. The next pope, Paul VI (r. 1963–1978), published an encyclical in 1968 entitled *Humanae vitae* (*On Human Life*) which repeated official teachings on sexuality as elaborated in Pope Pius XI's encyclical from 1930 (*Casti connubii*). Disregarding the existence of contraceptives and seemingly ignorant of lay Catholics' use of them, the Church maintained the sacredness of human reproduction. The first sentence of Paul VI's encyclical expressed it clearly: "The transmission of human life is a most serious role in which married people collaborate freely and responsibly with God the Creator". Although the pope acknowledged a number of new challenges like population growth and "a new understanding of the dignity of woman and her place in society" (*Humanae vitae* §2), his solution was conservative. On the one hand, the pope embraced technological solutions to augment food production and meet the demands of a fast-increasing world population, but, on the other hand, he refused to consider any technical solutions that would restrict population increase in the first place:

> The question of human procreation, like every question which touches human life, involves more than the limited aspects specific to such disciplines as biology, psychology, demography or sociology. It is the whole man and the whole mission to which he is called that must be considered … [H]usband and wife, through that mutual gift of themselves, which is specific and exclusive to them alone, develop that union of two persons in which they perfect one another, cooperating with God in the generation of new lives.
>
> *(Humanae vitae §7, 8)*

The encyclical caused strong reactions among liberal clergy, but the prohibition against contraception was blatantly ignored by ordinary people, as is evidenced by the Catholic countries at the bottom of the European birth statistics.[3] But Catholics are increasingly adopting the prevalent attitude towards sex and contraception in society. In this regard, Kristin Luker points to an authority crisis for the Catholic hierarchy, as the parish clergy who are closer to the lives of normal people are "tacitly in favour of birth control" (Luker 1984: 167).

Noting that the official teachings on contraception and abortion are not infallible, liberal Catholic theologians maintain that the issue is not closed and that it remains debatable. The official ban on abortion even in cases of rape points to a systematic refusal to engage women's perspectives. Hence, feminist criticisms of the Church's current stand on abortion are systematically ignored, and internal debates on abortion are absent. Where contraception is concerned, critics have been subjected to reprisals and what many would classify as censorship. One illustrative example is the case of Father Charles Curran, professor of theology at the Catholic University of America. In 1985, he was presented with an ultimatum by then Cardinal Joseph Ratzinger (the future Pope Benedict XVI), who was the head of the Vatican's Congregation for the Doctrine of the Faith (formerly, the Inquisition): He must either retract his liberal position on contraceptives or lose his job.[4]

The existence of lay Catholics who ignore the Church's prohibition against contraception and simply keep away from church or 'forget' to confess, as well as liberal clergy who receive harsh treatment when openly criticizing the official position, points to a deepening authority crisis in the Catholic Church. Sociologists of religion suggest that the Church's anachronistic view on gender and sexuality have increased secularizing tendencies and have undermined the Church's political and moral credibility. Somewhat contrary to this argument is Grace Davie's observation that women are more actively engaged in organized religion than men. Davie tentatively argues that this may have something to do with women's role in reproduction, which makes them closer to existential questions of life and death than men: "Might it be the case, in other words, that one reason for the disproportionate religiousness of men and women lies in the fact that women are closer, both physically and emotionally, to the sacred" (Davie 2007: 235). Since women are over-represented in jobs in health care and the low-paying service sector, as well as being more religious than men, these gender differences are indicative of strong cultural patterns. In this regard, Davie points to a tendency of self-denial among many (religious) women who seem to accept male superiority, defend patriarchal values, and embrace a subordinate position for women, often with enthusiasm. These attitudes are embedded in the con-servative values associated with Catholic and Evangelical churches. In their view, liberal values and feminism are intrinsically linked with secularization and are therefore to be regarded as a threat to (true) Christian faith. Arguing from a fundamentalist point of view, with frequent citations from the Bible, these conservative Christians form a formidable counter-force to those who promote liberal-democratic policies. In questions concerning women, family, and sexu-ality, conservative Christians share interests with other religious traditions. At the United Nations, conservative religious actors, notably the Catholic Church, Muslim countries, and Islamic and Evangelical Christian non-governmental organizations (NGOs) form ad hoc alliances to protect traditional, patriarchal family values against the influence of liberal-democratic and feminist values (Butler 2006, Vik, Moe, and Stensvold 2013).

The Christian conservative fight against liberal values started before the Second World War, when the Catholic Church and Protestant churches took a political stance against secularization and issued statements regarding the sanctity of mar-riage. Protestant churches categorically banned abortion, but unlike the Catholic Church they allowed for one exception, which was when the mother's life was in danger. Interestingly, the religious views were in tune with national laws in Western countries at the time, which punished abortion with prison sentences for the woman as well as the abortion providers. Nevertheless, abortion rates were high, and medical complications and mortality rates made abortion a major social problem. Although abortion was illegal by state law and morally condemned by religious authorities, thousands of abortions were performed clandestinely. Death rates were high, even for medically 'safe' abortions, but as a part of a general improvement in surgical techniques in the nineteenth century, abortion survival rates improved (Reagan 1997). If a woman sought to have an abortion on ther-apeutic grounds, she or her doctor would present her case in front of a medical committee which would make a decision on her behalf. Most abortions were performed illegally in consultant rooms or in the back of flower shops, depending on the woman's economic resources. Those with sufficient economic resources and good connections would often manage to find professional help, but the majority of poor unmarried women consulted so-called 'wise women' or used more desperate measures such as poisons or the infamous knitting needles, and they often died from infection. In countries where abortion is illegal, the same methods are used today, most notably in several countries in South America and Africa. Observing that since the 1950s countries have increasingly legalized abortion, Susan Cohen observes: "Since 1997, another 21 countries or populous jurisdictions have liberalized their laws, including Colombia, Ethiopia, Iran, Mexico City, Nepal, Portugal and Thailand. During this same period, only three countries – El Salvador, Nicaragua and Poland – have increased restrictions" (Cohen 2009: 2). Most abortions were performed on unmarried women. To give birth to a child out of wedlock was associated with shame, and unmarried women faced massive social scorn. If they chose to give birth, the local community would treat them with contempt, and so would their 'illegitimate' children. The fact that women chose such a high-risk procedure as illegal abortion says something about the social burden that single mothers faced and the courage it took for those unmarried mothers to face the moral scorn of the more fortunate.

In the 1960s, the contraceptive pill was launched and sexuality became a heated political issue. The battle for equality was fought by feminists with their strongest supporters coming from the political left (Hibbard 2010). National laws were gradually made to conform to liberal values. The most radical changes were made in the 1970s, when Western European countries, except Catholic Ireland, decriminalized abortion. Established Protestant churches (Anglican, Lutheran, Reformed Presbyterian) followed suit and adapted their teaching to liberal, more progressive views and condoned women's right to choose abortion for medical, psychological, or social reasons during the first trimester. When these Protestant churches accepted abortion, it was not because they endorsed feminism, as Mark Ellingsen explains, but because of "fidelity to the Christian tradition and humanitarian concerns" (Ellingsen 1990: 3). But the liberal waves of democratic reforms faced increasingly strong opposition from conservative Christians (Luker 1984). The ensuing debate was fierce; it was a verbal battle between irreconcilable values and world views, with liberal feminism facing off against conservative Christians fighting for patriarchal traditions. Together, they framed pregnancy as a female condition and treated abortion as something which concerned women's moral conscience; they both defined pregnancy as a particular function of the female body, but their understanding of the moral implications of abortion were radically different: Conservative Christians maintained that the pregnant woman had a moral duty towards the foetus, while liberal feminists held that her primary moral duty was to herself. The new liberal abortion laws that were adopted by Western countries in the 1970s reflected the latter understanding, defining abortion as a medical procedure. These new laws recognized the principle of individual autonomy and defined the pregnant woman as the ultimate authority where abortion was concerned. From a conservative point of view, the most provocative aspect of this legislation was that the foetus was defined as a part of the pregnant woman's body – a definition that was diametrically opposed to the traditional view, which effectively defined it as belonging to the man. This infringement on male patriarchal rights was seen as a provocation. Viewed like this, we may say that the conservative Christian fight against legal abortion is just as much about female subordination as it is about the foetus' individual rights.

What started the conservative Christian anti-abortion activism was the decriminalization of abortion in the United States. On 22 January 1973, the United States Supreme Court[5] ruled that abortion is legal under the Constitution. The case was brought to court by a single pregnant woman, Jane Roe, who challenged the State of Texas (district attorney Henry Wade) for its strict abortion law which only permitted therapeutic abortion to save the life of the mother. In a 7–2 vote, the Supreme Court ruled that the Texas law violated the 14th Amendment. It addressed pregnancy as a matter concerning the woman's body and approached abortion in terms of the woman's civil rights and liberties. The main argument was the importance of women's right to privacy and the medical distinction between a viable and unviable foetus. The court ruling stated that abortion was legal if performed before the foetus was viable, that is, dependent on the mother and unable to survive outside the womb. Interestingly, this distinction echoes the medieval Canonical provision which distinguished between abortion and infanticide when it came to punishment; it defined birth as the decisive moment, and capital punishment was reserved for infanticide. A few years after Roe v. Wade, abortion became a main target for conservative Christian activism. Disregarding the viable–unviable distinction, anti-abortion activists claimed that abortion – at any stage – was in fact homicide.

According to John J. Davis, the Roe v. Wade decision in 1973 created a conservative Christian reaction which forced several denominations to change their more liberal views on abortion. Before Roe v. Wade, anti-abortion campaigns had been a particular Catholic concern, whereas Protestant denominations were more concerned with other religio-political issues such as school prayer and Bible reading, which were closely associated with typically Protestant concerns about preaching the Word (Davis 1984). Citing an Evangelical theologian, William Martin explains the lack of pro-life engagement among Protestants by referring to the traditional animosity between the two wings of Western Christendom: "A lot of Protestants reacted almost automatically – If the Catholics are for it, we should be against it" (Martin 1996: 196). But within a decade of Roe v. Wade, a majority of Protestant denominations had renounced their former liberal attitudes and joined the Catholic Church in the fight against legal abortion.[6] Martin explains the massive mobilization of Evangelicals into anti-abortion activism as largely a result of books, films, and appeals made by leading religious figures like Billy Graham (Martin 1996: 156). And once Roe v. Wade made abortion into a right that women had rather than a help that society could give to weak women, they reacted. The rights argument went against the grain of the Christian tradition of female subordination; it was particularly provocative because it ignored the biblical relationship between man and woman. Conservative Protestants joined the Catholics when they realized that legal abortion had become a symbol of their resistance to secularization and what they saw as an increasingly immoral society. This conservative reaction means that abortion remains a contested issue as anti-abortion activists attempt to restrict access to abortion even where abortion is legal, as it is in the United States. In Britain, a parliamentary debate in the spring of 2008 saw anti-abortionists propose to reduce the time frame in which women could have access to legal abortion from 24 to 20 weeks. The amendment was rejected with a large majority vote. In the United States, the annual "March for Life" rally marks the anniversary (22 January) of the Supreme Court decision, Roe v. Wade, with demonstrations all over the country.

The mobilization of Protestant denominations into the pro-life movement is amply illustrated by the changing views of the Southern Baptist Convention, the largest of the American Evangelical denominations.[7] In 1968, the Southern Baptist Convention made a declaration in support of legal abortion in the first trimester. In 1971, this liberal view was expressed by a clear majority, which supported a resolution asking for "the possibility of abortion under such conditions as rape, incest ... and damage to the emotional, mental, and physical health of the mother". Other US denominations such as the United Presbyterian Church, the United Methodist Church, and the Protestant Episcopal Church adopted similar resolutions (Davis 1984: 3). In 1974, the Southern Baptist Convention confirmed the 1971 resolution, but soon after their policy changed and subsequent resolutions increasingly emphasized the need for legislation prohibiting abortion except for therapeutic abortions, which could be performed to save the life of the mother. On this point, the Southern Baptist Convention is in agreement with other Evangelicals, making the Catholic Church the exception. A similar divide between Catholics and Protestants has to do with contraception. While they all agree that sex outside marriage is a sin, only the Catholic Church has a ban on contraception. During the 1980s, the annual resolutions of the Southern Baptist Convention became increasingly conservative and started to include biblical references to underpin the belief that life begins at conception. There are repetitive references to the disastrous social effects of abortion and the high number of innocent, unborn babies that are murdered every day. Abortion was described as a "national sin" in 1984. The Southern Baptist Convention called for "appropriate legislation and/or constitutional amendment which will prohibit abortions except to save the physical life of the mother" and called for "legislative remedies for *this national sin*" (my italics). In 1996, the fight against abortion was expressed in sharp terms as a reason for "God's judgment": "Abortion in general, and partial-birth abortion in particular, continues as a blight upon our culture and surely deserves God's judgment".[8] In 2003, the Southern Baptist Convention denounced the 1971 and 1974 resolutions, blaming former leaders for blindly adopting unbiblical views on abortion.

It seems that the distinction between a viable and a non-viable foetus in Roe v. Wade is regarded as particularly problematic because it disregards the main argument of the anti-abortion advocates, namely, that the foetus is a human being. Moreover, the viable–non-viable distinction is uncertain, since premature care and life-saving techniques are constantly pushing the limit of when a foetus can survive outside the womb. For instance, over the past number of years the time frame for abortion has been reduced to 24 weeks (second trimester, six months). The anti-abortion advocates' most rigorous opponents on the feminist side are the defenders of the viability principle known under the label 'pro-justice', who argue for a strict understanding of women's autonomy and who categorically refuse to discuss any limitations to women's right to choose. This position is foremost associated with the US abortion debate. In other Western countries, where abortion laws tend to allow women the right to choose abortion during the first trimester, the debate is less polarized. Moreover, in countries where a majority of the population are members of the national Protestant church, which often take a liberal, pragmatic position in the matter, abortion is hardly a matter of political discussion. In Denmark, for instance, the Lutheran state church (reluctantly) accepted the abortion law of 1974, which allows women the choice to seek an abortion during the first trimester. Later in the pregnancy, abortion is decided by an expert committee. As mentioned earlier, Catholic Ireland is an exception, and, together with Poland, it has the strictest abortion laws in Europe. However, in July 2013 the Irish parliament passed a law granting the right to therapeutic abortion. The Protection of Life During Pregnancy Act allows abortion if the woman's life is in danger. The law was passed after a public uproar was caused by a tragic incident in which a 14-year-old pregnant girl was denied a therapeutic abortion, and died during pregnancy.[9]

In some countries, pro-life activists have turned to violence and have even committed murder. Most of these violent attacks on abortion clinics and murders of abortion providers have taken place in North America (United States and Canada).[10] Some anti-abortion groups are openly violent and undemocratic. The Army of God, for example, is a Christian anti-abortion group which sees itself as a group of warriors for life and which targets the US government, which it defines as irreligious and illegitimate. In connection with his book on religious terrorism, Mark Juergensmeyer interviews Reverend Michael Bray, who was convicted in 1985 for destroying seven abortion clinics (Juergensmeyer 2003). The last murder of a doctor performing abortions took place in a Reformed Lutheran church after the service at Pentecost 2009. The victim was George Tiller, who served as an usher at the church.[11] The Army of God sees violence as a necessary means to protect the innocent, and several members were convicted for a number of crimes between 1982 and 1997.[12] Another violent group, the American Association of Life Activists, was condemned in 2002 for advocating violence when they published wanted-style posters with the pictures, names, and home addresses of physicians working in abortion clinics. Using violence, they obviously defined their antagonists, the pro-choice and feminist groups, as something other than human. These are extremists at the fringe of the anti-abortion movement, but they are indicative of the uncompromising nature of these debates. However, opinion polls show a stable majority in support of legal abortion during the first three months of pregnancy: Gallup polls in 1996 and 2011 exhibit remarkable consistency, showing 64 per cent and 62 per cent in support of legal abortion, respectively.[13]

Abortion is also a contested issue in Europe. In the 1980s, two priests in the Norwegian state church, Børre Knudsen and Ludvig Nessa, used US methods to voice their views, arranging spectacular protest marches during which they would throw baby dolls splashed in ketchup at liberal-minded politicians. They did not muster much public support, however, and both eventually resigned from their church positions in protest (Stensvold 2005b). In general, anti-abortion protesters in Europe are few and far between and do not compare with pro-life activists in the United States – in size or in method. This may be due in part to differences in the legal situation of women giving birth. Most European countries have rather generous regulations for leave of absence after birth. Maternity leave arrangements usually involve economic compensation for a restricted period of time. The French state is among the least generous, paying for only a four-month leave of absence.[14] In Germany, women may stay home six weeks before birth and eight weeks after delivery, and they have the right to have unpaid leave for the first three years after birth.[15] Britain has more generous arrangements, with maternity allowance being six weeks before and eight months after birth.[16] Scandinavian countries are even more generous with their maternity arrangements. In Norway, for example, the state pays normal wages for a one-year leave of absence. The reason for this is not to adhere to Christian norms and values, but to facilitate women's careers and redefine traditional gender roles. Therefore, the leave of absence is divided between the parents, with nine months for the mother and three months reserved for the father. Similar arrangements exist in other northern European countries, countries which also have liberal abortion laws and free health care. At first glance, this may seem like a paradox: On the one hand, the state stimulates high birth rates, and on the other it facilitates access to abortion. But instead of forcing women to accept unwanted pregnancies, the state pays for every birth and provides safe abortions free of charge. Ironically, the net result of this policy is lower abortion rates and higher birth rates than other Western countries: 1.8 children per woman compared to 1.9 in the United States. Catholic countries are at the bottom of the list with countries like Poland and Italy, which have birth rates of 1.3 and 1.4 children per woman, respectively.[17]

Unlike abortion laws in European countries, the US abortion law is under constant pressure. Public debates and political discussions about abortion occur in every country, but the most heated and persistent debates take place in the United States, where abortion even influences presidential elections. According to Gallup Polls, a candidate's view on abortion was decisive for one in five voters in the 2004 presidential election.[18] Although opinion polls show that attitudes towards abortion are stable, the anti-abortion lobby has won several legal and political battles in recent years and has conjured enough political support to enforce stricter abortion laws in many states.[19] One reason why abortion is such a contested issue is probably the high degree of religiosity in the United States (Berger 1999) and the subsequent impact of theological and ethical arguments in favour of 'the unborn child'. Equally emotionally charged feminists defend women's right to decide over their own bodies. Both are popular grassroots movements, which cut across political party lines, although the new Christian right's association with the Republican Party from Reagan through George W. Bush's presidencies is the stronger party alliance (Hibbard 2010). Activists from the Catholic Church, the Mormon Church (The Church of Jesus Christ of Latter-Day Saints), Evangelical and Pentecostal denominations dominate the US abortion debate.[20] Varying in size from small groups to large and resourceful congregations with efficient organizations, Evangelical anti-abortionists are often politically adept after decades of activism. Having entered the debate as a part of the so-called 'new Christian right' in the Reagan era, they define themselves in opposition to the liberal theology of mainstream Protestantism and emphasize the final authority of the Bible and individual salvation, often through a conversion experience (being 'born again'). Abortion cuts across the Catholic and Protestant divide and invites collaboration on single issues according to how one's views relate to conservative and liberal values. In the abortion debate, pro-choice activism is connected with large feminist organizations and anti-abortion advocates have close ties with conservative Christian denominations (Luker 1984: 142). Inter-denominational collaborations started with the world famous evangelist Billy Graham, who openly praised Pope John Paul II for his anti-communism, his critique of secular society, and his ardent fight for the 'culture of life'. According to Jennifer Butler, the collaboration can be explained by common values and world views: "Conservative Catholics have more in common with conservative Evangelicals than with more liberal Catholics" (Butler 2006: 92). This single-issue orientation is also evident in the way they organize. Unlike the pro-choice movement, which has its roots in the national feminist movement and which mushroomed into local feminist groups, anti-abortion activism is locally based in churches and congregations across the United States.

Seeing abortion as a deadly sin, Christian anti-abortion activists cast themselves as lifesavers. Making no distinction between a fertilized egg and a full-grown foetus, they frame the debate about legal abortion as a question of obeying the fifth commandment: "You shall not kill". The pro-choice side, however, refuses to see the zygote, embryo, or foetus as human beings and reserves the status of human being for the pregnant woman. To them, abortion is not a breach of the fifth commandment, but an interruption of a *possible* human being – the beginning of something which under different circumstances could have become a human being. Primarily a position associated with feminism, the pro-choice movement also includes some individual Christian activists mainly from liberal Protestant denominations that condone women's right to autonomy. There is also an influential Catholic pro-choice organization with international reach,

Catholics for Choice,[21] a lay organization in open conflict with the Catholic establishment.

As already noted, the two sides in the US abortion debate are rooted in two kinds of civil organizations: the feminist movement and Christian churches and denominations. The abortion debate is not driven from the top, and the bulk of activities take place at the grassroots level. There is a marked dominance of conservative Christians in the anti-abortion camp, while the pro-choice camp is highly secular (Luker 1984: 188). Anti-abortion groups often maintain close relationships with local congregations, with pro-life activism as one among several optional activities. Pro-choice organizations, on the other hand, are local branches of national organizations. Both camps, however, rely on individual engagement and local activism. There are also international pro-life groups with local networks such as the Catholic Priests for Life organization.[22] The Evangelical Christian Coalition of America is an important actor on the national level. Started in 1988 by Evangelical preacher and Republican Party politician Pat Robertson, it is based on individual membership and combines conservative politics with Christian moral issues. Anti-abortion activism is just one among a number of conservative political rallying points.[23] Not all pro-life organizations have a Christian basis either. For instance, the national umbrella organization National Right to Life (1968) does not openly declare a Christian identity – despite the fact that its moral reasoning resonates with Christian values. Their homepage has no references to God or the Bible, but under the heading "the beginning of life", we find the following statement: "The life of a baby begins long before he or she is born. A new individual human being begins at fertilization, when the sperm and ovum meet to form a single cell". Clearly, this is a version of the Christian anti-abortion stance. A bit further on, we read a much repeated assertion: "In the United States over 40 million unborn babies have been killed in the 40 years since abortion was legalized and more than 1.2 million are killed each year".[24] This is recognizably conservative Christian argumentation, but it is stripped of theological references.

An important but often neglected aspect of conservative Christian anti-abortion activism is that it cuts across denominations. Inspired by Colin Campbell's theory of religious organizations (1972) and identity-building, we may say that anti-abortion activism creates a shared Christian awareness and agreement on what constitutes Christian values. Viewing the US anti-abortion movement from this angle, we see single-issue activism based on shared values and moral norms which de-emphasizes denominational barriers and constitutes a pool for potential political mobilization. Campbell's theory allows us to analyze the activities of lay grassroots activism as a loosely knit community with a shared culture of values and ideas. Defining itself in opposition to liberal (secular) values, anti-abortion activism may contribute to creating a pan-conservative Christian identity across denominational barriers.

Legal abortion was made possible by a combination of factors: the ability of feminists in the 1960s to muster political pressure, and ineffectual resistance. But since the end of the 1970s, anti-abortion activism has become a political force in US politics as Catholics, Baptists, Pentecostals, and Presbyterians unite in a fight for their shared values and ultimate concern.[25] This lay activism also points to a major change in Western Christianity, a change from professional–theological authority to lay power based on the moral concerns and emotional engagement of ordinary church members. While the professional (priestly) theological focus is on doctrine and rituals (professional disputes split Christianity into innumerable Churches), lay people focus on moral issues and political concerns.

Notes

1 For an updated overview of Evangelical denominations in the United States, see the website of the National Association of Evangelicals, which is available at https://www. nae.net/membership/current-members.
2 This letter is available (in Italian) at the Vatican website: http://w2.vatican.va/content/ pius-xii/it/speeches/1951/documents/hf_p-xii_spe_19511029_ostetriche.html.
3 On birth statistics in OECD countries, see Castles 2003.
4 See http://americamagazine.org/issue/100/charles-curran-case.
5 The text is available at http://www.law.cornell.edu/supremecourt/text/410/113.
6 John J. Davis lists the following: the Southern Baptist Convention, the Lutheran Church–Missouri Synod, the Church of the Nazarene, the General Association of Regular Baptist Churches, the Reformed Presbyterian Church of North America, the Presbyterian Church in America, the Free Methodist Church, the Reformed Presbyterian Church (Evangelical Synod), the Mennonite Church at General Assembly, the Church of God (Cleveland, Tennessee), and the Fellowship of Grace Brethren Churches (Davis 1984: 3).
7 Resolutions available at the Southern Baptist Convention's website: http://www.sbc. net/resolutions/search/. I am indebted to Hanne Trangerud for this information.
8 See "Resolution on Abortion". *Southern Baptist Convention*. June 1984. Available at http://www.sbc.net/resolutions/21; and "Resolution on the Partial-Birth Abortion Ban". *Southern Baptist Convention*. June 1996. Available at http://www.sbc.net/resolutions/26, respectively.
9 http://www.bbc.com/news/world-europe-25566657.
10 The National Abortion Federation, an interest group on the pro-choice side, lists cases of anti-abortion violence on its website: http://prochoice.org/education-and-advocacy/violence/.
11 See http://www.ncregister.com/site/article/the_shooting_of_george_tiller/.
12 It is possible that this group still exists. Information downloaded from the University of Maryland's National Consortium for the Study of Terrorism and Responses to Terrorism website (http://www.start.umd.edu/start/data_collections/tops/terrorist_organi zation_profile.asp?id=28) on 19 February 2012.
13 http://www.gallup.com/poll/1576/abortion.aspx.
14 http://www.famili.fr/,droit-du-travail-pendant-la-grossesse-connaissez-vous-vos-droits,638,398146.asp.
15 http://www.babycenter.de/a8974/elternzeit.
16 For British maternity arrangements, see http://www.patient.co.uk/health/maternity-benefits.
17 http://www.indexmundi.com/facts/indicators/SP.DYN.TFRT.IN/rankings.

18 http://www.gallup.com/poll/13786/abortion-issue-guides-one-five-voters.aspx.
19 The Guttmacher Institute has a monthly update on abortion policy developments on its website at http://www.guttmacher.org/sections/abortion.php.
20 *Religion and Public Life*. January 2013. Pew Research Project. "Religious Groups' Official Positions on Abortion". Available at http://www.pewforum.org/2013/01/16/religious-groups-official-positions-on-abortion/.
21 http://www.catholicsforchoice.org/.
22 http://www.priestsforlife.org/plgroups/atoesites.html.
23 http://www.cc.org/.
24 http://www.nrlc.org/.
25 See German theologian Paul Tillich's famous definition of religion as ultimate concern in his *Dynamics of Faith* (Tillich 1957).

14

FOETUS OR CHILD?

Christian reactions to feminism

Feminists have long argued that legal abortion gave women the right to control their bodies and restored to them the autonomy which men had always enjoyed. Legal abortion was logically grounded in a medical approach to the body, which sees the body as an assembly of organs. In the same manner as laryngitis is a condition pertaining to the throat, pregnancy is a condition pertaining to the uterus. Since the foetus is attached to one of the pregnant woman's organs, it must be up to her, the owner of the organ, to make the choice – abortion or birth. From a conservative Christian viewpoint, however, abortion is homicide and legal abortion is a sign of an unchristian society. When women gain equal rights, having aspired to be treated like men, who will look after the children and keep the family together? To these conservatives, the feminists' claim to equality relied on a radical reformulation of ownership of the foetus and, by association, of children. In their minds, the foetus is the fruit of male procreation; it was the man's responsibility and it therefore belonged to him. In the medical logic of contemporary abortion laws, however, the foetus is implicitly defined as belonging to the woman. This attack on traditional male dominance may to some extent account for the stark reactions of conservative Christians.

Catholics as well as Evangelicals have described legal abortion as an attack on God's creation and Christian values. The feminists' arguments in support of legal abortion only affirm their abhorrence, especially when feminists insist on treating the foetus as a part of the woman's body. To conservative Christians, the foetus is an individual human being. Although it relies on its mother, they regard it as categorically distinct from her. This split between woman and foetus is expressed through a refusal to see pregnancy as a process. In the feminists' view, the foetus' humanity cannot be compared to that of the pregnant woman, who is an individual human being in every respect – a legal subject, a morally responsible person, and an individual entangled in human relationships with others – a wife, friend, colleague, daughter, sister, and neighbour.

According to WHO estimates, around 40 million abortions take place each year, most of them in developing countries under unsafe conditions. Thirteen per cent end in maternal death. According to Gilda Sedgh et al, "in 2008, six million abortions were performed in developed countries and 38 million in developing countries, a disparity that largely reflects population distribution" (Sedgh et al. 2012: 325). Ironically, the percentage is lower in countries with liberal abortion laws. Among the Scandinavian countries, where abortion has been legal since the late 1970s and where abortion is performed cost-free in state hospitals, Sweden has significantly higher abortion rates than Norway and Denmark. In Norway, abortion rates have dropped since the 1980s.[1] These are uncontested facts that both sides in the abortion debate agree on. However, they have different explanations as well as solutions to the problem. Those who support legal abortion and defend the pregnant woman's right to choose focus on the consequences of an unwanted pregnancy and point to health, psychological, and economic consequences for the women. For anti-abortion activists, unwanted pregnancies are problematic for religious and moral reasons. Their solution is to try and put a stop to it altogether by teaching young people more religion and more respect for moral norms. Should an unwanted pregnancy occur, it is due to a sin, as they see it, and women should accept the consequences and bring the pregnancy to its natural conclusion – in obedience to God and his creation. The most favoured contraception 'technique' among conservative Christians is sexual abstinence. Insisting on a causal link between marriage and sex, there are many cross-denominational initiatives to promote sexual abstinence among teenagers. One organization, The Silver Ring Thing (1995), promotes virginity as a way to avoid teen pregnancy. It involves a ceremony (a quasi-wedding), where girls promise to remain virgins and dance with their fathers after receiving a silver ring as a sign of their pledge. The organization has international reach and has received US government funding during George W. Bush's presidency and Barrack Obama's first term until 2010.[2]

Pro-choice activists are less optimistic. Taking statistical facts and historical evidence into account, they draw the conclusion that unwanted pregnancy is a permanent problem which cannot be solved by more rules and ceremonies. Abortion cannot be eradicated because "women who are determined to avoid an unplanned birth will resort to unsafe abortions if safe abortion is not readily available" (Sedgh et al. 2012: 631). Taking a pragmatic view on sex before marriage and unwanted pregnancy as facts of life, feminists propose three measures to bring down abortion numbers: sex education, easy access to contraception, and safe abortion procedures. The problem, as they see it, is not abortion in terms of ending the foetus's life, but women's health and survival.

Although most conservative Protestants accept contraception, they have strong reservations against sex education. Since they only accept sex within marriage, they feel that sex education for teenagers and schoolchildren would stir unwanted interest and ultimately lead to more unwanted pregnancies. Together with the Catholic Church, they want a total ban on abortion – though the latter is alone in its prohibition against all use of contraceptive devices. This is clearly a position which is more concerned with moral rules than with solving real-life problems. These two prohibitions, anti-abortion and anti-contraception, effectively cancel each other out and deny the problem of unwanted pregnancy altogether. As Rosemary Ruether points out, if the real problem is women, not abortion, then the position makes sense: "Since the most effective way to avoid abortion would be to promote contraception, the double band indicates that the real battle is not over the lives of foetuses or their mothers but over the rights of women to be moral agents in the reproductive capacities of their own bodies" (Ruether 1985: 860).

Although abortion debates in the United States are both harsh and intense, the percentage of public support for one side or the other is surprisingly stable (Reagan 1997). Gallup Polls in 1996 and 2011 show a slight fall in this majority from 64 per cent to 62 per cent in support of legal abortion.[3] A larger majority of them approve of abortion in the first trimester (Jelen and Wilcox 2003). Interestingly, this attitude reflects the traditional Christian distinction of the status of the foetus before and after quickening and shows that a majority of people in the United States support a gradual approach to abortion: they support women's right to choose abortion in the first trimester, but start to oppose abortion in the second trimester; finally, they support an outright ban on abortion in the third trimester (Jelen and Wilcox 2003: 491). This gradual approach is shared by the majority of established Protestant churches. The Methodist Church in Britain is representative of this view. A carefully phrased statement explains its views on abortion as follows (2013):

> The result of the coming together of human sperm and ovum is obviously human. The appearance of the 'primitive streak' (the beginning of the neurological system) after some fourteen days is an important stage. However for many weeks after this event, natural abortion will continue to bring about the termination of over 50% of embryos. Fertilisation, implantation and subsequent development are parts of a continuous process. It is simply not possible to identify the single moment when a new human person begins. The right of the embryo to full respect clearly increases throughout a pregnancy.[4]

The reference to 50 per cent embryo deaths includes fertilized eggs that are expelled – for unknown reasons – within the first couple of weeks without the woman even suspecting a pregnancy plus the stipulated 20 per cent spontaneous abortions, which mainly occur during the first trimester.[5] This uncertainty is reflected in the Methodist Church's reference to the impossibility of identifying "the exact moment when a new human person begins". While the Catholics draw the opposite conclusion and count the fertilized egg as a human being, the Methodists conclude that the humanity of the foetus "increases throughout pregnancy". This, I dare say, reflects better the female experience of pregnancy, namely, as a gradual increase of confidence and hope for a full-born baby. The Catholic Church has the most extreme and also the most consistent view, banning all intrusions into the natural processes regarding pregnancy from the very start:

> Human life must be respected and protected absolutely from the moment of conception. From the first moment of his existence, a human being must be recognized as having the rights of a person – among which are the inviolable right of every innocent being to life.
>
> (Catechism of the Catholic Church §2270)

Thus, the zygote is defined as a human being with full human rights. Interestingly, this implies that the pregnant woman's rights are set aside. Although seemingly simple, the position is logically problematic when taking into consideration that 20 per cent of pregnancies end in spontaneous abortion and a stipulated 30 per cent of conceived eggs are expelled within the first days (at the zygote stage). Logically, these 'deaths' should be just as upsetting to pro-life advocates as the relatively much lower number of abortions performed at abortion clinics. Another consequence of this position is that birth is no longer seen as a decisive event. If ensoulment happens at the moment of fertilization, this is a sacred moment and fertilization is a much more important event than the moment of birth. In fact, birth does not even represent a decisive change – a viewpoint which is effectively expressed when anti-abortionists refer to 'the child' regardless of whether it is inside or outside the womb. Obviously, this 'child' is fully human and furnished with a soul from the start. Another consequence of this position is that the manner of conception does not matter. Regardless of whether it is conceived by married parents, the result of rape, or produced in a laboratory, the fertilized egg is a human being equivalent to a full-born baby. To equate a fertilized egg with a human being seems absurd, but it is sustained by belief in immediate ensoulment and the sanctity of life. Now, the soul is a religious concept and therefore cannot be proven on principle. But as for the idea of the sanctity of life, everyone can agree that fertilization marks the beginning of life; however, to grant a fertilized cell with sanctity because it is alive is problematic. Even bacteria have life.

The immediate ensoulment thesis (the belief that human beings are endowed with a soul from the moment of conception, that is, when the egg is fertilized) is the dominant position among anti-abortionists who usually refer to themselves as 'pro-life' activists. In their view, fertilization and ensoulment happen at the same time, a view which is founded on the belief that 'life' and 'soul' are indistinguishable qualities. This is the position held by the Catholic Church and conservative Protestants (mostly Evangelicals and Pentecostals). One of the consequences of this belief is that the contraceptive coil or IUD (Intrauterine Device) as well as the so-called 'morning-after pill', or regret pill, are classified as abortion devices and therefore banned. The traditional view on human ensoulment was formulated by Thomas Aquinas in the thirteenth century and stated that the foetus was infused with a human soul when it had developed a human form. It is usually referred to as "delayed ensoulment" or "delayed hominization" (making human). This is the understanding held by the traditional Protestant churches (Lutheran, Calvinist, Methodist).

Both the anti-abortionists, who believe in immediate ensoulment, and their opponents bolster their arguments by referring to medical research. John Haldane and Patrick Lee, two of the most prominent pro-life scientists, refer to DNA when they argue that the fertilized egg is a human being. Their arguments frame the egg as a unique individual with its own genetic make-up already in place: "The structure of the embryo's DNA is distinct from that of the mother or of the father, and it remains in this organism throughout the whole life" (Haldane and Lee 2003: 271). In their argument, "the structure of the DNA" becomes something comparable to the soul: an individual essence, the person's inner core which God or nature assigns to them at the beginning of life.

A striking feature of Haldane and Lee's rendering of genetics is their depiction of genes as static features. Genetic researchers no longer speak of genes as constituting a constant and stable essence. DNA structures are rather more complex than Haldane and Lee let on and are far more sensitive to environmental changes than formerly believed (epigenetics). When Haldane and Lee argue that abortion in the first trimester is the moral equivalent of abortion at a later stage, they presuppose that the growth process of the embryo does not produce any fundamental changes in the DNA, when in fact epigenetics has established that our genes are not static qualities, but act more like a reservoir of possibilities that can be turned on and off when responding to their environment. When Haldane and Lee relate to "the structure of the DNA" as something static, it is because they need it in order to defend their belief in immediate ensoulment. Their main concern is not genetics, however, but the sacredness of human life and the moral status of the foetus.

The conservative Christian anti-abortion stance relies, as we have seen, on the belief in immediate ensoulment. Haldane and Lee try to legitimize this belief by referring to a biogenetic model, but are unable to integrate the processual insights of epigenetics. In this regard, it is worth noting that Haldane and Lee's position stands in opposition to the traditional Christian doctrine (Aquinas) of delayed ensoulment. According to this belief, the soul is infused into the foetus at a later stage (ca. three months), and therefore it is only abortion after the first trimester that is regarded as murder. An updated version of this position is the delayed hominization model. Robert Pasnau, one of the most influential philosophers in support of this thesis argues against Haldane and Lee's argument for immediate ensoulment. To define the fertilized egg as a human being endowed with a human soul cannot be logically sustained by biological data, he claims, because it means that one is equating DNA with the soul: "If to be human is to have a God-given soul, then the presence of the human genetic code at conception shows nothing about whether the embryo is a human being" (Pasnau 2002: 109).

According to Pasnau, anti-abortion activists who endorse the idea of immediate ensoulment typically make selective use of genetics when attempting to find scientific arguments in support of their position. This is in itself an unscientific enterprise – using science to give credibility to a religiously motivated conclusion. Disregarding the importance of foetal development is absurd: It is to equate a potential being (an egg) with an actual creature (a chick) and disregard the basic laws of nature. His position largely corresponds to the pro-choice position and is shared by most of the established Protestant churches. It is worth noting, however, that Pasnau's arguments are founded in traditional Catholicism and that the woman's perspective is therefore conspicuously absent from his argument – much like it is from Haldane and Lee's rhetoric.

Christians in the anti-abortion camp share a strong belief in immediate ensoulment, that is, that ensoulment coincides with conception. As Pasnau argues, this implies that they equate the concept of life with the concept of the soul. But this does not mean that they hold every kind of life to be sacred. Not all human life is equally sacred, as becomes evident in cases where women who get pregnant after rape are denied abortion, as dictated by official Catholic teaching. To anti-abortionists, the human foetus is the issue, and it is the foetus' life which is precious because it is innocent and helpless and in need of their protection. According to Christian anthropology, it is the soul which distinguishes the human being from the rest of creation and it is because of the God-given soul that the foetus must be saved – at any cost. The ultimate goal and meaning of life is to be saved in a Christian sense, namely, to reestablish the relationship to God which was destroyed by Adam's original sin. Anti-abortionists argue that the foetus already stands in a relationship to God because it has a soul. Like all human beings, the foetus can be saved. But since you must be a Christian to be saved, it is of paramount importance that the foetus be born in order to be made into a Christian. There are two ways that may lead to salvation, and the Christian community is divided on the matter. According to Catholics, baptism is necessary, but to Evangelicals you must "accept Jesus". The latter means conversion and requires a certain age and level of cognitive development. For Catholics, the main point is that the foetus is born so that the ritual of baptism can be performed. For Evangelicals, however, survival at birth is not enough; the child must grow up in a Christian environment in order to receive the Gospel.

The logic behind both positions is a Christian world view which defines the ultimate purpose of a human life as salvation. The goal is not to establish human relationships or to live happily ever after, but to restore the ruptured relationship to God. When seen in this light, the importance of saving the foetus' life becomes evident, as expressed in the Catholic prohibitions against abortion even after rape and even if the mother's life is in danger. The logical basis for the preference of the foetus over the mother rests on the idea of innocence; it is innocent life which is sacred and which should be protected. This is a position which the Catholic Church supports on its own. Protestants allow abortion in these cases for therapeutic reasons. Despite the cruelty of such laws, the purpose is not to punish the unlucky woman for her sin but to save a human soul (the foetus). The Catholic Church sees itself as the gateway to salvation, and human souls are what it saves. The ultimate concern of the Church is not the sanctity of biological life per se. If a pregnant woman chooses abortion she hinders the Church from saving an innocent soul. It is within this simple scheme of innocence versus guilt that a particularly cruel provision in the official Catholic view on abortion makes some sort of sense: It is because the foetus is innocent, always more innocent than the woman, that the foetus must be saved, even if the mother should die in the process. Comparing sin with innocence is logical, but such a comparison is possible if and only if you accept the premise that the foetus has the same human status as the mother. The disregard for the woman's humanity that is inherent in this position is all the more surprising, since her death is obviously the greater evil since it affects so many people: her other children, her husband, and her parents. But this does not come into the official Catholic equation. Comparing the foetus to its mother and finding that she is infinitely more sinful because she has already lived for many years as a common sinner – the foetus is itself a decisive proof of that. The main point is the salvation of the foetus. The mother has already had her chance: She has lived for several years, made her own moral decisions, and has had the possibility of becoming a Christian (baptism or conversion). If the mother won't protect the foetus, then someone (the pro-life advocates) must do it for her. Thus, they implicitly define the pregnant woman as a potential enemy of the unborn child. When conservative Protestant churches disagree and allow therapeutic abortion, it is perhaps because women are not such estranged creatures in their eyes: Protestant clergy have wives and daughters, and even some female theologians whom they count among their rank to remind them of women's humanity.

Both positions in the abortion debate seem locked in a traditional Eve/Mary confrontation, where the pro-lifers desperately seek to suppress the egotistical Eve and forcefully replace her with a caring Mary, while their feminist opponents embrace Eve's initiative and see her as an ambassador of free will. According to Charles Bellinger, the two positions are united in a (contradictory) struggle against tyranny (Bellinger 1992). Analyzing the contemporary abortion debate as a US phenomenon, he sees each position as a fight against oppression in the proud moral tradition of the Abolitionists. The pro-life position identifies the foetus as the oppressed and defines the modern US state as the tyrant, whereas the pro-choice position sees anti-abortion activists as tyrants. Bellinger's analysis stops here, but it is possible to argue that these two tyrannies correspond to two incompatible fields of interest, namely, the private sphere and the state, the family versus politicians, patriarchy versus modern legislature. A more systematic analysis of the different protagonists and their personal backgrounds, value systems, and moral ideals would be needed in order to throw light on Bellinger's final question, which has to do with why pro-life advocates would "struggle against easy access to abortion when they are not being personally oppressed by it" (Bellinger 1992: 7). Bellinger's observation is supported by Kristin Luker's study. Among the more than one hundred anti-abortion activists she interviewed, none had undergone an abortion or had directly experienced it. Instead, a good third had experienced problems related to parenthood: inability to conceive, miscarriage, or child dead due to congenital disease. By comparison, more than half of the pro-choice activists reported having experienced abortion themselves or among their close relations, whereas only 6 per cent of them had experienced problems associated with parenthood (Luker 1984: 151–52). So it would seem that at some level the two opposite positions in the abortion debate are both grounded in personal experience.

Disregarding social facts like poverty and leaving the father totally out of the picture, anti-abortionists see abortion as a sign of moral destitution: First, she has sex, and then she runs away from the consequences. What she should do is to accept that her body was made for nurturing and bringing forth a new life. She could give the child up for adoption, if needed, but under no circumstances should she place herself under the surgeon's knife. Strangely, adoption is not promoted as a serious alternative to abortion, neither by the Catholic Church nor by any of the major Evangelical churches. Instead, they speak as if unwanted pregnancies happen to women who are married, although statistics show that the majority of abortions in Western countries involve single women. They identify women as the problem, accusing those who are unwilling to go through with an unwanted pregnancy for being egotistical. The stereotypical idea of the egotistical abortion-seeker is presented in different ways. One influential anti-abortion NGO, The Susan B. Anthony List, does it by selective use of research data. This is not the typical grassroots anti-abortion group, but an organization based in Washington, DC working for the election of pro-life politicians.[6] Their elite status also shows in their more sophisticated arguments. For instance, they use data from the renowned Guttmacher Institute, which is associated with the pro-choice side, but use it selectively in such a manner as to show that women who have abortions are egotistic and immoral: Twenty-five per cent of all abortion-seekers stated that the reason for seeking an abortion was that the timing was wrong. The second most frequent reason (23 per cent) was that they couldn't afford a baby at the time.[7] Although the percentages are correct, the figures that are left out from the statistics give a different explanation of why women seek abortion: poverty. In 2009, more than 60 per cent of abortion-seekers were unmarried mothers.[8] Obviously aware of the statistical connection between poverty and abortion, another actor on the anti-abortion scene, the American Adoption Agency, targets pregnant women and lists several economic arguments against abortion in order to persuade them to choose adoption instead.[9]

The current abortion debate is a worldwide phenomenon which combines Christian concerns for morality with an elaborate theory of the sacredness of traditional gender roles. Because they condone the use of contraception, Protestants seem more in tune with real-life problems than the Catholics, but conservative Protestants join the popes in praising traditional gender roles and marriage. For instance, Focus on the Family, an international organization with national branches on all continents promotes a traditional patriarchal family model. Its founder, James Dobson, an Evangelical minister with a background working in the Church of the Nazarene, is an influential religious entrepreneur.[10] In what follows, he gives an illustrative account of the conservative Evangelical family model:

> For what reason is man to marry a wife? Because woman was originally a constituent part of man, she must return to become one with him again, so that the full expression and design of God's image in human beings can be revealed ... (T)here is a profound and awesome reason for the way God ordered the creation of man – one that is commented on throughout Scripture, and one that we must observe if we are to find the fulfillment of our very being as humans. It is ordered as the union of a man and a woman in marriage – heterosexual and monogamous.[11]

Here, the woman is construed as a subordinate being as well as the missing piece of the man: "She must return to become one with him again". What about the woman, one may ask: If she is a "constituent part of man", is the man not the missing piece of the woman? The question is of course rhetorical and inspired by the lopsided male perspective so prominent in this citation. Viewed from this perspective, the feminist demand for individual autonomy and free choice in sexual matters is beside the point when a woman is defined by her relation to her husband. The pro-choice arguments for legal abortion, which are based on the idea of (bodily) autonomy, clearly fall outside the scope of such a world view.

Another conservative understanding of Christian marriage is explained in detail by Pope John Paul II (r. 1978–2005). In his encyclical *Evangelium vita* (*The Gospel of Life*) published in 1995, on a symbolically suitable day – 25 March, the feast of the Annunciation (the conception of Christ) – he repeated the ban on contraception, defined abortion (even for therapeutic reasons) as illegal, and praised traditional marriage. A small, but interesting change in Catholic rhetoric occurred in a speech by Pope Benedict XVI (r. 2005–2013) during his visit to Africa in 2009, which gave rise to a (false) rumour that the pope, when seeing the horrors of the AIDS epidemic had in fact condoned the use of condoms. It turned out to be a misunderstanding: What the pope said was that "condoms reduce the risk of HIV infection".[12] Referring to homosexual relations, he did not speak about contraception at all because homosexuals evidently cannot make children and may use condoms as much as they like since they do it for health reasons. This does not mean that heterosexual couples could use condoms to protect themselves from HIV, however, since that would impede on human reproduction. In a book consisting of interviews with the pope, *Light of the World*, by the German journalist Peter Seewald published in 2010, the pope underlined once again the sanctity of marriage as the only moral framework for sexual activity. So when, in another section of the book, he recommended condoms for male prostitutes, this was not an acceptance of sex between homosexuals or of prostitution, but a pragmatic expression of a Christian concern for the health of homosexuals. Thus, it would seem that the pope acknowledged the importance of good health for homosexual men, but not for heterosexual couples. The press took the pope's statement as a small concession towards allowing the use of condoms to combat the HIV epidemic. Taking into account the Catholic Church's categorical rejection of homosexual acts, this was a logical conclusion. But no such declarations followed.

The Catholic Church's acceptance of contraception would undermine the moral reason for marriage and ultimately challenge the ideal of chastity. The Catholic ban on contraception may seem both heartless and unrealistic, but it is also strictly logical because it is based on the premise that the Church's ideal is an ascetic, monastic life secluded from sin. For the Church, marriage remains a less desirable but morally acceptable way of life because God created human reproduction. Seen from this point of view, contraception is an absurdity because procreation is the only legitimate motivation for indulging the sexual drive. According to this logic, homosexuality is an abhorrence, as is sex outside marriage. The current pope, Francis I (r. 2013–), has yet to make his own declarations on the matter, but he has repeated his predecessors' teachings. In an interview with the US Jesuit journal *America Magazine* on 30 September 2013, Pope Francis explained his apparent lack of interest in issues related to homosexuality, contraception, and abortion:

> We cannot insist only on issues related to abortion, gay marriage and the use of contraceptive methods. This is not possible. I have not spoken much about these things, and I was reprimanded for that. But when we speak about these issues, we have to talk about them in a context. The teaching of the church, for that matter, is clear and I am a son of the church, but it is not necessary to talk about these issues all the time.

By expressing satisfaction with his predecessors and diverting the attention to poverty, his chosen cause, the current pope is attempting to set his own agenda.[13] It is possible to say that when the pope underlines the necessity of seeing things in their proper context that he is preparing the way for social and economic arguments favouring families with fewer children. Nevertheless, in the remainder of the interview he defines context much more narrowly, referring to the confessional when he and other clerics are confronted with a woman who repents for her sins and wishes to "move forward in her Christian life". On the other side of the confessional wall sits a woman, who, unlike the priest, is only in church for a brief time. When the confession is over and the penalty meted out, she returns to ordinary life.

Although the personal experience of abortion seems to play an important role for pro-choice activism, the happy experiences of birth and parenthood are not the underlying causes for anti-abortion activism. In addition to a conservative Christian background and strong ties to a specific church, the most significant difference between pro-choice and anti-abortion activists in Kristin Luker's study was the social difference between the two camps: The typical pro-choice activist was a single, professional woman with a college or university degree, whereas the majority of anti-abortion activists were housewives with high school diplomas (Luker 1984: 194). This socio-economic difference largely corresponds with a Christian–secular divide: A large majority of anti-abortion advocates were active Christians, whereas the pro-choice side was massively secular and irreligious. According to Luker, 63 per cent of pro-choice activists had no religion and 29 per cent described themselves as "vaguely Protestant". Among anti-abortion advocates, however, the majority were practicing Catholics and 5 per cent described themselves as non-religious (Luker 1984: 196). Although thirty years have passed since this study was published, the correlation between one's view on abortion and one's world view persists.

The unequal distribution of active Christians between the two sides in the abortion debate underscores the impression of a cultural divide in the midst of US society. The split is captured in the Christian–secular divide, but also cuts across the Christian community along a conservative–liberal axis. From a Christian perspective, the latter is problematic because it places Christians on opposite sides of the political spectrum and points to an internal struggle within Christian churches and denominations. Over the past few decades, the conservatives have strengthened their position, and liberal Protestant churches have increasingly lost ground to more conservative (Evangelical and Pentecostal) denominations. Peter Beyer explains this as a side-effect of identity politics in a secularized society where conservative religious beliefs and practices have an advantage because they are more easily distinguishable from the secular than their liberal counterpart (Beyer 1994). Without going further into Beyer's theory, it is worth noting that it ties in well with the conservative Christian exclusivist claim that theirs is the only valid religious view. For them, abortion is simple: Life starts at conception; human life is sacred; and you cannot take someone's life unless you do so in self-defence.

The current abortion debate can be seen as a confrontation between traditional patriarchal family values and contemporary ideals of gender equality. The existence of such blatantly opposed value systems in the midst of modern (US) society is intriguing. It can of course not pass unnoticed that the kind of religion involved here is conservative Christianity (official Catholicism, Evangelical churches). With Christianity's origins in patriarchal cultures (antiquity), this comes as no surprise. In antiquity, women had no place in society outside the private sphere and were essentially defined as either daughter or wife. Christianity continued the pattern and postponed the promised equality between the sexes to eternity. However, religion is not a stable and fixed system of meaning. Like everything else, religious interpretations evolve. Religious symbols and ideas of sacredness are always in a dialectical relationship with society. Peter Berger explains it by referring to changing needs brought on by new ways of living (Berger 1990). The ability of a religion to create belief relies on its capacity to address peoples' needs. This is what Berger refers to as a religion's plausibility structure. Put bluntly, it means that in a patriarchal society like that of feudal Europe, where the feudal lord ruled over his land and folk, his authority was reflected in medieval Catholicism, which venerated an authoritarian, awe-inspiring creator-God who resembled the social authority structure people were familiar with in their daily lives. Like the feudal lord who decided over them, God demanded obedience. For a modern, democratic society built on egalitarian principles, something else is required – but not, it would seem, for conservative Christians, who still value male control and female subordination, and equate obedience with piety.

If we compare contemporary Christian attitudes towards abortion, two if not three basic interpretations emerge. First, the Catholic position which is dictated by an authoritative tradition, and regards any change that is imposed from the outside with deep scepticism. Here, gender equality, which today is a political reality for Catholics living in the West, is brushed off as irrelevant. Marriage between man and wife, and the complementary and hierarchical relationship between them, remains unchallenged. Second, although conservative Protestants refer to the Bible rather than church tradition to legitimize their views, they arrive at the same conclusion: God's plan for humanity was to assign man and woman different roles, and this difference is symbolized by their sexual difference and their ability to procreate. Third, the liberal Christian model differs from this assessment in its basic understanding of Christianity as a religion of love and compassion, and fights against everything that goes against egalitarian values. Hence, it favours gender equality and supports women's political rights. Obviously, all three positions are based on faith and hence cannot be decided in principle. Instead, we have a power struggle between various shades of conservative and liberal Christianity, which is framed as a fight about women's role in society, motherhood, pregnancy, and abortion. The fight is political, and, for the most part, it is played out in public debate about women, gender relations, and the female body. But the various positions are also presented in more subtle ways in fiction, advertising, and popular culture.

Notes

1 This data is available at the Norwegian Institute of Public Health (Folkehelseinstituttet) at http://www.fhi.no/eway/default.aspx?pid=239&trg=List_6212&Main_6157=6263:0:25, 5713&MainContent_6263=6464:0:25,5714&List_6212=6218:0:25,5723:1:0:0:0:0.
2 https://www.silverringthing.com/.
3 http://www.gallup.com/poll/1576/abortion.aspx.

4 http://www.methodist.org.uk/who-we-are/views-of-the-church/abortion-and-contra ception.

5 'Abortion' is here understood as a spontaneous end to a known pregnancy. "(W)e estimated that spontaneous pregnancy losses equaled 20% of all births plus 10% of all abortions" (Sedgh et al. 2012: 628).

6 http://www.sba-list.org.

7 http://www.sba-list.org/suzy-b-blog/why-do-women-really-have-abortions.

8 http://www.guttmacher.org/sections/abortion.php.

9 http://www.americanadoptions.com/pregnant/adoption_abortion_parenting.

10 For an informative journalistic account of Focus on the Family, see Gilgoff 2007.

11 From *The Divine Order to Marriage* by David Kyle Foster, here cited from the Focus on the Family website (http://www.focusonthefamily.com/).

12 See BBC News, 10 November 2010, on http://www.bbc.co.uk/news/world-europe-11804398.

13 http://americamagazine.org/pope-interview.

15

OBJECTIFICATION

Women in contemporary culture

The battle over abortion and gender equality is played out as a drama of values in political fora and in the legal system, but over the last number of decades the mass media have become an increasingly important arena. This is where society holds up a mirror to itself, to paraphrase Shakespeare's maxim about the theatre – the popular culture of his time. Although school, family, and local community (church) are places where we learn our basic values, mass media also play a crucial role in framing cultural ideas. Tracing the emergence of collective identity (nationalism), Benedict Anderson argues historically for a causal relationship between the emergence of mass media (the cheap printing press), the spread of literacy, and nationalism (Anderson 1989). Mass media (film, television, the Internet, and the press) is where we receive information and learn, often unwittingly, our society's dominant views – what French sociologist Pierre Bourdieu named *doxa* (Bourdieu 1977). A modern democratic society cannot be envisaged without a free press and a shared public domain where citizens can participate in free and open debates (Habermas 1962). In contemporary society, mass media also serve other functions, not least commercial interests (advertising), which shape our shared and often standardized ideas and notions to a larger extent than Habermas' emphasis on rational communication would allow. In some areas, notably in the cultural construction of women and the female body, mass media sustain traditional ideas and exhibit a paradoxical tendency to oppress women – in traditional as well as in rather subtle ways.

Although Western women have acquired legal equality and access to the public sphere – to education, work, and political position, traditional gender roles and the power distribution still remain much the same as before: She is associated with submission and passivity, and He is the dominant party in control. The resilience of traditional ideas can be seen in contemporary popular culture, where women are presented largely as mute objects to be desired and manipulated. In stark opposition to dominant political views which recognize women as equals by law, cultural norms seem strangely unaffected by modernity. Applying the critique of Church hierarchy made by Elisabeth Schüssler Fiorenza to contemporary society, this apparent contradiction makes more sense (Schüssler Fiorenza 1992). Schüssler Fiorenza understands patriarchy as the will to dominate and calls for structural change. What we have today is just superficial gender equality. What is needed is the abolishment of all suppression; dominance stands in the way of liberation, equality, and a fair society. In her critique of the (Catholic) Church, she refers to this as *kyriarchal* power. Her alternative is the Church of women – a metaphor for an egalitarian society. As long as the power to dominate (kyriarchal power) is allowed to operate on an institutional level, all efforts to renegotiate the power of men over women, rich over poor, white over black, can only produce superficial changes. Schüssler Fiorenza's call for fundamental change is directed at religion, or more specifically the Catholic Church, which has – so far – been left unscathed by feminism. And this is not only because women are excluded from the hierarchy and are therefore easy to overlook. The strength of religious patriarchy is also a result of liberal ideals of tolerance. In this regard, it should be noted that all Western democracies, out of respect for religious ideas and values, allow religious organizations to remain havens for patriarchal power. Unlike other parts of society, religious institutions are granted autonomy and the right to follow their own internal norms. Thus, society sanctions violation of gender equality laws and discriminates against homosexuals and lesbians when it happens in the name of religion. Taking popular culture at face value, it would seem that it too is exempt from official gender policies, albeit for other reasons. According to Susan Sontag, the reason for this may have something to do with contemporary popular culture's emphasis on visualization: "A capitalist society requires a culture based on images. It needs to furnish vast amounts of entertainment in order to stimulate buying and anesthetize the injuries of class, race and sex … Cameras define reality in two ways essential to the workings of an advanced industrial society: as a spectacle (for the masses) and as an object of surveillance (for the rulers)" (Sontag 1977: 178). The criticism of consumer culture aside, it would seem that popular culture operates according to its own logic and continues to present women as mute and passive objects in a male-dominated world. Instead of giving a voice to women, popular culture places the female body at centre stage. In other words, it seems that popular culture does not reflect the legal and practical equality that women have achieved over the last decades, but repeats and enforces traditional ideas of women and the female body.

In 1991, the famous picture of a pregnant Demi Moore created havoc. More than two decades later, pregnancy has perhaps become an even more contested issue. When surrogate mothers and IVF techniques have become part of mainstream culture, new questions about women's bodies and ownership of the foetus are raised. Whose body is it? When pregnancy no longer implies motherhood (surrogacy), and fertilization takes place in laboratories (IVF), the cultural meaning of women's role in reproduction is put under strain. Meanwhile, the cultural representation of the female body – in advertising and art as well as abortion debates – shows it as an object to be dominated, manipulated, and desired by somebody else.

In a study of covers on the *Rolling Stone* magazine (1967–2009), Erin Hatton and Mary Nell Trautner found an increase in sexualized images of women and a growing tendency of depicting women as "hypersexualized", whereas the same cannot be said for men: "These findings not only document changes in the sexualization of men and women in popular culture over time, they also point to a narrowing of the culturally acceptable ways for 'doing' femininity as presented in popular media" (Hatton and Trautner 2011: 256). Women are increasingly presented as sex objects and are dissociated from other roles. Thus, mass media repeat and multiply traditional patterns and fail to reflect new (official) norms and values. So far, the new interactive media seem not to have changed anything in this regard. Instead the cultural construction of women continues along traditional paths, repeating a pattern of male dominance which women as well as men learn to take for granted. Obviously, the effect is radically different on men and women: While men learn to objectify women and thereby legitimize (male) power and traditional sexual hierarchies, women learn to see themselves not as subjects but through the eyes of others.

Slimming classes, beauty parlours, and cosmetic surgery can be seen as symptomatic of this culture. Although not exclusively for women, body and beauty enhancement procedures remain primarily associated with (young and middle-aged white middle-class) women. And even if fitness classes and body sculpting are increasingly popular with (young) men, body manipulation techniques remain in the female domain, pointing to a dissatisfaction with the body, which is markedly more prominent among women. In fact, it would seem that body consumerism indicates an increased level of shame associated with the female body. In this regard, Jean-Paul Sartre's argument that objectification of the self is linked to the knowledge of being observed by someone else is different from becoming aware of oneself through inner contemplation. To see oneself like that, as someone who is seen through the eyes of the Other, means being stripped of one's subjectivity. Moreover, it creates a feeling of shame, a feeling Sartre compares to being caught when spying: "The recognition of the fact that I am indeed that object that the Other is looking at and judging".[1] If this is indeed the way that culture teaches women to relate to themselves, the logical (or least damaging) solution open to women is to create a mental split and relate to the body as something totally detached from themselves. Although beauty operations, body sculpturing, and slimming regimes are promoted as ways of self-improvement and largely associated with something positive, these techniques do in fact rely on a violent division of body and self (Grogan 2008). This is not women's fault; rather, it is due to attitudes imposed by consumerism and modern mass media. As Teresa de

Lauretis claims, the Hollywood dream factory has socialized women into seeing the world through the camera's gaze (De Lauretis 1984).[2] David Morgan makes a similar point when he compares the camera's eye with any kind of instrument which extends the human gaze, like microscopes and ultrasound machines, and points out that these instruments are used by science in its objectifying and manipulative approach to the human body (Morgan 2012: 13).

Judging their bodies by cultural standards set out by mass media and the entertainment industry, women relate to their own bodies as objects to be looked at and evaluated by others: admired and desired, but never, never, it would seem, to be regarded as an integral part of one's being.[3] Only a radical split between the body and the self can allow someone to talk about 'getting myself into shape' or saying 'I finally have the figure I deserve'. In extreme cases, self-objectification may lead to fatal illness such as *anorexia nervosa*. As one anorexic 19-year-old girl put it when asked to explain her illness, "I just wanted to be seen, at the same time as I wished to be invisible. And I had to purge my body from all the small devils that possessed it".[4] These self-objectifying trends also include pregnancy, which from the body-image perspective is extremely challenging. Preoccupation with weight gain is a major issue on innumerable blogs, but more telling is the preoccupation with workout regimens during pregnancy.[5] Even more serious, perhaps, is the rise in caesarean sections over the last couple of decades. Between 1996 and 2009, caesarean sections increased 60 per cent in the United States: from 20.7 per cent of births in 1996 to 32.9 per cent in 2009.[6] In many countries, women are given the choice between a natural vaginal delivery or a caesarean, but from a medical point of view the choice is not sound, since the caesarean section is a major surgery and should be avoided except for medical reasons. A possible explanation for the increase is a myth spread in magazines and blogs that it is easier to resume sexual relations after a caesarean section. Although the decision is ultimately a medical one, there is certainly room for the woman to influence the decision; fear of natural birth is one reason why she would opt for a caesarean. And since they make it possible to time the delivery within normal working hours, caesarean sections are also a convenient solution for clinics. To counter this trend, the American College of Obstetricians and Gynecologists has developed "clinical guidelines for reducing the occurrence of non-medically-indicated caesarean delivery and labour induction prior to 39 weeks".[7] It is also possible to see the increase in caesarean sections as a sign of a more general trend associated with IVF and surrogacy which plays down the foetus' (biological) dependence on the mother and de-emphasizes the importance of pregnancy and birth for the relationship between mother and child.

The invention of surrogacy does nothing to counter the cultural objectification of women. Surrogate mothers are women who donate their wombs to nurture other people's foetuses. The invention created controversy when it first emerged in the 1980s. Illustratively called the 'rent-a-womb industry', surrogacy was initially seen as offensive and immoral, and the Catholic Church condemned the practice.

What kind of women would get pregnant for money? Protesters questioned the morals of the surrogate mother, but the infertile couple who created the demand in the first place was treated with respect. But initial protests soon subsided when the media started to run stories about altruistic sisters who sacrificed themselves and put their wombs at disposal for the happiness of others. Thus, surrogacy was painted as an act of unselfish love. In fact, it was presented as an ideal 'job' for housewives, since it allowed them to stay at home and look after their own children. But when commercial agencies tapped into the surrogacy market in the 1990s and started outsourcing (India), protests arose again after the media started to run stories about the exploitation of vulnerable women. This time, the protesters were mainly liberals and feminists who sided with poor Indian women who were forced into surrogacy by their unemployed husbands. Evangelical groups had been critical from the start, although the altruistic sister-in-law solution had some support among them; they did not join the protesters until surrogacy became increasingly associated with homosexual couples. Their criticism was not rooted in solidarity with poor women, but with their concern for traditional family values, a concern they shared with the Catholic Church. Jennifer Butler points to 2004 as the start of a new joint initiative between Catholic and Evangelical activists, who started collaborating on this and other women's issues (Butler 2006: 69). This was the Catholic "Year of the Family" and the tenth anniversary of the UN Cairo Conference on Population and Development (1994), where conservative Christians with the Catholic Church in the lead had managed to muster support from authoritarian Muslim states and hinder Western secular initiatives to control fertility rates and monitor population growth.

What made surrogacy possible was the fact that modern medicine saw the body as a machine. The same logic informs the legal system, as illustrated in court cases where surrogate egg donors (women) are treated the same way as sperm donors (men), that is, with the same legal rights to the surrogate child (biological offspring). The surrogate mother who (only) provides the uterus (not egg) has no such rights. She has 'rented her womb' and is therefore not a mother because she is bound to the child by a legal contract and has "no biological links to the child" (Raymond 1993: 66). The underlying premise is of course that pregnancy and birth are understood as technical necessities in the production of a child. The child is therefore defined by its biological roots (parents) and not by its links to the surrogate mother, as the court sees it. The result is a radical dissolution of pregnancy into discrete parts: egg, sperm, uterus, birth. Needless to say, it implies a dehumanization of the pregnant woman. By treating it as an industrial process and focusing on the end product, the child, pregnancy becomes detached from motherhood and women become more like men: as providers of building material, that is, DNA. Although surrogacy may be regarded as a scientific achievement and a public good, because it allows infertile couples to become parents, from a feminist point of view the practice is hugely problematic because it relies on a split between women (subject) and their bodies (object). It would seem that the

Catholic Church comes to women's rescue when it bans all sorts of interference with the egg. But it is not a concern for women's integrity that motivates the Church's categorical refusal of any kind of tampering with the human reproductive process:

> Techniques that entail the dissociation of husband and wife, by the intrusion of a person other than the couple (donation of sperm or ovum, surrogate uterus), are gravely immoral. These techniques (heterologous artificial insemination and fertilization) infringe the child's right to be born of a father and mother known to him and bound to each other by marriage. They betray the spouses' right to become a father and a mother only through each other.
> (Catechism of the Catholic Church, §2376)

As stated in the quote above, "heterologous artificial insemination" is not accepted because it entails insemination by a donor – a stranger – into the wife's vaginal tube. The procedure is not allowed because it violates the marriage. By the same token, the Catholic Church does in fact accept "homologous artificial insemination", that is, assisted insemination with sperm from the husband. The logic behind this distinction is the sacramental character of marriage, which makes it the only acceptable institution for procreation.[8] From this point of view, the Catholic Church forbids all kinds of IVF treatment because it involves the manipulation of eggs and sperm by a third party and brings what belongs to the intimate sphere of marriage into the public realm. For the same reason, it also bans surrogacy, which is an even greater violation of marriage, since it brings a third party into every stage of the process. Within this framework, then, surrogate mothers are excluded by definition. And surrogacy for homosexual couples is equally banned – because the Church does not allow same-sex marriage.

When the majority of Western states changed their abortion laws in the 1970s, they made their decision on the logical premise that the foetus was a part of the woman's body. Anti-abortion activism claims the opposite, defining the foetus as a human being – they demand that society treat it as a separate being, which, in principle, is independent of the mother. Surrogacy relies on the same distinction: Defining the foetus as the legal property of the parents, it belongs to someone other than the pregnant woman whose body it shares. Laws which allow artificial insemination and research on embryos and fertilized egg cells are based on a different logic, which defines the egg as comparable to sperm and treats both as separate from their biological origins. Like abortion, artificial fertilization techniques have remained a highly controversial issue, with conservative Christian voices in the forefront warning against inhuman medical research methods. In addition to arguing that it is almost impossible for legislators to keep up with rapid developments in fertility research, anti-abortionists protest against IVF because it allows homosexual and lesbian couples to become parents. Since the protesters are the same, there is good reason to see the anti-abortionists' fight for the foetus and the fight against IVF as mirror images: One aims to protect human life, and the other argues against creating new human life. The position is based on the following logic: Just as abortion is wrong because it interferes with God's creation, so IVF is wrong because scientists play God.

The two positions – for and against IVF – are associated with two radically different interest groups: Those who rally against IVF are conservative Christians, whereas fertilization activism is promoted by a wide range of non-religious actors: political parties, lesbian and homosexual groups, research institutes and economic interests from private IVF providers. These are formidable opponents, and may to some extent explain why the fight against IVF finds little popular and media support. The conservative Christian repudiation of IVF is logically linked to their anti-abortion stance. Both positions rely on the notion that God is directly involved in human procreation and that the act of fertilizing the egg (conception) is a creative act by God. And since God intends to make a human being when he fertilizes the egg, it should be regarded as one. These beliefs are summed up in the idea that human life is sacred "because from its beginning it involves the creative action of God" (*Catechism of the Catholic Church*, §2258). This is also the logic behind the categorical repudiation of IVF. It trespasses on God's privilege; scientists should not manipulate fertilized eggs. By approaching conception as God's creative act, the Catholic Church and other conservative Christians see God as the true parent, and themselves as morally responsible for the foetus (in lieu of the parents).

Abortion and IVF represent radically opposite solutions to the problem of human procreation and point to an inherent ambiguity in modern legislation. On the one hand, we have legal abortion, which grants women the right *not* to have children, and, on the other hand, there are laws which grant married couples the right to have their own biological children and consult professional help if they have problems conceiving. Put bluntly, we may say that the modern laws which regulate procreation are based on two mutually exclusive principles, namely, the sanctity of biological offspring on the one hand and the autonomy of the individual woman on the other. This leaves ample room for ethical debates and religious activism.

Like other fertility techniques, surrogacy was the result of medical research which was developed into a treatment. Since the 1990s, surrogacy has turned into a profitable business. Most conservative Christians share this view and see IVF and surrogacy as attacks against traditional family values. Both techniques challenge the unique function of the marital union between husband and wife (reproduction), and they are seen as morally wrong because they interfere with God's creation. In popular propaganda, the Dr. Jekyll and Mr. Hyde is evoked as a mythical illustration of the dangers inherent in man's attempts to 'play God'.

What we mean by 'human being' varies. Suffice it to recall that slavery was not abolished by the Christian West until the nineteenth century, and racist theories which distinguished between more or less perfect human beings were generally accepted in the first part of the twentieth century. What we mean by a human being is a cultural construction and constantly negotiated, questioned, and revised. Therefore, all abortion rhetoric comes at a cost. When pro-choice advocates argue for women's right (absolutely) to choose, the argument feeds into the anti-abortionists' stereotypical idea of egotistical feminists (career women) who sacrifice innocent children on the altar of self-realization. It should be noted that this allegation does not hold. Statistics show that 45 per cent of women in the United States who chose to have an abortion were unmarried, and that 61 per cent of them were already single mothers with sole responsibility for one or more children (Jones and Singh 2010). In a similar vein, the anti-abortion rhetoric of conservative Christians referring to "immediate ensoulment" and the sanctity of human life is met with prejudice. First, since these are religious claims they are impossible to sustain unless you accept the basic premise of a creator-God. Second, the position strikes them as deeply immoral, since it relies on a correlation between a foetus and a full-born child, which cannot be sustained in practice. What is morally more important – saving a starving child or stopping an abortion?

The Christian association between soul and life is hard to understand and is incessantly challenged by medical inventions and improvements in modern medicine that blur the distinction between life and death. In antiquity, it was the breath that decided the matter ('last breath'); after the invention of the stethoscope (1816); it was the heart ('the last heartbeat'). Today, the EEG (electroencephalogram) measures brain activity. Lacking a reliable definition, medical professionals are left to draw the line between life and death and decide who shall receive curative treatment on a life-support machine and who cannot benefit from treatment. Treatment is usually withdrawn when the patient has no brain activity (brain-dead). Only a few countries (Netherlands and Switzerland) have legalized so-called life-shortening procedures (euthanasia), but most countries will allow a person today to opt out of life support if the person in question has left a testament which explicitly requests that life-prolonging procedures be avoided. Based on the soul–life belief, the Catholic Church and other conservative Christians have intervened in a number of cases to ensure that brain-dead patients remain on life-prolonging treatment. Interestingly, these activist groups largely overlap with anti-abortion activists. Since the 1990s, activist groups have rallied against the cessation of life support with the same fervour as they have fought for the foetus' life.

Reflecting on the existential status of human beings, Richard Gist, a Methodist pastor, points out that what defines a human being is a capacity for interaction and an ability to form relationships (Gist 1981). He points to the painful experience of trying to relate to a loved one after he or she has fallen into a vegetative state (coma). A life sustained by technical equipment may be defined biologically as life, but Gist refuses to accept such a division. To speak of the soul as something different from the body, as an *it*, is just as wrong as to define a human life just by its biological presence.

In 2004, President George W. Bush gave a new reality to the anti-abortion activists' claim that the foetus is a human being. He proposed a new law, popularly known as the Unborn Victims of Violence Act, which stated that a person who kills a pregnant woman should face two separate charges: taking the life of the woman and taking the life of the foetus (Unborn Victims of Violence Act, §1841):

> Protection of unborn children (a)(1) Whoever engages in conduct that violates any of the provisions of law listed in sub-section (b) and thereby causes the death of, or bodily injury (as defined in section 1365) to, a child, who is in utero at the time the conduct takes place, is guilty of a separate offense under this section.[9]

The enacting of this law was an important legal step towards granting the foetus an independent legal status. To pro-choice activists, it may seem absurd, but Kristin Luker, who interviewed more than 200 activists, explains that the underlying motivation of anti-abortionists is a firm conviction that the foetus is a real baby. Abortion then is indeed understood as "killing unborn babies". This belief was "not an explicit or salient part of their upbringing; it was simply something they had always taken for granted", but it was all the more powerful for that (Luker 1984: 128). This idea of the foetus as an unborn baby gets implicit support from daily usage (expectant mothers are more prone to refer to the contents of their wombs as "a child" rather than as "a foetus"), and from the mass media, where references to the "unborn baby" abound.

The term 'foetus', on the other hand, has a strong scientific connotation and is reserved for medical usage and unwanted pregnancies. The idea of the foetus as ready made baby was more powerfully enforced by an image – a clean and clear colour photo of a human foetus in the womb which appeared on the cover of *LIFE* magazine in 1965 and which immediately became a standard image in popular culture. It started out as a book, *Ett barn blir till* (*A Child Is Born*), by the Swedish photographer Lars Nilsson. It became an immediate success, and several photos were published in *LIFE* magazine in March of that year, selling 8 million copies. This photo of an embryo in the womb was the cover of *LIFE* from 30 April 1965 and helped create the idea of the foetus as a baby:

> Manipulation was crucial too in the construction of the famous cover image. By placing the embryo against the background of a starry sky and isolating it almost completely from its maternal environment, Nilsson created an iconic image of the embryo as spaceman, a heroic figure of pure potential. The physical reality of the maternal body was elided and in its place was a figuration of the womb as empty space, ready for inspection and colonisation.

> *(Hanson 2004: 156)*

The idea of pregnancy as an unborn baby in the womb was also effectively proffered by the introduction of the ultrasound. Intended as a diagnostic instrument and introduced as a part of normal pregnancy check-ups in the 1980s, ultrasound soon reached symbolic proportions: It opened up the mother's body to external inspection and even allowed photographic documentation of its contents. It gave form to an idea, so to speak. In fact, we may say that the ultrasound image was given artificial support from the Lars Nilsson photo. When we look at the blurry, indistinct ultrasound image they give us at the hospital, what we see in our mind's eye is Lars Nilsson's beautiful photo. Superimposed on the blurry ultrasound image, it turns it into something more than a documentation of the foetus' medical condition – it turns it into an imaginary portrait of a real baby.

Today, ultrasound has become a part of the ritual of pregnancy and birth.[10] It makes visible something which is hidden and serves to establish the foetus as an individual being. As Clare Hanson notes, the ultrasound has become a *rite de passage* in pregnancy, "the point at which the embryo becomes (at 11–13 weeks) a 'real baby'" (Hanson 2004: 158). Although these images are unclear and hard to read, and although an image of a foetus at four months has little resemblance to a baby and lacks individual characteristics (making it impossible to distinguish 'my' foetus from yours), the ultrasound image serves as proof and a promise of life. These images, the *LIFE* foetus and the ultrasound, both feed into the idea of the foetus as 'an unborn baby' and help visualize abortion as an atrocity – a bloody sacrifice on the altar of female egotism. Inspired by Nilsson's perfect baby–foetus

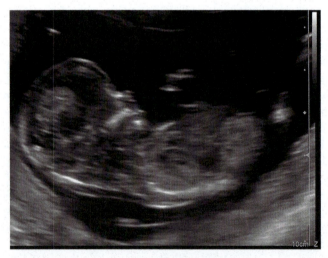

FIGURE 15.1 A foetus about ten weeks old. Ultrasound images are hard to interpret for the untrained eye. Lacking individual characteristics, it can hardly serve as a portrait, but functions rather as an x-ray – as a sign in need of interpretation by professionals. Shutterstock/©IgorMitrovic88.

pastiche, anti-abortion activists speak of the "unborn child" long before an ultrasound image can even document its existence. Unlike traditional Christian ideas about pregnancy that see it as a process of gradual development, these activists see a perfect child from the start.

"I didn't realize I looked so sexy", said actress Demi Moore commenting on the famous pregnancy picture on the cover of *Vogue*. But the photograph did not just portray a sexy woman, it was also an intervention in an ongoing debate about gender roles. In 1991, when the picture was published, US society was marked by heated abortion debates. The image belonged aesthetically as well as politically to the pro-choice side, signalling a woman in control of her own sexuality and future motherhood. From an anti-abortion perspective, the image had another, more sinister meaning. Mixing sex and procreation gave it a disturbingly ambiguous quality. Moreover, it depicted pregnancy as a female affair represented by a career woman who, by virtue of her profession (actress), has a body which somehow belongs in the public domain. Considering the fact that there was not even a hint of a man in it, the image of a naked and pregnant Demi Moore appeared to conservative Christians as a transgression of all that is associated with family values and the private sphere.

But even if conservative Christians are critical of the commercial exploitation of women's bodies in film and advertising, their own ideas about women cannot exactly be said to be the exact opposite. Since they are critical of female emancipation and gender equality, they do not worry about exploitation and objectification of women, but the indecent exposure of female bodies in film and television upsets them. And this worry is not for the sake of the woman, but for the fact that she may incite sexual desire in men. Feminists, for their part, react to female passivity portrayed in popular culture, in advertising, and in film, and are critical of the conservative Christian idea of gender complementarity (which implies the hierarchical supremacy of the male) because it too allows for the exploitation of women – except that it takes place 'behind closed doors' in the private sphere (home). Marriage is where life begins, and the private family circle is where children are nurtured and grow. But even if conservative Christians maintain that the family as they see it is a sacred institution that was created by God in the beginning of time, marriages and family life are not immune to historical change. Even a biological phenomenon like pregnancy is culturally construed.

Notes

1 Jean-Paul Sartre in *Being and Nothingness* (1966, 350), here cited from Morgan 2012: 18.
2 Women's attitudes towards the body have been treated extensively in feminist studies over the last several decades. The first bulk of feminist studies appeared in the 1980s, a decade when feminist perspectives were also included in other fields. However, after the turn of the millennium there has been a marked decrease in new important work. For an excellent overview of this topic, see Price and Shildrick 1999.

3 There is a vast literature on women and objectification which has primarily been a concern in psychology. For an excellent introduction to this topic, see Szymanski, Moffitt, and Carr 2011.

4 Interview in *Aftenposten*, 20 September 2009. My translation.

5 A search for 'baby bump' on the internet will give you a glimpse into this universe and will show that 'baby bump' is a preferred metaphor among middle-class women and commercial actors. See http://babyandbump.momtastic.com/.

6 National Center for Health Statistics (NCHS) Data Brief 124. June 2013. Available at http://www.cdc.gov/nchs/data/databriefs/db124.htm.

7 See note 6.

8 Sacraments are a special category of rituals that purport to create real change when they are performed. There are seven sacraments: marriage, which makes man and woman into one flesh ("Therefore a man leaves his father and his mother and clings to his wife, and they become one flesh" (Genesis 2:24)); the Eucharist, which involves a metamorphosis of objects (bread and wine); the ritual which marks the entrance into the priesthood, where the priest is 'infused' with the Holy Spirit through the laying on of hands; baptism, which transports the infant to the realm of the saved (the Church); confirmation; penance; and the anointment of the sick (last rites traditionally performed on one's death bed). These ritual effects rely on two criteria: First, the priest must be officially ordained in the Catholic Church, and, second, the rituals must be performed correctly.

9 Available at http://www.gpo.gov/fdsys/granule/USCODE-2010-title18/USCODE-2010-title18-partI-chap90A-sec1841.

10 Robbie Davis-Floyd analyzes birth as a modern *rite de passage* (Davis-Floyd 2003).

AFTERTHOUGHTS

What we today refer to as making a child or creating offspring, medieval Christians called procreation or generation. Deeply ensconced in an agricultural world, offspring to them literally meant 'offspring': a new twig on a tree. Today, we frequently call it reproduction. The word creates a striking parallel to industrial production and a new way of conceptualizing pregnancy: as if it were no longer a process of growth within the female body but a process which starts with raw material (fertilized egg) plus work (the nutritive activity of the womb) and results in a finished product (child). In this industrial model, the child becomes something which in principle is detached from the mother (although it is dependent on her body for a while). Thus, the industrial model serves to dehumanize the relationship between mother and child, and objectify the female body. This is a final farewell to the vegetative model of antiquity, which compared the pregnant woman to fertile soil. As illustrated by contemporary abortion debates, both sides see the foetus (product) as completely distinct from the mother (labourer). Anti-abortionists do so by effectively denying the mother her humanity (autonomy), and pro-choice advocates do so by strictly defining the foetus as a potential human being.

In Christianity, creation is God's privilege. The best that man can do is to cooperate with God and procreate. But if human procreation can be conceived as a mechanical process whereby man reproduces himself, this is more than a mere conceptual change. Rather, it points to an entirely new (unchristian) idea of the human being and what we are capable of. Christian pro-life activists pretend that the foetus springs alive in the mother's womb like a miracle: It's a ready-made miniature baby just waiting to be born. Pro-choice activists have no such faith. They believe that the foetus is a product of natural processes (growth) and gradual development between conception and birth. Take for example, this quote from Richard Gist: "I do not take abortion lightly. When a foetus is destroyed, I moan, 'life has been taken', and feel a troubled regret. I do not like it. But I also recognize another truth: real life has not been taken. Rather, promise has been denied; the vehicle of life has been aborted; an individual will not be realized" (Gist 1981: 2023).

Gist's reflections propose a fresh way of approaching a modern dilemma. Medical research has developed methods of artificially manipulating the human body, a development which has blurred the line between life and death and which has created a moral vacuum in its wake. When it is possible to perform surgery on unborn foetuses and new organs can be developed from stem cells and implanted in another body, it makes the human body into something else. In stark opposition to traditional Christian views about the human body as an integral part of the individual human being, medical science relies on another approach to the body, treating it as somehow separated from the self or mind – which is situated (vaguely) in the brain. It seems, however, that this radical split between body and mind is restricted to medical practice, since legally the individual remains a unit of body and mind/self. The idea of the autonomous individual is part of the stockpile of taken-for-granted ideas which seem surprisingly resilient in the face of change. When new ways of thinking emerge – like the industrial model of pregnancy during the Enlightenment – they do not necessarily replace older (Christian) ways of understanding. Historical development is not a simple process of replacing old understandings with better and more logical explanations. It is rather more like a haphazard adding on to the ever-growing stockpile of available models. The persistence of established patterns of thought is particularly evident when it comes to procreation and pregnancy. Many of the ideas that were developed in antiquity are still around today; even though they have lost their explanatory value, they still colour the way we understand the world. So we still talk about female fertility in the same manner as we speak about fertile soil, and we still refer to men's sperm or seed, even though embryology has long since made this model redundant. Inspired by Ludwig Wittgenstein's argument that the "meaning of a word is its use in language" (Wittgenstein 1957, §43), we can identify three ways of conceptualizing pregnancy in contemporary usage, which correspond to three life-worlds or clusters of meaning: First, there is the metaphors we use which associate procreation with vegetative growth (seed, soil) – a reminiscence of ancient Greek models. Second, the tendency to speak of pregnancy as an almost automatic process by using mechanistic metaphors from the Enlightenment, which is often combined with words associated with industrial production (as discussed above). Here, pregnancy is envisaged as a process initiated when the sperm 'manages' to fertilize the egg (note the agency assigned to the sperm). Third, there is pregnancy conceptualized in terms of fate and the will of God. This conceptualization is obviously associated with religious – but not necessarily Christian – world views. When it comes to biology, the genetic link between both parents and their offspring is taken as a self-evident fact. For instance, when we talk about how a child inherits exactly half of its traits from each parent – although the distribution admittedly can be somewhat unjust: the beautiful eyes from one, the bad back from the other – we disregard the finer aspects of hereditary rules as well as the recent findings of epigenetics, and we speak as if the child were an ideal combination of mother and father.

The wide range of metaphors related to pregnancy points to a lack of common understanding. Apart from conservative Christians, there is a striking inconsistency in the way that pregnancy is understood: One may speak of fate and mystical coincidence, while the other understands pregnancy as an almost mechanical occurrence. Interestingly, neither model leaves much room for female autonomy and women's right to choose. From a feminist perspective, pregnancy is understood as an intrinsically personal experience and therefore as one that is open to individual interpretation – and, consequently, also to individual solutions. With Charles Taylor's analysis of contemporary culture in mind, we may say that the feminist framing of pregnancy as a personal experience reflects the cultural turn from transcendent authority to immanence and the positing of the individual as the ultimate source and judge of truth (Taylor 2007). The habit of referring to the embryo or foetus as a baby is a case in point. Apart from anti-abortion advocates who refer to the 'unborn child' as a rhetorical strategy, women who welcome their pregnancy also tend to refer to the foetus as a child. This is probably because 'foetus' is perceived as a technical term, whereas 'baby' is perceived as a term that is warm and closer to life. Because the woman who welcomes her pregnancy and wants the foetus to grow into a full-born child, the reference to 'the child', I will suggest, points to another level of meaning. It is no longer an instance of descriptive language, but an evocation, an expression of wishful thinking, if not an attempt at magically forcing the future and an attempt to make the uncertain real – as if the foetus were already a baby.

To conservative Christian critics, modern developments like IVF, surrogacy, same-sex couples, and gender equality are signs that traditional Christian moral standards are under attack (secularism). These are not isolated cases, but are a part of a larger scheme which threatens religion and Christian moral standards in Western society. In order to understand their motivational fear, Kristin Luker cites an anti-abortion activist and allows us to catch a glimpse of her concerns:

> One woman made the point clearly: "God is the creator of life, and I think all sexual activity should be open to that (creation). That does not mean that you have to have a certain number of children or anything, but it should be open to Him and His will. The contraceptive mentality denies his (God's) will. It's my will, not your will. And here again, the selfishness comes in".
>
> *(Luker 1984: 186)*

The statement is made by a conservative Christian woman whose religiosity is centred on obedience to God, religious rules, church authorities, and accepting women's subordination to men. To her, submission to God's will is valued much higher than individual autonomy. Her values and ideals are radically different from the feminist ideal of the independent, rational, and creative individual who is free to make his or her own choices and take responsibility for his or her life. The Christian ideal instead refers everything back to *one* source, God, the creator who has ultimate ownership of the world. In this scenario, *choice* is not an honorary concept, but a signal of disobedience.

Although Western women have obtained legal equality, the cultural construction of gender roles remains surprisingly stable. Forms and expressions change with fashion, but it seems that the subordination and objectification of women in popular culture remains much the same as before. Hence, in spite of secularization, traditional gender relations are sustained and transmitted elsewhere. But unlike Christianity, the subordination of women in contemporary culture is not sustained by an elaborately intertwined world view and anthropology, or by theories about the world and human life within it. On the contrary, scientific theories give no grounds for a gender hierarchy, and technical control of human reproduction (contraception) has removed the practical impediments to women's social participation on an equal footing with men. What still remains a strictly female plight is pregnancy – the nurturing of human offspring – but this, I suggest, should not be regarded as a strictly bodily matter; it should be celebrated, rather, as women's voluntary gift and their contribution, body and soul, to the future.

BIBLIOGRAPHY

Ackerknecht, Erwin H. 1976. "Midwives as Experts in Court". *Bulletin of the New York Academy of Medicine* 52: 1224–28. Available at http://www.ncbi.nlm.nih.gov/pmc/articles/PMC1807280/pdf/bullnyacadmed00156–0070.pdf.
——. 1982. *A Short History of Medicine*. Baltimore: Johns Hopkins University Press.
Albert, Jean-Pierre. 1990. *Odeurs de saintité. La mythologie chrétienne des aromates*. Paris: Éditions de l'EHESS.
——. 1997. *Le sang et le ciel*. Paris: Aubier.
Alberti, Leon Battista. 2004. *On Painting*. Translated by Cecil Grayson. London: Penguin.
Albrecht, Gloria H. 2003. "Contraception and Abortion within Protestant Christianity". In Daniel C. Maguire (ed.), *Sacred Rights: The Case for Contraception and Abortion in World Religions*. Oxford: Oxford University Press.
Anderson, Benedict. 1989. *Imagined Communities: Reflections on the Origins and Spread of Nationalism*. London: Verso.
Ankum, W.M., H.L. Houtzager, and O.P. Bleker. 1996. "Reinier de Graaf (1641-1673) and the Fallopian Tube". *Human Reproduction Update* 2 (4): 365–69.
Aquinas, Thomas. 1975. *Summa contra gentiles (Summa de veritate catholicae fidei contra gentiles) Book Two: Creation*. Translated by J.F. Anderson. Notre Dame: University of Notre Dame Press. Available at http://dhspriory.org/thomas/ContraGentiles2.htm#88.
——. 2010. *Summa Theologica I*. Translated by Alfred Freddoso. Notre Dame: University of Notre Dame Press. Available at http://www3.nd.edu/~afreddos/summa-translation/TOC-part1.htm.
Aristotle. 1993. *De anima*. Edited by Michael Durrant. London: Routledge.
——. 1994–2009. *Politics*. Translated by Benjamin Jowett. Available at http://classics.mit.edu/Aristotle/politics.html.
——. 1994–2009. *History of Animals*. Translated by D'Arcy Wentworth Thompson. Available at http://classics.mit.edu/Aristotle/history_anim.html.
Arvidsson, Stefan. 2006. *Aryan Idols: Indo-European Mythology as Ideology and Science*. Chicago: University of Chicago Press.
Augustine. 1955. *Enchiridion*. Available at http://www.tertullian.org/fathers/augustine_enchiridion_02_trans.htm.
——. 1984. *The City of God (Gudsstaten)*. Harmondsworth: Penguin Classics.
De Beauvoir, Simone. 1989 (1949). *The Second Sex*. New York: Vintage Books.

Bellinger, Charles K. 1992. "Questions on Abortion and the Struggle against Tyranny". *The Crucible: A Journal for Christian Graduate Students* 3: 3–8. Available at http://www. religion-online.org/showarticle.asp?title=1777.

Berger, Peter. 1990 (1967). *The Sacred Canopy: Elements of a Sociological Theory of Religion.* New York: Anchor Books.

———. (ed.). 1999. *The Desecularization of the World: The Resurgence of Religion in World Politics.* Grand Rapids, MI: Eerdmans.

———. 2010. *Between Relativism and Fundamentalism: Religious Resources for a Middle Position.* Grand Rapids, MI: Eerdmans.

Beyer, Peter. 1994. *Religion and Globalization.* London: Sage.

Biondi, Stefano. 2009. "Can Good Law Make Up for Bad Politics? The Case of Eluana Englaro". *Medical Law Review* 17(4): 447–56.

Bob, Clifford. 2012. *The Global Right Wing and the Clash of World Politics.* Cambridge: Cambridge University Press.

Børresen, Kari. 1968. *Subordination et equivalence: Nature et rôle de la femme d'après Augustin et Thomas Aquin.* Oslo: Universitetsforlaget.

———. (ed.). 1995. *The Image of God: Gender Models in Judaeo-Christian Tradition.* Minneapolis: Fortress Press.

———. 2002. *From Patristics to Matristics: Selected Articles on Christian Gender Models.* Edited by Øivind Norderval and Katrine Ore. Rome: Herder.

———. 2004. "Religion Confronting Women's Human Rights: The Case of Roman Catholicism". *North and South: Gender Views from Norway. Special edition of Kvinneforskning.* Available at http://eng.kilden.forskningsradet.no/artikkel/vis.html?tid=54096&within_tid=54080.

Bourdieu, Pierre. 1977. *Outline of a Theory of Practice.* Cambridge: Cambridge University Press.

Brind'Amour, Katherine. 2007. "Pope Sixtus V". *The Embryo Project Encyclopedia.* Available at http://embryo.asu.edu/handle/10776/1727.

Brown, Elizabeth A.R. 1990. "Authority, the Family, and the Dead in Late Medieval France". *French Historical Studies* 16(4): 803–32.

Brown, Peter. 1988. *The Body and Society: Men, Women and Sexual Renunciation in Early Christianity.* New York: Columbia University Press.

———. 2000. *Augustine of Hippo: A Biography.* Berkeley: University of California Press.

Brown, Steven P. 2002. *Trumping Religion: The New Christian Right, the Free Speech Clause and the Courts.* Tuscaloosa, AL: University of Alabama Press.

Brundage, James A. 1995. *Medieval Canon Law.* Harlow, UK: Longman.

Buettner, Kimberly A. 2007a. "John Charles Rock". *Embryo Project Encyclopedia.* Available at http://embryo.asu.edu/handle/10776/1725.

———. 2007b. "Karl Ernst von Baer". Embryo Project Encyclopedia. Available at http://embryo.asu.edu/pages/karl-ernst-von-baer.

Butler, Jennifer S. 2006. *Born Again: The Christian Right Globalized.* London: Pluto Press.

Bynum, Caroline Walker. 1992. *Fragmentation and Redemption.* New York: Zone Books.

Caine, Barbara and Glenda Sluga. 2000. *Gendering European History 1780–1920.* London: Leicester University Press.

Campbell, Colin. 1972. "The Cult, the Cultic Milieu and Secularization". *Sociological Yearbook of Religion in Britain* 5: 119–36.

Carlen, Claudia (ed.) 1990. *Syllabus of Errors.* (1864) in *The Papal Encyclicals*, 5 vols. 1740–1981. Raleigh, NC: McGrath. Available at http://www.papalencyclicals.net/Pius09/p9syll.htm.

Carlson, Allan. 2007. "Children of the Reformation: A Short and Surprising History of Protestantism and Contraception". *Touchstone Online Journal* (Evangelical). Available at http://www.touchstonemag.com/archives/article.php?id=20-04-020-f.

Casanova, José. 1994. *Public Religions in the Modern World.* Chicago: University of Chicago Press.

Casti connubii 1930. Encyclical. Pius XI. *Acta Apostolicae Sedis* 22.

Castles, Francis G. 2003. "The World Turned Upside Down: Below Replacement Fertility, Changing Preferences and Family-Friendly Public Policy in 21 OECD Countries". *Journal of European Social Policy* 13(3): 209–27.

Catechism of the Catholic Church. 1993. Città del Vaticano: Libreria Editrice Vaticana. Available in English at http://www.vatican.va/archive/ENG0015/_INDEX.HTM.

Chadwick, Owen. 1990 (1964). *The Reformation.* Harmondsworth, UK: Penguin.

Christian, William A. 1984. "Religious Apparitions and the Cold War in Southern Europe". In Eric R. Wolf (ed.), *Religion, Power and Protest in Local Communities.* Berlin: Walter De Gruyter.

Clark, Elizabeth A. (ed.). 1996. *St. Augustine on Marriage and Sexuality.* Selections from the Fathers of the Church, Vol. 1. Washington, DC: The Catholic University of America Press.

Clark, Michael and Catherine Crawford (eds.). 1994. *Legal Medicine in History.* Cambridge: Cambridge University Press.

Cobb, Matthew. 2000. "Reading and Writing the Book of Nature: Jan Swammerdam (1637–1680)". *Endeavour Magazine* 24(3): 122–28.

——. 2002. "Malpighi, Swammerdam and the Colourful Silkworm: Replication and Visual Representation in Early Modern Science". *Annals of Science* 59: 111–47.

——. 2006. *The Egg and the Sperm Race: The Seventeenth-Century Scientists who Unravelled the Secrets of Sex, Life and Growth.* London: The Free Press Pocket Books.

Code of Canon Law. 1983. Available at http://www.vatican.va/archive/ENG1104/_INDEX.HTM.

Cohen, Susan B. 2009. "Facts and Consequences: Legality, Incidence and Safety of Abortions Worldwide". *Guttmacher Policy Review* 12(4): 2–6. Available at http://www.guttmacher.org/pubs/gpr/12/4/gpr120402.html.

Cohn, Norman. 1970 (1961). *The Pursuit of the Millennium.* Oxford: Oxford University Press.

Corea, Gerardo. 1998. *Un medico legale tra salassi e torture.* Roma: Aldo Primerano Editrice.

Cottingham, J., R. Stoothoff, and D. Murdoch. 1984. *The Philosophical Writings of Descartes.* Vol. 1. Cambridge: Cambridge University Press.

Council of Vienne. Decree 1. Available at http://www.ewtn.com/library/COUNCILS/VIENNE.HTM.

Cunningham, Andrew. 1997. *The Anatomical Renaissance: The Resurrection of the Anatomical Projects of the Ancients.* Aldershot, UK: Scolar Press.

Darmon, Pierre. 1977. *Le mythe de la procréation à l'âge baroque.* Paris: Éditions du Seuil.

Davie, Grace. 1994. *Religion in Britain since 1945: Believing without Belonging.* Oxford: Basil Blackwell.

——. 2007. *The Sociology of Religion.* Los Angeles: Sage.

Davis, John Jefferson. 1984. *Abortion and the Christian: What Every Believer Should Know.* Phillipsburg, NJ: Presbyterian and Reformed Publishing Company.

Davis-Floyd, Robbie E. 2003. *Birth as an American Rite of Passage.* Berkeley: University of California Press.

Dean-Jones, Lesley A. 1994. *Women's Bodies in Classical Greek Science.* Oxford: Clarendon Press.

De Lauretis, Teresa. 1984. *Alice Doesn't: Feminism, Semiotics, Cinema.* Bloomington, IN: Indiana University Press.

DeMarco, Donald and Benjamin Wiker. 2004. *Architects of the Culture of Death.* San Francisco: Ignatius Press.

Derbes, Anne. 1996. *Picturing the Passion in Late Medieval Italy.* Cambridge: Cambridge University Press.

De Renzi, Silvia. 2004. "Women and Medicine". In Peter Elmer (ed.), *The Healing Arts: Health, Disease and Society in Europe, 1500–1800.* Manchester: The Open University.

Descartes, René. 1649. *Les passions de l'âme.* Amsterdam: Lodewijk Elsevier. Available at http://www.ac-grenoble.fr/PhiloSophie/file/descartes_passions.pdf.

Desmond, Adrian and James Moore. 1991. *Darwin.* Harmondsworth, UK: Penguin.

Division of Christian Education of the National Council of Churches of Christ in the USA. 1989. *The Bible. New Revised Standard Version (NRSV)*. Available at http://www. devotions.net/bible/00bible.htm.

Douglas, Mary. 1966. *Purity and Danger: An Analysis of Concepts of Pollution and Taboo*. London and New York: Routledge.

——. 1986. *How Institutions Think*. New York: Syracuse University Press.

——. 1996 (1970). *Natural Symbols: Explorations in Cosmology*. London: Routledge.

Duby, Georges. 1992. "The Courtly Model". In Christiane Klapisch-Zuber (ed.), *A History of Women in the West: Silence in the Middle Ages*. Cambridge: The Belknap Press of Harvard University Press.

Duffin, Jacalyn. 1999. *History of Medicine: A Scandalously Short Introduction*. Toronto: University of Toronto Press.

——. 2011. "Questioning Medicine in Seventeenth-Century Rome: The Consultations of Paolo Zacchia". *Canadian Bulletin of Medical History* 28(1): 149–70.

Duffy, Eamon. 1997. *Saints and Sinners: A History of the Popes*. New Haven: Yale University Press.

Dupont, Ellen M. 2008. "Regnier de Graaf". *Embryo Project Encyclopedia*. Available at http://embryo.asu.edu/handle/10776/1746.

Eberl, Jason T. 2005. "Aquinas' Account of Human Embryogenesis and Recent Interpretations". *Journal of Medicine and Philosophy* 30: 379–94.

Eco, Umberto. 1985. "How Culture Conditions the Colours We See". In Marshall Blonsky (ed.), *On Signs*. Baltimore: Johns Hopkins University Press.

Ellingsen, Mark. 1990. "The Church and Abortion: Signs of Consensus". *Christian Century*: 3–10. Available at http://www.religion-online.org/showarticle.asp?title=749.

Elmer, Peter. 2004. "Chemical Medicine and the Challenge to Galenianism: The Legacy of Paracelsus, 1560–1700". In Peter Elmer (ed.), *The Healing Arts: Health, Disease and Society in Europe, 1500–1800*. Manchester: The Open University.

Eriksen, Anne and Anne Stensvold. 2002. *Maria-kult og helgendyrkelse i moderne katolisisme*. Oslo: Pax.

Esler, Philip F. 1994. *The Early Christian World*. London: Routledge.

Evangelium vitae. 1995. Encyclical. Pope John Paul II. Available at http://w2.vatican.va/ content/ john-paul-ii/en/encyclicals/documents/hf_jp-ii_enc_25031995_evangelium-vitae.html.

Ferlaino, Franco. 1990. *Vattienti: Osservazione e riplasmazione di una ritualità tradizionale*. Milano: Jaca Book.

Filippini, Nadia. 1990. "Il medico e la levatrice". *Quaderni Storici* 25: 291–97.

Finocchiaro, Maurice A. 1997. *Galileo on the World Systems*. Berkeley: University of California Press.

Fitzgerald, A.D. 1999. *Augustine Through the Ages: An Encyclopedia*. Grand Rapids, MI: Eerdmans.

Fornaciari, Antonio et al. 2008. "The Blessed Christina of Spoleto: A Case of 15th Century Artificial Mummy from Umbria". In P. Atoche et al. (eds.), *Proceedings of Congress "Mummies and Science: World Mummies Research"*: 521–27.

Freud, Sigmund. 1990. *The Origins of Religion*. Harmondsworth, UK: Penguin.

Frugoni, Chiara. 1992. "The Imagined Woman". In Christiane Klapisch-Zuber (ed.), *A History of Women in the West: Silences in the Middle Ages*. Cambridge: The Belknap Press of Harvard University Press.

Frye, Northrop. 1982. *The Great Code: The Bible and Literature*. San Diego: Harvest-Harcourt Brace.

Geary, Patrick. 1978. *Furta Sacra: Thefts of Relics in the Central Middle Ages*. Princeton: Princeton University Press.

Geels, Antoon and Owe Wikström. 2006. *Den religiösa människan: En introduktion til religionspsykologin*. Stockholm: Natur ock Kultur.

Gilbert, Scott F. 2013. *Developmental Biology*. 10th ed., Sunderland, MA: Sinauer Associates.

Gilgoff, Dan. 2007. *The Jesus Machine: How James Dobson, Focus on the Family and Evangelical America Are Winning the Culture War*. New York: St. Martin's Griffin.

Gilhus, Ingvild. 1997. *Laughing Gods, Weeping Virgins: Laughter in the History of Religion*. London: Routledge.

——. 2006. *Animals, Gods and Humans: Changing Attitudes to Animals in Greek, Roman and Early Christianity*. London: Routledge.

Gilhus, Ingvild et al. 2009. *Farsmakt og moderskap i antikken*. Oslo: Spartacus.

Gist, Richard. 1981. "Soul and the Person: Defining Life". *Christian Century*: 2022–24. Available at http://www.religion-online.org/showarticle.asp?title=1701.

Glendon, Mary Ann. 2001. *A World Made New: Eleanor Roosevelt and the Universal Declaration of Human Rights*. New York: Random House.

Glock, H.-J. 1996. *A Wittgenstein Dictionary*. Oxford: Blackwell.

Grambo, Ronald. 1979. *Norske trollformularer og magiske formler*. Oslo: Universitetsforlaget.

Graves, Dan. 1996. *Scientists of Faith: Forty-Eight Biographies of Historic Scientists and their Christian Faith*. Grand Rapids, MI: Kregel Resources.

Green, Monica. 2002. *The Trotula: An English Translation of the Medieval Compendium of Women's Medicine*. Philadelphia: University of Pennsylvania Press.

Grell, Ole Peter. 2004. "Medicine and Religion in Sixteenth-Century Europe". In Peter Elmer (ed.), *The Healing Arts: Health, Disease and Society in Europe, 1500–1800*. Manchester: The Open University.

——. 2007. "Between Anatomy and Religion: The Conversion to Catholicism of the two Danish Anatomists Nicolaus Steno and Jacob Winslow". In Ole Peter Grell and Andrew Cunningham (eds.), *Medicine and Religion in Enlightenment Europe*. Aldershot, UK: Ashgate.

Grogan, Sarah. 2008. *Body Image: Understanding Body Dissatisfaction in Men, Women and Children*. New York: Routledge.

Grøndahl, Cathrine. 2009. *Jeg satte mitt håp til verden*. Oslo: Gyldendal.

Gross, Clover F. 2006. *Margaret Sanger: Feminist Heroine, Public Nuisance, or Social Engineer?* M.A. thesis. Humboldt State University.

Habermas, Jürgen. 1962. *Strukturwandel der Öffentlichkeit: Untersuchungen zu einer Kategorie der bürgerlichen Gesellschaft*. Darmstadt: Luchterhand.

Hadley, D.M. (ed.). 1999. *Masculinity in Medieval Europe*. London: Longman.

Haldane, John and Patrick Lee. 2003. "Aquinas on Human Ensoulment, Abortion and Value of Life". *Philosophy* 78(2): 255–78.

Hanegraaff, Wouter J. 1996. *New Age Religion and Western Culture*. Leiden: Brill.

Hankinson, R.J. 1991. "Galen's Anatomy of the Soul". *Phronesis* 36(2): 197–233.

Hanson, Clare. 2004. *A Cultural History of Pregnancy: Pregnancy, Medicine and Culture, 1750–2000*. Basingstoke, UK: Palgrave Macmillan.

Harris, Ruth. 1999. *Lourdes: Body and Spirit in the Secular Age*. London: Penguin.

Hatfield, Gary. 2014. "René Descartes". In Edward N. Zalta (ed.), *The Stanford Encyclopedia of Philosophy* (Spring 2014 Edition). Available at http://plato.stanford.edu/archives/spr2014/entries/descartes/.

Hattab, Helen. 2001. "Experience and Experiment in Early Modern Europe". National Endowment for the Humanities Summer Institute from 24 June to 2 August 2001 (directed by Professors Pamela Long and Pamela Smith). Washington, DC: Folger Library.

Hatton, Erin and Mary Nell Trautner. 2011. "Equal Opportunity Objectification? The Sexualization of Men and Women on the Cover of *Rolling Stone*". *Sexuality & Culture* 15(3): 256–78.

Haynes, Jeffrey (ed.). 2009. *Routledge Handbook of Religion and Politics*. New York: Routledge.

Herman, Arthur. 2001. *The Scottish Enlightenment: The Scots' Invention of the Modern World*. London: Harper Perennial.

Hibbard, Scott W. 2010. *Religious Politics and Secular States: Egypt, India and the United States*. Baltimore: Johns Hopkins University Press.

Hill Fletcher, Jeannine. 2013. *Motherhood as Metaphor: Engendering Interreligious Dialogue.* New York: Fordham University Press.

Hock, Ronald F. (ed.). 1996. *The Infancy Gospels of James and Thomas.* Salem, OR: Polebridge Press.

Høystad, Ole Martin. 2007. *A History of the Heart.* Chicago: University of Chicago Press.

Humanae vitae. 1968. Encyclical. Pope Paul VI. Available at http://w2.vatican.va/content/paul-vi/en/encyclicals/documents/hf_p-vi_enc_25071968_humanae-vitae.html.

Hunt, Stephen. 2003. *Alternative Religions: A Sociological Introduction.* Aldershot, UK: Ashgate.

Huntington, Samuel. 1993. "The Clash of Civilizations?". *Foreign Affairs* 72(3): 22–49.

I Dizionari TEA. 1989. *Dizionario dei santi.* Milano: Editori Associati.

James, M.R. 1926. *The Apocryphal New Testament.* Oxford: Clarendon Press.

James, William. 1997 (1902). *The Varieties of Religious Experience.* New York: Touchstone.

Jelen, Ted G. and Clyde Wilcox. 2003. "Causes and Consequences of Public Attitudes Towards Abortion: A Review and Research Agenda". *Political Research Quarterly* 56(4): 489–500.

Jones, R.K. and S. Singh. 2010. *Characteristics of U.S. Abortion Patients, 2008.* New York: Guttmacher Institute.

Juergensmeyer, Mark. 2003. *Terror in the Mind of God: The Global Rise of Religious Violence.* Berkeley: University of California Press.

Jungmann, Josef A. 1986. *The Mass of the Roman Rite: Its Origins and Development (Missarum Sollemnia).* Westminster, UK: Christian Classics.

Juschka, Darlene M. (ed.). 2001. *Feminism in the Study of Religion: A Reader.* London: Continuum.

Jütte, Robert. 2008. *Contraception: A History.* Cambridge: Polity Press.

Kermit, Hans. 1998. *Niels Stensen: Naturforsker og helgen.* Tromsø: Ravnetrykk.

Kevles, Daniel J. 1985. *In the Name of Eugenics: Genetics and the Uses of Human Heredity.* Cambridge: Harvard University Press.

King, Ursula (ed.). 1995. *Religion and Gender.* Oxford: Blackwell.

Kirkeordinansen av 1539: Lover og forordninger 1537–1605. 1988. Oslo: Norsk lokalhistorisk institutt.

Kirkeordinansen av 1607 og Forodninger om eksteskapssaker gitt 1582. 1985. Oslo: Den rettshistoriske kommisjon.

Knödel, Natalie. 1997. "Reconsidering an Obsolete Rite: The Churching of Women and Feminist Liturgical Theology". *Feminist Theology* 5(14): 106–25.

Koyré, Alexandre. 1968 (1957). *From the Closed World to the Infinite Universe.* Baltimore: Johns Hopkins University Press.

Kristeva, Julia. 1983. *Histoires d'amour.* Paris: Denoël.

——. 1986. "Stabat Mater". Translated by León Roudiez. In Toril Moi (ed.), *The Kristeva Reader.* New York: Columbia University Press.

Kuhn, Thomas. 1962. *The Structure of Scientific Revolutions.* Chicago: University of Chicago Press.

Kuriyama, Shigehisa. 1999. *The Expressiveness of the Body and the Divergence of Greek and Chinese Medicine.* New York: Zone Books.

Kusukawa, Sachiko. 2004a. "Medicine in Western Europe in 1500". In Peter Elmer (ed.), *The Healing Arts: Health, Disease and Society in Europe, 1500–1800.* Manchester: The Open University.

——. 2004b. "The Medical Renaissance of the Sixteenth Century: Vesalius, Medical Humanism and Bloodletting". In Peter Elmer (ed.), *The Healing Arts: Health, Disease and Society in Europe, 1500–1800.* Manchester: The Open University.

Lakoff, George and Mark Johnson. 1980. *Metaphors We Live By.* Chicago: University of Chicago Press.

Lambeth Conference Resolution. 1930. Available at: http://www.lambethconference.org/index.cfm.

Laqueur, Thomas. 1987. "Orgasm, Generation, and the Politics of Reproductive Biology". In Catherine Gallagher and Thomas Laqueur (eds.), *The Making of the Modern Body: Sexuality and Society in the Nineteenth Century*. Berkeley: University of California Press.

Lawrence, Cera R. 2008. "Marcello Malpighi (1646–1694)". *Embryo Project Encyclopedia*. Available at: http://embryo.asu.edu/handle/10776/6239.

Lee, Becky R. 1996. "The Purification of Women after Childbirth: A Window into Medieval Perceptions of Women". *Florilegium* 14: 43–55.

LeGates, Marlene. 2001. *In Their Time: A History of Feminism in Western Society*. New York: Routledge.

Legenda Aurea. Iacopo da Varazze. 1995. Torino: Einaudi.

Lévi-Strauss, Claude. 1963. "The Structural Study of Myth". In *Structural Anthropology*. Vol. 1. New York: Basic Books.

———. 1989 (1969). *The Raw and the Cooked*. Chicago: University of Chicago Press.

Liebman, Robert and Robert Wuthnow. 1983. *The New Christian Right: Mobilization and Legitimation*. New York: Aldine.

Lokhorst, Gert-Jan. 2014. "Descartes and the Pineal Gland". In Edward N. Zalta (ed.), *The Stanford Encyclopedia of Philosophy* (Spring 2014 Edition). Available at http://plato.stanford.edu/archives/spr2014/entries/pineal-gland/.

Lopata, Alex. 2009. "History of the Egg in Embryology". *Journal of Mammalian Ova Research* 26: 2–9.

Lopez, Angel. 2012. "Pope Gregory XIV". *Embryo Project Encyclopedia*. Available at http://embryo.asu.edu/pages/pope-gregory-xiv.

Luebke, David M. (ed.). 1999. *The Counter-Reformation*. Oxford: Blackwell.

Luhmann, Niklas. 1982. *The Differentiation of Society*. New York: Columbia University Press.

Luker, Kristin. 1984. *Abortion and the Politics of Motherhood*. Berkeley: University of California Press.

Lund, P.J. 2006. "Semmelveis – en varsler". *Tidsskrift for den norske lægeforening* 126: 1776–79.

Maguire, Daniel C. (ed.). 2003. *Sacred Rights: The Case for Contraception and Abortion in World Religions*. Oxford: Oxford University Press.

Mangham, Andrew and Greta Depledge (eds.). 2011. *The Female Body in Medicine and Literature*. Liverpool: Liverpool University Press.

Martin, Emily. 2001. *The Woman in the Body: A Cultural Analysis of Reproduction*. Boston: Beacon Press.

Martin, William. 1996. *With God on our Side: The Rise of the Religious Right in America*. New York: Broadway Books.

McNeill, John T. and Helena M. Gamer. 1974. *Medieval Handbooks of Penance*. New York: Octagon Books.

Meli, Domenico Bertoloni. 2011. *Mechanism, Experiment, Disease: Marcello Malpighi and Seventeenth-Century Anatomy*. Baltimore: Johns Hopkins University Press.

Mingazzini, Paolo. 2010. "Leonardo e l'anatomia". *Il Bassini* 30: 62–74.

Moi, Toril. 1998. "What is a Women? Sex, Gender and the Body in Feminist Theory". In *What is a Woman? And Other Essays*. Oxford: Oxford University Press.

Morgan, David. 2012. *The Embodied Eye: Religious Visual Culture and the Social Life of Feeling*. Berkeley: University of California Press.

Mosse, George. 1964. *The Crisis of German Ideology: Intellectual Origins of the Third Reich*. London: Weidenfeld and Nicolson.

Mundal, Else. 1989. "Barneutbering". In Hedda Gunneng, Beata Losman, Bodil Møller Knudsen (eds.), *Kvinnors Rosengård: Medeltidskvinnors liv och hälsa, lust och barnefödande*. Stockholm: Centrum för kvinnoforskning vid Stockholms Universitet.

Naldini, Mario (ed.) 1986. Niccolò Stenone. *Conversione e attività pastorale*. Scritti scelti. Firenze: Nardini Editore.

Newman, Karen. 1996. *Fetal Positions: Individualism, Science, Visuality*. Stanford: Stanford University Press.

Noonan, John T. Jr. 1970. "An Almost Absolute Value in History". In *The Morality of Abortion: Legal and Historical Perspectives*. Cambridge: Harvard University Press.

Onians, Richard Broxton. 1988. *The Origins of European Thought about the Body, the Mind, the Soul, the World, Time, and Fate*. Cambridge: Cambridge University Press.

Ortner, Sherry B. 1973. "On Key Symbols". *American Anthropologist* 75(5): 1338–46.

——. 1974. "Is Female to Male as Nature is to Culture?". In M.Z. Rosaldo and L. Lamphere (eds.), *Women, Culture, and Society*. Stanford: Stanford University Press.

Otto, Rudolph. 1958. *The Idea of the Holy – An Inquiry into the Non-Rational Factor in the Idea of the Divine and Its Relation to the Rational*. Oxford: Oxford University Press.

Ovid. 1955. *Metamorphoses*. Translated by Mary Innes. London: Penguin.

Pardo-Tomás, José and Alvar Martinez-Vidal. 2007. "The Ignorance of Midwives: The Role of Clergymen in Spanish Enlightenment Debates on Birth Care". In Ole Peter Grell and Andrew Cunningham (eds.), *Medicine and Religion in Enlightenment Europe*. Aldershot, UK: Ashgate.

Pasnau, Robert. 2002. *Thomas Aquinas on Human Nature: A Philosophical Study of Summa Theologiae, 1a 75–89*. Cambridge: Cambridge University Press.

——. 2007. "The Mind-Soul Problem". In Paul Bakker and Johannes Thijssen (eds.), *Mind, Perception, and Representation: The Tradition of Commentaries on Aristotle's De anima*. Aldershot, UK: Ashgate.

Pastore, Alessandro and Giovanni Rossi (eds.). 2008. *Paolo Zacchia: Alle origini della medicina legale 1584–1659*. Milano: Franco Angeli.

Pinto-Correia, Clara. 1997. *The Ovary of Eve: Egg and Sperm and Preformation*. Chicago: University of Chicago Press.

Pius XII. 1963. *Allocution to Midwives, October 29, 1951*. In the Benedictine Monks of Solemnes (eds.), *Papal Teachings on Matrimony*. Boston: St. Paul Editors. Available at http://w2.vatican.va/content/pius-xii/it/speeches/1951/documents/hf_p-xii_spe_19511029_oste triche.html.

Pollitt, Katha. 1997. "Abortion in American History". *The Atlantic Monthly* 273(5): 111–15.

Poovey, Mary. 1987. "'Scenes of an Indelicate Character': The Medical 'Treatment' of Victorian Women". In Catherine Gallagher and Thomas Laqueur (eds.), *The Making of the Modern Body: Sexuality and Society in the Nineteenth Century*. Berkeley: University of California Press.

Porter, Roy. 2003. *Flesh in the Age of Reason: How the Enlightenment Transformed the Way We See our Bodies and Souls*. London: Penguin.

Powell, Hilary. 2012. "The 'Miracle of Childbirth': The Portrayal of Parturient Women in Medieval Miracle Stories". *Social History of Medicine* 25(4): 795–811.

Preus, Samuel J. 1987. *Explaining Religion: Criticism and Theory from Bodin to Freud*. New Haven: Yale University Press.

Price, Janet and Margrit Shildrick (eds.). 1999. *Feminist Theory and the Body: A Reader*. New York: Routledge.

Ragan, Bryant and Elizabeth Williams (eds.). 1991. *Re-Creating Authority in Revolutionary France*. New Brunswick, NJ: Rutgers University Press.

Raymond, Janice G. 1993. *Women as Wombs: Reproductive Technologies and the Battle over Women's Freedom*. Melbourne: Spinifex Press.

Reagan, Leslie. J. 1997. *When Abortion Was a Crime: Women, Medicine and Law in the United States, 1867–1973*. Berkeley: University of California Press.

Riddle, John M. 1997. *Eve's Herbs: A History of Contraception and Abortion in the West*. Cambridge: Harvard University Press.

Roberts, Jon H. 1988. *Darwin and the Divine in America: Protestant Intellectuals and Organic Evolution 1859–1900*. Notre Dame: University of Notre Dame Press.

Roger, Jacques. 1997. *Life Sciences in Eighteenth-Century French Thought*. Edited by Keith R. Benson. Stanford: Stanford University Press.

Rubin, Miri. 1991. *Corpus Christi: The Eucharist in Late Medieval Culture*. Cambridge: Cambridge University Press.

Ruestow, E.G. 2010. "Anton von Leeuwenhoek and his Perception of Spermatozoa". In Scot F. Gilbert (ed.), *Developmental Biology*. Sunderland, MA: Sinauer Associates Publishers. Available at http://10e.devbio.com/article.php?id=65.

Ruether, Rosemary. 1983. *Sexism and God-Talk: Toward a Feminist Theology*. Boston: Beacon Press.

———. 1985. "Catholics and Abortion: Authority vs. Dissent". *The Christian Century*. Available at http://www.religion-online.org/showarticle.asp?title=1926.

Saller, Richard P. 1999. *"Pater familias, mater familias*, and the Gendered Semantics of the Roman Household". *Classical Philology* 94: 182–97.

Saracino, Michele. 2011. *Being about Borders: A Christian Anthropology of Difference*. Collegeville, MN: Liturgical Press.

Schiebinger, Londa. 1987. "Skeletons in the Closet: The First Illustrations of the Female Skeleton in Eighteenth-Century Anatomy". In Catherine Gallagher and Thomas Laqueur (eds.), *The Making of the Modern Body: Sexuality and Society in the Nineteenth Century*. Berkeley: University of California Press.

Schott, Robin May (ed.). 2010. *Birth, Death and Femininity: Philosophies of Embodiment*. Bloomington, IN: Indiana University Press.

Schüssler Fiorenza, Elisabeth. 1983. *In Memory of Her: A Feminist Theological Reconstruction of Christian Origins*. London: SCM Press.

———. 1992. *But She Said: Feminist Practices of Biblical Interpretation*. Boston: Beacon Press.

Sedgh, Gilda et al. 2007. "Induced Abortion: Estimated Rates and Trends Worldwide". *Lancet* 370: 1338–45.

Sedgh, Gilda et al. 2012. "Induced Abortion: Incidence and Trends Worldwide from 1995 to 2008". *Lancet* 379: 625–32.

Shapin, Steven. 1996. *The Scientific Revolution*. Chicago: University of Chicago Press.

Sharp, Jane. 1999 (1671). *The Midwives Book. Or the Whole Art of Midwifry Discovered*. Edited by Elaine Hobby. Oxford: Oxford University Press.

Shaw, Brent D. 1993. "The Passion of Perpetua". *Past and Present* 139: 3–45.

Siraisi, Nancy G. 1990. *Medieval and Early Renaissance Medicine*. Chicago: University of Chicago Press.

Slights, William W.E. 2008. *The Heart in the Age of Shakespeare*. Cambridge: Cambridge University Press.

Smail, Daniel Lord and Kelly Gibson (eds.). 2009. *Vengeance in Medieval Europe: A Reader*. Toronto: University of Toronto Press.

Solberg, Berge. 2009. "Embryo, stamcelle og foster". De nasjonale forskningsetiske komiteer. Available at http://www.etikkom.no/FBIB/Temaer/Forskning-pa-menneskelig-materiale/Embryo-stamcelle-og-forster/.

Solheim, Jorun. 1998. *Den åpne kroppen. Om kjønnssymbolikk i moderne kultur*. Oslo: Pax.

Sommers, Sheena. 2011. "Transcending the Sexed Body: Reason, Sympathy and 'Thinking Machines' in Debates over Male Midwifery". In Andrew Mangham and Greta Depledge (eds.), *The Female Body in Medicine and Literature*. Liverpool: Liverpool University Press.

Songe-Møller, Vigdis. 1989. "The Definition of 'Male' and 'Female' – An Unsolved Problem". *Studia Theologica* 43: 91–98.

———. 2002. *Philosophy without Women: The Birth of Sexism in Western Thought*. London: Continuum.

Sontag, Susan. 1977. *On Photography*. London: Penguin.

Steinberg, Leo. 1996. *The Sexuality of Christ in Renaissance Art and Modern Oblivion*. Chicago: University of Chicago Press.

Steinsland, Gro. 2005. *Norrøn religion. Myter, riter, samfunn*. Oslo: Pax.

Stenone, Niccolo. 1986. *Conversione e attività pastorale*. Firenze: Nardini Editore.

Stensvold, Anne. 2005a. "Kulturkamp – religiøs kultur og motkultur". In A.B. Amundsen (ed.), *Norges religionshistorie*. Oslo: Universitetsforlaget.
——. 2005b. "Statskirke uten stat – folkekirke uten folk". In A.B. Amundsen (ed.), *Norges religionshistorie*. Oslo: Universitetsforlaget.
Stevens, Scott Manning. 1997. "Sacred Heart and Secular Brain". In David Hillman and Carla Mazzio (eds.), *The Body in Parts: Fantasies of Corporeality in Early Modern Europe*. New York: Routledge.
Stoeffler, F. 1973. *German Pietism in the Eighteenth Century*. Leiden: Brill.
Stroumsa, Gedaliahu G. 1990. "*Caro Salutis Cardo:* Shaping the Person in Early Christian Thought". *History of Religions* 30(1): 25–50.
Supreme Court of the United States. 1973. Roe v. Wade. Available at http://www.law.cornell.edu/supremecourt/text/410/113.
Szymanski, Dawn, Lauren Moffitt, and Erika Carr. 2011. "Sexual Objectification of Women: Advances to Theory and Research". *The Counselling Psychologist* 39(1): 6–38.
Taylor, Charles. 2007. *A Secular Age*. Cambridge: The Belknap Press of Harvard University Press.
Telste, Kari. 1999. *Brutte løfter. En kulturhistorisk studie av kjønn og ære 1700–1900*. Ph.D. thesis. University of Oslo.
Tessiore, Giorgio. 1994. *Sindone: "segno" di Cristo?* San Rocco, IT: Arti Grafiche.
Thomas, Yan. 1992. "The Division of Sexes in Roman Law". In Pauline Schmitt Pantel (ed.), *A History of Women: From Ancient Goddesses to Christian Saints*. Cambridge: The Belknap Press of Harvard University Press.
Tillich, Paul. 1957. *Dynamics of Faith*. New York: Harper.
Turner, Victor. 1967. "Betwixt and Between: The Liminal Period in Rites of Passage". In *The Forest of Symbols*. Ithaca: Cornell University Press.
Vernant, Jean-Pierre. 1982. *The Origins of Greek Thought*. London: Methuen.
Vik, Ingrid, Christian Moe, and Anne Stensvold. 2013. *Lobbying for Faith and Family: A Study of Religious NGOs at the United Nations*. NORAD Report July 2013. Oslo: Norwegian Ministry of Foreign Affairs. Available at http://www.norad.no/no/resultater/publikasjoner/norads-rapportserie/publikasjon?key=401801.
Vauchez, André. 1987. *Les laïcs au Moyen Age: Pratiques et expériences religieuses*. Paris: Éditions Cerf.
Von Rad, Gerhard. 1972. *Genesis: A Commentary*. London: SCM Press.
Warner, Marina. 1990. *Alone of all Her Sex: The Myth and the Cult of the Virgin Mary*. London: Picador.
Weber, Max. 1946. "Religious Rejections of the World and their Directions". In *From Max Weber: Essays in Sociology*. New York: Oxford University Press.
——. 1965. *The Protestant Ethic and the Spirit of Capitalism*. London: Allen & Unwin.
——. 1993. *The Sociology of Religion*. Boston: Beacon Press.
Weinstein, Donald and Rudolph M. Bell. 1982. *Saints and Society*. Chicago: University of Chicago Press.
Wemple, Suzanne Fonay. 1992. "Women from the Fifth to the Tenth Century". In Christiane Klapisch-Zuber (ed.), *A History of Women: Silence in the Middle Ages*. Cambridge: The Belknap Press of Harvard University Press.
Wiedemann, Thomas. 1989. *Adults and Children in the Roman Empire*. London: Routledge.
Wilson, Bryan. 1982. *Religion in Sociological Perspective*. Oxford: Oxford University Press.
Wire, Antoinette Clark. 1990. *The Corinthian Women Prophets: A Reconstruction through Paul's Rhetoric*. Minneapolis: Fortress Press.
Witt, Charlotte. 2012. "Feminist History of Philosophy". In Edward N. Zalta (ed.), *The Stanford Encyclopedia of Philosophy* (Fall 2012 Edition). Available at http://plato.stanford.edu/archives/fall2012/entries/feminism-femhist/.
Witte, John. 1986. "The Reformation of Marriage Law in Martin Luther's Germany: Its Significance Then and Now". *Journal of Law and Religion* 4(2): 293–351.

Wittgenstein, Ludwig. 1957. *Philosophical Investigations*. Oxford: Oxford University Press.
Wright, Thomas. 2013. *Circulation: William Harvey's Revolutionary Idea*. London: Vintage.
Young, Katherine. 1987. "Introduction". In Arvind Sharma (ed.), *Women in World Religions*. Albany: State University of New York Press.
Zacchia, Paolo. 1621–1655. "Consilium 39". In Ada Lepp (tr.), *Quaestiones Medico-Legales*. Available at http://meds.queensu.ca/medicine/histm/zacchia%20latin%20list.htm.
Zimdars-Swartz, Sandra L. 1991. *Encountering Mary: From La Salette to Medjugorje*. Princeton: Princeton University Press.

INDEX

CPSIA information can be obtained
at www.ICGtesting.com
Printed in the USA
LVOW01s1603150317

527324LV00010B/940/P

9 780415 857598